Dubai

Lou Callan

LONELY PLANET PUBLICATIONS
Melbourne • Oakland • London • Paris

Dubai
1st edition – April 2000

Published by
Lonely Planet Publications Pty Ltd A.C.N. 005 607 983
192 Burwood Rd, Hawthorn, Victoria 3122, Australia

Lonely Planet Offices
Australia PO Box 617, Hawthorn, Victoria 3122
USA 150 Linden St, Oakland, CA 94607
UK 10a Spring Place, London NW5 3BH
France 1 rue du Dahomey, 75011 Paris

Photographs
All of the images in this guide are available for licensing from
Lonely Planet Images.
email: lpi@lonelyplanet.com.au

Front cover photograph
View of the Arabian Tower, Jumeira Beach Hotel (Christine Osborne)

ISBN 1 86450 131 6

Printed by Colorcraft Ltd, Hong Kong

Contents – Text

Contents – Maps

The Author

Lou Callan

After finishing a degree in languages, Lou wandered from publishing pillar to printing post while completing further studies in publishing and editing. After lots of long lunches and strenuous book launch parties as publicity manager at Oxford University Press Australia, she found work as a contributing editor on *Australian Bookseller & Publisher*. With her affinity for languages and a hankering for travel, Lou fell into the job of phrasebooks editor at Lonely Planet Publications in 1994.

After a brief stint as guidebooks editor she packed up and followed her husband Tony to a life among the red dunes of Al-Ain in the UAE in 1998. As a natural progression, Lou found herself writing this book and LP's *Oman & the UAE*.

FROM THE AUTHOR

For their invaluable help during the update of this book and for putting up with all my queries and phone calls, I'd like to thank the following: Loay M Shadid and Naji Alaeddine; everyone at the Department of Tourism & Commerce Marketing and the Dubai International Arts Centre.

Extra special thanks goes to Tony Cleaver, my tireless travel companion and darling husband, whose help with this book was indispensable.

This Book

From the Publisher

This 1st edition was edited at Lonely Planet's Melbourne office by Dan Goldberg with assistance from Bethune Carmichael and Michelle Glynn. Sarah Sloane designed the book with cartographic assistance from Maree Styles; Indra Kilfoyle designed the cover. Thanks to Quentin Frayne for providing the Language chapter and Rowan McKinnon for technical assistance.

A special thanks to Alem Goshime, a local Dubai artist whose illustrations are throughout this book, and also to Pam Rhodes, from the Dubai International Arts Centre, for helping to get the illustrations from Dubai to Australia in one piece.

Foreword

ABOUT LONELY PLANET GUIDEBOOKS

The story begins with a classic travel adventure: Tony and Maureen Wheeler's 1972 journey across Europe and Asia to Australia. Useful information about the overland trail did not exist at that time, so Tony and Maureen published the first Lonely Planet guidebook to meet a growing need.

From a kitchen table, then from a tiny office in Melbourne (Australia), Lonely Planet has become the largest independent travel publisher in the world, an international company with offices in Melbourne, Oakland (USA), London (UK) and Paris (France).

Today Lonely Planet guidebooks cover the globe. There is an ever-growing list of books and there's information in a variety of forms and media. Some things haven't changed. The main aim is still to help make it possible for adventurous travellers to get out there – to explore and better understand the world.

At Lonely Planet we believe travellers can make a positive contribution to the countries they visit – if they respect their host communities and spend their money wisely. Since 1986 a percentage of the income from each book has been donated to aid projects and human rights campaigns.

Updates Lonely Planet thoroughly updates each guidebook as often as possible. This usually means there are around two years between editions, although for more unusual or more stable destinations the gap can be longer. Check the imprint page (following the colour map at the beginning of the book) for publication dates.

Between editions up-to-date information is available in two free newsletters – the paper *Planet Talk* and email *Comet* (to subscribe, contact any Lonely Planet office) – and on our Web site at www.lonelyplanet.com. The *Upgrades* section of the Web site covers a number of important and volatile destinations and is regularly updated by Lonely Planet authors. *Scoop* covers news and current affairs relevant to travellers. And, lastly, the *Thorn Tree* bulletin board and *Postcards* section of the site carry unverified, but fascinating, reports from travellers.

Correspondence The process of creating new editions begins with the letters, postcards and emails received from travellers. This correspondence often includes suggestions, criticisms and comments about the current editions. Interesting excerpts are immediately passed on via newsletters and the Web site, and everything goes to our authors to be verified when they're researching on the road. We're keen to get more feedback from organisations or individuals who represent communities visited by travellers.

> Lonely Planet gathers information for everyone who's curious about the planet – and especially for those who explore it first-hand. Through guidebooks, phrasebooks, activity guides, maps, literature, newsletters, image library, TV series and Web site we act as an information exchange for a worldwide community of travellers.

Research Authors aim to gather sufficient practical information to enable travellers to make informed choices and to make the mechanics of a journey run smoothly. They also research historical and cultural background to help enrich the travel experience and allow travellers to understand and respond appropriately to cultural and environmental issues.

Authors don't stay in every hotel because that would mean spending a couple of months in each medium-sized city and, no, they don't eat at every restaurant because that would mean stretching belts beyond capacity. They do visit hotels and restaurants to check standards and prices, but feedback based on readers' direct experiences can be very helpful.

Many of our authors work undercover, others aren't so secretive. None of them accept freebies in exchange for positive write-ups. And none of our guidebooks contain any advertising.

Production Authors submit their raw manuscripts and maps to offices in Australia, USA, UK or France. Editors and cartographers – all experienced travellers themselves – then begin the process of assembling the pieces. When the book finally hits the shops, some things are already out of date, we start getting feedback from readers and the process begins again ...

WARNING & REQUEST

Things change – prices go up, schedules change, good places go bad and bad places go bankrupt – nothing stays the same. So, if you find things better or worse, recently opened or long since closed, please tell us and help make the next edition even more accurate and useful. We genuinely value all the feedback we receive. Julie Young coordinates a well travelled team that reads and acknowledges every letter, postcard and email and ensures that every morsel of information finds its way to the appropriate authors, editors and cartographers for verification.

Everyone who writes to us will find their name in the next edition of the appropriate guidebook. They will also receive the latest issue of *Planet Talk*, our quarterly printed newsletter, or *Comet*, our monthly email newsletter. Subscriptions to both newsletters are free. The very best contributions will be rewarded with a free guidebook.

Excerpts from your correspondence may appear in new editions of Lonely Planet guidebooks, the Lonely Planet Web site, *Planet Talk* or *Comet*, so please let us know if you *don't* want your letter published or your name acknowledged.

Send all correspondence to the Lonely Planet office closest to you:

Australia: PO Box 617, Hawthorn, Victoria 3122
USA: 150 Linden St, Oakland, CA 94607
UK: 10A Spring Place, London NW5 3BH
France: 1 rue du Dahomey, 75011 Paris

Or email us at: talk2us@lonelyplanet.com.au

For news, views and updates see our Web site: www.lonelyplanet.com

HOW TO USE A LONELY PLANET GUIDEBOOK

The best way to use a Lonely Planet guidebook is any way you choose. At Lonely Planet we believe the most memorable travel experiences are often those that are unexpected, and the finest discoveries are those you make yourself. Guidebooks are not intended to be used as if they provide a detailed set of infallible instructions!

Contents All Lonely Planet guidebooks follow roughly the same format. The Facts about the Destination chapters or sections give background information ranging from history to weather. Facts for the Visitor gives practical information on issues like visas and health. Getting There & Away gives a brief starting point for researching travel to and from the destination. Getting Around gives an overview of the transport options when you arrive.

The peculiar demands of each destination determine how subsequent chapters are broken up, but some things remain constant. We always start with background, then proceed to sights, places to stay, places to eat, entertainment, getting there and away, and getting around information – in that order.

Heading Hierarchy Lonely Planet headings are used in a strict hierarchical structure that can be visualised as a set of Russian dolls. Each heading (and its following text) is encompassed by any preceding heading that is higher on the hierarchical ladder.

Entry Points We do not assume guidebooks will be read from beginning to end, but that people will dip into them. The traditional entry points are the list of contents and the index. In addition, however, some books have a complete list of maps and an index map illustrating map coverage.

There may also be a colour map that shows highlights. These highlights are dealt with in greater detail in the Facts for the Visitor chapter, along with planning questions and suggested itineraries. Each chapter covering a geographical region usually begins with a locator map and another list of highlights. Once you find something of interest in a list of highlights, turn to the index.

Maps Maps play a crucial role in Lonely Planet guidebooks and include a huge amount of information. A legend is printed on the back page. We seek to have complete consistency between maps and text, and to have every important place in the text captured on a map. Map key numbers usually start in the top left corner.

Although inclusion in a guidebook usually implies a recommendation we cannot list every good place. Exclusion does not necessarily imply criticism. In fact there are a number of reasons why we might exclude a place – sometimes it is simply inappropriate to encourage an influx of travellers.

Introduction

Imagine, just for a moment, that you were transported in a time capsule back to Dubai as it was in the early 20th century. There are no roads, running water, electricity or hospitals. In fact, there's no infrastructure at all. Instead, palm frond huts and windtower houses made from sea rock and gypsum dot the coastline, inhabited predominantly by Iranian and Indian merchants, sheikhs and their sheikhas. Bedouin and their camels wander nomadically from wadi to oasis. Traders come and go, bearing herbs and spices, sandalwood and frankincense, pearls and gold. In this small coastal hamlet, silence and serenity walk hand in hand along the banks of the tranquil Creek.

Today, the scene is vastly different. Dubai is no longer a Middle Eastern backwater; in less than a century, it has been transformed into a modern metropolis, the commercial hub of the region and an internationally renowned shoppers' paradise. When you first see the glistening, modern buildings lining Dubai Creek, or sip French wine well into the night at one of the city's many nightclubs, it's hard to believe that this was once an empty, arid desert inhabited by more camels than people.

Contemporary Dubai is a fascinating crossroads where the past meets the future, where tradition has embraced modernity. Where else in the world would you find a sheikh, replete with a 4WD and a mobile phone peaking out of his *dishadasha* (shirt-dress) pocket, cruising into the desert sunset while negotiating a business transaction?

Architecturally, Dubai is a treasure-trove of contrasting styles. Rubbing shoulders with the postmodern, glass, metal and steel skyscrapers sprouting from the sandy coastal flats are traditionally designed mosques, courtyard houses and windtowers. Feast your eyes on the incongruity of these traditional and modern styles, which provide a fascinating portal to the past and the future.

Contrary to popular belief, the city's bountiful wealth was founded on trade, not oil. Dubai is one of the last bastions of unrestrained capitalism: it's Hong Kong meets the Middle East. What opium was to the growth of Hong Kong in the late 19th century, gold was to Dubai in the 1960s. Oil, when it was discovered in 1966, merely exacerbated trade profits and accelerated modernisation.

Nowadays, everyone comes to Dubai for a piece of the action – prosperity is the name of the game. Pakistani labourers, Indian taxi drivers, Sri Lankan maids, English businessmen, Australian engineers, Jordanian teachers, Filipino waitresses – they're all here, lured like magnets by the prospect of affluence.

Over the last decade, business and tourism have oiled Dubai's runaway economy. Designer shops, luxury hotels, exclusive beach clubs and some of the world's richest sporting events have succeeded in wresting fistfuls of tourist dollars from well-to-do travellers, long-term expat workers and business people keen to ply their trade – and their bank accounts.

Culturally, too, Dubai is a fascinating showcase of traditional Arab and Bedouin lifestyles. And its tolerance of westerners, in contrast to the rest of the Gulf States, is an additional incentive for travellers and tourists who crave to see the charms of Arabia through First World spectacles.

Dubai is a cosmopolitan melting pot of people standing at the crossroads of time – and the quintessential home of sand, sea, sun and shopping.

Facts about Dubai

HISTORY
Early Settlement

Less is known about the early history of this area than about most other areas of the Gulf. It is certain, however, that this part of Arabia has been settled for millennia, and archaeological remains found in Al-Qusais, on the north-eastern outskirts of Dubai, corroborate the claim that there was human settlement here as far back as 3000 BC.

Archaeological evidence also suggests that the area known today as the United Arab Emirates (UAE) and Oman was closely associated with the mysterious Magan civilisation during the Bronze Age. Though precious little is known about the Magan civilisation, it is thought that they dominated the ancient world's copper trade, exploiting the rich veins of copper in the hills near Sohar (in Oman); it is also likely that they traded pearls in Mesopotamia (contemporary Iraq).

If the rise of the Magan civilisation is shrouded in mystery, so too is its decline. All records ceased after the second millennium BC and some historians have speculated that the desertification of the area signalled its demise; others have argued that its importance may have been diminished by the growing reliance on iron for the manufacture of weapons and tools.

The next major occupation of the area does not seem to have occurred for another two millennia. Archaeological excavations at Jumeira, about 10km south of the Dubai Creek, have revealed a 6th century AD caravan station.

The Sassanids, a dynasty that ruled in Persia from 224 to 636 AD, inhabited the area until they were uprooted by an Islamic tribe called the Umayyads in the 7th century. Archaeologists have surmised that the buildings at the outpost were restored and extended by the Umayyad dynasty, making it the only site in the UAE to span the pre-Islamic and Islamic periods.

Over the next few centuries, the Gulf experienced a boom in maritime trade due to

Pearling

Memories of the heyday of pearling are laden with romanticism. But, for those who took to the sea for the summer months, it was a life of hardship as well as pride. For those who dived the depths the rewards were no match for the dangers involved. Most of the divers were slaves from East Africa and the profits of the industry went straight to their master, the owner of the boat.

The only equipment the divers used was a rope tied around the waist, a turtle-shell peg on their nose and leather finger gloves to protect their hands from the sharp coral and shells. At certain times of the year they would wear an all-over muslin bodysuit to protect them from jellyfish stings. The best pearls were found at depths of up to 36m and divers would be under the water for around three minutes. To reach this depth, divers used a rope weighted with a stone that was tied to the boat and thrown overboard.

Pearl merchants would grade pearls according to size by using a number of copper sieves, each with different sized holes. The greatest market for pearls was originally India, but in the early 20th century the UK and the US became keen buyers of this fashionable jewel. Today the advent of artificially cultured pearls has triggered the demise of the industry. The Dubai Museum and Dubai Village feature significant displays on pearling.

its location between the Mediterranean Sea and the Indian Ocean. Trade soon became the backbone of the local economy as seafarers travelled as far as China, returning laden with silk and porcelain.

The earliest recorded accounts of settlement in Dubai itself came from two Italian explorers: Gasparo Balbi and Marco Polo. In 1580 Polo described Dubai as a prosperous town, largely dependent on pearl fishing.

European Presence

In the late 16th century, Portugal, attempting to dominate the lucrative trade routes, became the first European power to take an interest in this part of the Gulf coast. Its power lasted until the 1630s and eventually extended as far north as Bahrain. The only evidence of its presence today, however, is the two Portuguese cannons on display at the Dubai Museum.

The area was subsequently infiltrated by the French and the Dutch in the 17th and 18th centuries, both of whom also aspired to control the trading routes to the east. The British were equally intent on ruling the seas in order to protect their route to India, and in 1766 the Dutch finally gave way to Britain's seemingly omnipresent East India Company, which had already established trading links with the Gulf as early as 1616.

Throughout this time Dubai remained a small and rather insignificant fishing and pearling hamlet, perched precariously on a perpetually disputed border between the two local powers of the region – the Qawasim of what are now Ras al-Khaimah and Sharjah to the north, and the Bani Yas tribal confederation of what is now Abu Dhabi to the south. Dubai also had to contend with rivalries between other regional powers – the Wahhabi tribes of what is now Saudi Arabia, the Ottoman Empire and the British.

The Bani Yas

The Bani Yas was the main power among the Bedouin tribes of the Gulf interior and was originally based in Liwa, an oasis on the edge of the desert known as the Empty Quarter (Rub al-Khali in Arabic) in the south of the UAE. They engaged in the traditional Bedouin activities of camel herding, small-scale agriculture, tribal raiding and extracting protection money from merchant caravans passing through their territory.

At the turn of the 19th century, Dubai was led by Mohammed bin Hazza who remained Ruler of Dubai until the Al Bu Fasalah, a branch of the Bani Yas tribe from Abu Dhabi, came to dominate the town in 1833, severing it from Abu Dhabi.

About 800 people from this tribe settled by the Creek in Bur Dubai under the leadership of Maktoum bin Butti, who established the Al-Maktoum dynasty of Dubai which still rules the emirate to this day. For Maktoum bin Butti, good relations with the British authorities in the Gulf were essential to safeguard his new and small sheikhdom against attack from the larger and more powerful sheikhdoms of Sharjah to the north and Abu Dhabi to the south.

In 1841 the Bur Dubai settlement extended to Deira on the southern side of the Creek, though throughout the 19th century Dubai largely remained a tiny enclave of fishermen, pearl divers, Bedouin and Indian and Persian merchants.

Things began to change, however, around the end of the 19th century. In 1892, the British, keen to impose their authority on the region, extended their power through a series of Exclusive Agreements under which the sheikhs accepted formal British protection and, in exchange, promised to have no dealings with any other foreign power without British permission. (As a result of these treaties, Europeans took to calling the area the Trucial Coast, a title it retained until 1971.)

Concomitantly, at the end of the 19th century, Sharjah, the area's main trading centre, began losing its trade prosperity to Dubai. In 1894 Dubai's ruler, Shaikh Maktoum bin Hasher al-Maktoum, permitted tax exemption for foreign traders. Around the same time Lingah, in what is now Iran, lost its status as a duty-free port, and the Al-Maktoum family made a concerted effort to lure Lingah's disillusioned traders to Dubai while also managing to convince some of Sharjah's merchants to relocate.

At first the Persians who came here believed that it would just be a temporary move, but by the 1920s, when it became evident that the high import duties and trade restrictions in southern Iran were there to stay, they brought their families to Dubai and took up permanent residence.

More good news for the town came in the early 20th century, when the Al-Maktoums, probably with the assistance of the newly arrived Persian traders, prevailed on a British steamship line to switch its main port of call in the lower Gulf from Lingah to Dubai. When this was accomplished in 1903, it gave Dubai regular links with both British India and the ports of the central and northern Gulf (ie the ports of Bahrain, Kuwait, Bushire and Basra).

This marked the beginning of Dubai's growth as a trading power, and prosperity quickly blossomed.

The Expanding City

By the turn of the 20th century, Dubai was well established as an independent town with a population of some 10,000 people. Deira was the most populous area at this time with about 1600 houses, inhabited mainly by Arabs but also by Persians and Baluchis (who came from parts of what are now Pakistan and Afghanistan). By 1908 there were about 350 shops based in Deira and another 50 in Bur Dubai, where the Indian community was concentrated. To this day the Dubai Souq is very Indian oriented and is still home to the largest Hindu temple in Dubai.

The next key event in Dubai's expansion occurred in 1939 when Shaikh Rashid bin Saeed al-Maktoum took over as regent from his father, Shaikh Saeed. (Rashid only formally succeeded to the leadership when his father died in 1958.) He quickly moved to bolster the emirate's position as the lower Gulf's main trading hub. At about the same time, the rulers of Sharjah made the near fatal mistake of allowing their harbour to silt up. This was even more costly for them than it might otherwise have been because, in Dubai, Rashid was improving facilities along the Creek.

The Re-Export Trade

Dubai came to specialise in the 're-export trade'; its merchants imported goods, then sold them to other ports rather than peddle them at home. In practice, this usually meant smuggling in general, and smuggling gold to India in particular. It needs to be said that these goods left Dubai perfectly legally; it was the countries at the *other* end of the trade that looked on it as smuggling.

WWII also played a role in the growth of the re-export trade. The war brought much of the trade to a standstill and on top of this there was a shortage of basic food supplies. The British government supplied the Trucial Sheikhdoms with plenty of rice and sugar. Dubai merchants who had bought these goods cheaply, but found themselves oversupplied, shipped them off to the black market in Iran.

It was around the time of the flourishing re-export trade that modern Dubai began to take shape. During the 1950s, Shaikh Rashid became one of the earliest beneficiaries of Kuwait's Fund for Arab Economic Development, which loaned him money to dredge the Creek (which had become badly silted up, reducing the volume of Creek traffic) and to build a new breakwater near its mouth. The project was completed in 1963, and gold smuggling took off like a rocket.

Gold smuggling peaked in 1970, when 259 tons of gold flowed through the Emirate, on its way mainly to the huge market in India. In the early 1970s the Indian government began to crack down on gold smugglers, but before this occurred Dubai's merchants had already laid the foundations of today's enormous re-export trade in consumer goods bound for the rest of the Arabian peninsula and the Indian Subcontinent.

Dubai's days as a smuggler's paradise are not over. The trade now supposedly focuses on Iran: dhows take such cargo as VCRs and Levis jeans to Iranian ports and return laden with caviar and carpets.

The development of Dubai as a major trading centre was also spurred on by the collapse, around 1930, of the pearling trade, which had been the mainstay of Dubai's economy for centuries. The pearling trade fell victim both to the worldwide depression of 1929 and to the Japanese discovery, around the same time, of a method by which pearls could be cultured artificially. Sheikh Rashid concluded that the pearling industry was probably never going to revive and looked for alternative forms of revenue. This chain of events heralded a new era in Dubai's trade – re-exporting (see the boxed text 'The Re-Export Trade').

The rise of the re-export trade, whereby merchants imported goods and then immediately exported them, was spurred on by WWII and continued to flourish thereafter. The end of the war, India's independence and the decline of the British Empire saw the end of Britain's presence in the region.

In 1951 the Trucial States Council was founded, bringing the leaders of what would become the UAE together. The Council comprised the rulers of the sheikhdoms and was the direct predecessor of the UAE Supreme Council. It met twice a year under the aegis of the British Political Agent in Dubai.

The British decision to withdraw from all areas east of Suez prompted the establishment of the UAE and the modernisation of the region which had just been accelerated by the discovery of oil (see the boxed text 'Oil, Trade & Infrastructure').

However, before withdrawing from the region, the British set in motion the means by which the borders that now make up the UAE were drawn. Incredibly, this involved a British diplomat spending months riding a camel around the mountains and desert asking village heads, tribal leaders and Bedouin which sheikh they swore allegiance to.

Modern Dubai

When Dubai became one of the seven Emirates of the UAE in 1971, the emirs agreed to a formula under which Abu Dhabi and Dubai (in that order) would carry the most weight in the federation, but which would leave each emir largely autonomous. Shaikh Zayed bin

Oil, Trade & Infrastructure

Oil was first discovered near Dubai in 1966 and oil exports began three years later. However, a building boom had already begun along the Creek well before Dubai struck oil. Even after oil revenues began coming in, trade remained the foundation of the city's wealth, though oil has played its part in building Dubai since 1969.

The first bank (The British Bank of the Middle East) was established in 1946, and when Al-Maktoum Hospital was built in 1949 it was the only centre for modern medical care on the Trucial Coast until well into the 1950s. When Shaikh Rashid officially came to power in 1958 he set up the first Municipal Council. He also established a police force and basic infrastructure including electricity and water supply.

Until the early 1960s the only means of transport in town was donkey or camel. As is still the case today, *abras* were used to transport people across the Creek. Roads and bridges appeared in the early 60s; construction of the airport began in 1958 and the British Overseas Airways Corporation (BOAC) and Middle East Airlines (MEA) launched regular flights to Dubai soon after.

The ambitious UK£23 million Port Rashid complex was begun in 1967 after it became obvious that the growing maritime traffic could no longer be managed by the current facilities. It was completed in 1972.

The mid-70s saw the beginnings of a massive program of industrialisation that resulted in the construction of Jebel Ali Port, said to be the largest artificial port in the world, and the adjacent industrial centre, which was to become a free trade zone. At the time, the port was one of only two artificial structures in the world that was visible from space (the other being the Great Wall of China).

All of these developments brought to life Rashid's vision of Dubai as one of the Mid-

Sultan al-Nayan of Abu Dhabi became the Supreme Ruler of the UAE and Shaikh Rashid of Dubai became Vice President.

Since 1971, Dubai has been one of the most stable cities in the Arab world. This does not mean, however, that political life has been devoid of controversy. Border disputes between the Emirates continued throughout the 1970s and 80s, and the degree to which 'integration' among the seven sheikhdoms should be pursued has been the subject of constant debate.

In 1979, Shaikh Zayed and Shaikh Rashid sealed a formal compromise under which each gave a little ground on his respective vision of the country. The result was a much stronger federation in which Dubai remained a bastion of free trade while Abu Dhabi imposed a tighter federal structure on the other Emirates. Rashid also agreed to take the title of prime minister as a symbol of his commitment to the federation.

Shaikh Rashid, the driving force behind Dubai's phenomenal growth, died in 1990 after a long illness and was succeeded as emir by his son, Shaikh Maktoum. For several years prior to Rashid's death, Maktoum had been regent for his father in all but name, and the new emir has continued to follow in his father's footsteps.

The core of his policies has been to promote Dubai whenever and wherever possible. By the mid-90s, the Dubai Desert Classic had becosme a well established stop on the annual Professional Golfer's Association (PGA) tour, placing the city firmly on the world sporting map. The same logic is behind the staging of the world-class tennis tournaments, boat and horse racing, desert rallies and the air show (one of the four largest in the world).

High profile events, such as the Dubai Shopping Festival and the Dubai Summer Surprises, attract hoards of tourists mainly from other Gulf countries, and have catapulted Dubai's tourism into the league of the city's other major industries – trade and oil.

The history of Dubai reads like a tale of rags to riches, a chronicle which has witnessed a small coastal hamlet transform into a major commercial hub – a Hong Kong of the Arabian Gulf. It is hard to imagine anywhere else in the world that has developed at such pace, in such a short space of time, for so many different people.

GEOGRAPHY

Dubai sits on the Arabian Gulf, in the northwestern region of the UAE. This city is the capital of the emirate of the same name, which is the second largest of the seven Emirates which comprise the UAE. The emirate of Dubai is 3,885 sq km and the constantly expanding city is roughly 35 sq km. Dubai Creek, which extends 12km inland from the coast, divides the city in two.

Prior to settlement, this area was a flat coastal desert, characterised only by clumps of desert grasses and a small area of swampland at the eastern end of the Creek.

Travelling east of Dubai city, the flat sands slowly give way to the rugged foothills of the Hajar Mountains where you can find gorges and waterholes. A vast sea of sand dunes covers the area south of the city, becoming more and more imposing as it stretches into the desert known as the Empty Quarter that makes up the southern region of the UAE and the western region of Saudi Arabia. Farther north along the coast the land slowly becomes greener until you reach the mountainous northern Emirates.

CLIMATE

For most of the year Dubai's weather is warm and humid; the sky is rarely cloudy. The summer months are extremely hot with daytime temperatures from May to September in the low to mid 40s (Celsius). July and August are the hottest months with average temperatures around 43°C with 85% humidity. Sometimes the heat reaches 48°C and the humidity 95%. The sea temperature in the height of summer is about 37°C, which provides no relief, and hotel swimming pools have to be cooled during summer so that they don't turn into steaming hot baths.

During October, November, March and April the weather is much more bearable with temperatures in the low to mid 30s. In winter (December to February) Dubai enjoys perfect weather with an average temperature of 24°C, though it can get quite windy. Unlike the desert area inland, Dubai doesn't get too cold on winter nights, the lowest temperature hovering around 15°C. It doesn't rain often, or heavily, but when the weather does turn foul (usually in December or January) getting around can suddenly become difficult with streets turning into rivers and traffic becoming chaotic. Drivers here are not used to wet road conditions.

Sandstorms can occur during March and April, although Dubai is protected from much of the swirling dust and sand by its many buildings.

The Real Liquid Gold

Water is without doubt the most precious commodity in Dubai. Most of the water consumed in Dubai comes from the two desalination plants just out of the city. In 1997, of the 33.3 million gallons of water consumed in Dubai, 31 million came from these plants. Underground wells supplied the rest. Water is a fast diminishing resource: experts estimate that there will be a serious shortage in the next 10 years. With an average rainfall of 115mm each year, and scorchingly high temperatures, you can imagine the amount of water required to keep parks, gardens and people alive.

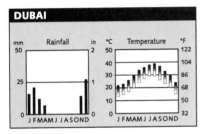

ECOLOGY & ENVIRONMENT

Other than the wind-blown sand and dust one would expect in an arid desert environment, Dubai is a very clean city. It doesn't yet have most of the environmental problems that a burgeoning population brings to a growing city. The Creek, however, overburdened by ever-increasing marine traffic, is polluted.

The greening of Dubai is part of the afforestation of the entire UAE, and the battle to thwart desertification, which threatens to envelop the Gulf, is ongoing. There are a number of well-established parks and gardens around the city and some major roads are lined with palm trees, shrubs, flowers and manicured lawns.

Although things are much better than they were a few years ago, you will still see rubbish left on beaches, in parks or thrown out of car windows, regardless of the effort by government agencies and Non Governmental Organisations (NGOs) to educate the community about protecting the environment. As a result, an enormous number of workers have been employed to make sure that the rubbish on the street does not get the chance to offend for too long, and the municipality has imposed a Dh500 fine for littering. Cleanup days are common and advertisements in newspapers alert people to the necessity of recycling and keeping the city clean.

Nevertheless, despite the cleanup efforts, Dubai generates one of the highest per capita volumes of waste in the world, and the Emirates Environmental Group has opened a number of recycling centres around the city.

Additionally, there is a high risk and incidence of oil spills off the coast. Over the years the devastation caused by these environmental spills has prompted a concerted effort by government agencies to monitor and control marine pollution. Oil companies are required to spend money on the protection of the coast. Dubai is also a member of the Regional Organisation for the Protection of the Marine Environment.

Local Environmental Organisations

The Federal Environmental Agency legislates on environmental issues and encourages communication between the Emirates. The Environmental Research and Wildlife Development Agency (☎ 02-414 131, PO Box 45553, Abu Dhabi) is a federal government body that monitors air pollution and waste disposal and imposes certain environmental standards on factories in Dubai.

There are also many NGOs concerned with the environment. The Arabian Leopard Trust (☎ 06-444 871, PO Box 24444, Sharjah) is a nonprofit volunteer organisation concerned with protecting endangered species. You can visit its web site (www .fujairah.com/leopard.htm) for further information. The Emirates Environmental Group (☎ 331 8100, PO Box 7013, Dubai) organises educational programs in schools and businesses as well as community programs, such as clean up drives. Its Web site (www.eeg-uae.com) provides further information. The Environment Friends Society(☎ 668 854, PO Box 4940, Dubai) is a community group that receives an annual budget from the Ministry of Labour & Social Affairs.

FLORA & FAUNA

In Dubai's parks you will see indigenous plant species such as the date palm and the neem, and a large number of imported species including the eucalyptus. The sandy desert surrounding the city is home to wild grasses and the occasional date-palm oasis.

In the salty scrublands along the coast, you will see the desert hyacinth. It has bright yellow and deep-red dappled flowers and tends to emerge in all its glory after heavy rains. It is not common in the city, but you'll see it a little farther out, around the beaches near the Jebel Ali Hotel.

Decorating the flat plains that stretch away from the foothills of the Hajar Mountains, around Hatta, is the acacia. This is a flat-topped, rather scraggly, incredibly hardy tree. In this area you will also come across the ghaf, a big tree that looks a little like a weeping willow. It survives so well because its roots stretch down for about 80m, allowing it to tap into deep water reserves. You will recognise the ghaf by its lower foliage, which is usually trimmed flat by grazing camels and goats.

The Date Palm

If you visit Dubai in early summer, one of the things you will be struck by is the enormous number of date clusters hanging off the huge number of date palms that line many of the streets and parks. The ubiquitous date palm has always held a vital place in the life of Emiratis. For centuries dates were one of the staple foods of the Bedouin, along with fish, camel meat and camel milk. Not a great deal of variety you may say, but consider the fact that there are 80 different kinds of dates in the UAE.

The reason the date palm can survive in such a harsh climate is because its fruit is roughly 70% sugar. This stops the rot and makes the date edible for a longer period than other tropical fruits.

Apart from providing a major foodstuff, the date palm was also used to make all kinds of useful items. Its trunk was used to make columns and ceilings for houses, while its fronds were used to make roofs and walls (called *areesh*). The date palm provided the only shade available in desert oases. Livestock were fed with its seeds and it was burned as fuel. The palm frond was, and still is, used to make bags, mats, boats (called *shasha*), shelters, brooms and fans.

There is no doubt that the Bedouin could not have survived as well as they have without the help of the date palm.

❀❀❀❀❀❀❀❀❀❀❀❀❀❀❀❀❀❀❀❀

As in any major city, you are not likely to come across any exotic wildlife in Dubai, unless you go to the zoo. The encroachment of urbanisation, combined with zealous hunting, has ensured the virtual extinction of many species. These include the houbara bustard (a common prey of falcons; see the boxed text 'Falconry' under Traditional Culture later in this chapter), the Arabian oryx (also called the white oryx), the striped hyaena and Gordan's wildcat.

The city is a hot spot for bird-watchers, however, being on the migration path between Europe, Asia and Africa and the parks, gardens and golf courses have large populations of resident and migratory birds. Indigenous species include the crab plover, the Socotra cormorant and the purple sunbird. Other species include the ring-necked parakeet, the pintail snipe, the palm dove and the Indian silverbill.

Artificial nests have been built to encourage flamingos to breed at the Khor Dubai Wildlife Sanctuary at the eastern end of Dubai Creek. Visitors are not permitted here, unless they are part of a bird-watching tour.

In addition to flamingos, the sanctuary has ducks, marsh harriers, spotted eagles, broad-billed sandpipers and ospreys. Bird-watching tours are available for those who desire (see Organised Tours in the Getting Around chapter).

On the fringes of the city, where the urban sprawl gives way to the desert, a desert fox, sand cat or falcon may be seen if you are very lucky. Otherwise, the only animals you are likely to encounter are camels and goats.

The waters off Dubai teem with around 300 different types of fish. Diners will be most familiar with the hamour, a species of grouper, but the Gulf is also home to an extraordinary range of tropical fish and several species of small sharks.

GOVERNMENT & POLITICS

There are no political parties or general elections in Dubai. Power rests with the ruling royal family, the Al-Maktoums (see the boxed text over the page). Though the UAE has a federal government, over which one of the seven emirs presides (in practice this is always Shaikh Zayed), each of the rulers is absolutely sovereign within his own emirate.

Shaikh Maktoum bin Rashid al-Maktoum is the ruler of Dubai and the Vice President of the UAE. He rules Dubai with two of his brothers who also hold ministerial positions within the federal government: Shaikh Mohammed is the Crown Prince and Minister of Defence, Shaikh Hamdan is the Deputy Ruler and Minister of Finance & Industry.

The degree of power which the seven emirs cede to the federal government has been one of the hottest topics of debate in government circles since the founding of the UAE in 1971. Over the years, Dubai has fought hardest to preserve as much of its independence and to minimise the power of the country's federal institutions.

Politics in the UAE tends to be rather opaque, but the relative interests of the various emirs are fairly clear. Abu Dhabi is the largest and wealthiest emirate and has the biggest population. It is, therefore, the dominant member of the federation and is likely to remain so for some time. Dubai is a reasonably wealthy emirate with an equally obvious interest in upholding its free-trade market and domination of the tourism industry. Sharjah and Ras al-Khaimah both have relatively small oil revenues and they, and the other Emirates, are dependent on subsidies from Abu Dhabi, though the extent of this dependence varies widely.

The forum where these issues are discussed is the Supreme Council, the highest legislative body in the country. The council, which tends to meet informally, comprises the seven emirs. On an official level, its main duty is to elect one of the emirs to a five year term as the country's president. In 1996, Shaikh Zayed was elected to his sixth term as president, a position he seems likely to hold for life.

There is also a Cabinet and the posts are distributed among the Emirates. Most of the federal government's money comes from Abu Dhabi and Dubai so members of these governments hold most of the important cabinet posts.

The Cabinet and the Supreme Council are advised, but cannot be overruled, by the Federation Council of Ministers, a 40-member consultative body whose members are appointed by the respective emirs. Abu Dhabi and Dubai hold almost half of the council's seats, and all the council's members come from leading merchant families.

ECONOMY

Dubai is the second richest emirate in the UAE, after Abu Dhabi. It has been the most successful in diversifying its economy, based on its desire to reduce its reliance on a slowly depleting resource – oil.

The Al-Maktoum Dynasty

The ruling family of Dubai has successfully managed to blend its private interests with public politics.

The current ruler of Dubai is Shaikh Maktoum bin Rashid al-Maktoum. Shaikh Ahmed, his uncle (Rashid's brother), holds the federal position of Chairman of the UAE, but Shaikh Zayed bin Sultan al-Nayan, the ruler of Abu Dhabi, is the Supreme Ruler of the UAE.

Maktoum's second brother, Shaikh Hamdan, is the Deputy Ruler of Dubai and the Federal Minister of Finance and Industry.

Shaikh Mohammed, the third brother, is the Crown Prince of Dubai and the Defence Minister of the UAE. He is probably the most well known of all the ruling family, and is constantly in the public eye with regards to his public policies and his private pastime: horse-racing. His dramatic Web site at www.sheikmohammed.com features photographs as well as greeting cards with some of the Crown Prince's own poetry and is further evidence of his public presence.

Indeed, horse racing is a hobby of all the members of the ruling family and they are well respected in the international community. Shaikh Maktoum owns the largest racing stables in the world; Shaikh Hamdan is known as a leading breeder of race horses and Shaikh Mohammed owns several champion race horses.

Among the women of the family, Shaikha Hessah bint Maktoum al-Maktoum, the eldest daughter of the ruler, is a well known artist whose vibrantly coloured, abstract paintings have been exhibited in Paris and London. Shaikha Hessah herself is not as prominent as her paintings, due to the fact that society requires her to shun public life.

DUBAI'S RULING DYNASTY
The Al-Maktoum Family Tree

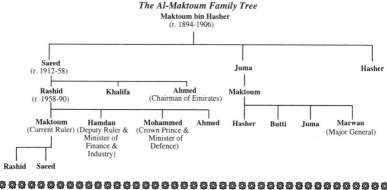

But it has never had to worry about being too reliant. In the decades before oil was discovered in the Gulf, Dubai had already established itself as the main trading (and smuggling) port in the region. Just one look at the dhows that line the Creek loaded with all kinds of merchandise – from jeans to plastic buckets – gives you an idea of the bustling commercialism of the city. The discovery of oil in the mid-60s only boosted the economic modernisation program already implemented by Dubai's ruler at the time, Shaikh Rashid bin Saeed Al-Maktoum.

Dubai's main exports are oil, natural gas, dates and dried fish; top export destinations are Japan, Taiwan, the UK, the US and India. Imports are primarily minerals and chemicals, base metals (including gold), vehicles and machinery, electronics, textiles and foodstuffs; the main importers into

Dubai are the US, China, Japan, the UK, South Korea and India. The re-export trade in Dubai makes up about 80% of the UAE's total re-export business. Many of Dubai's imports are shipped right out of the country again and they go mainly to Iran, India, Saudi Arabia, Kuwait and Afghanistan.

NONOIL TRADE FIGURES

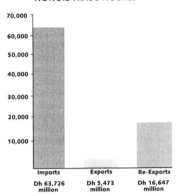

[These figures were correct at the time of writing.]

Dubai is also the home of a huge dry-dock complex, one of the Middle East's busiest airports and duty-free operations, the best road system in the country, the national airline of the UAE and large free-trade zones at Jebel Ali, 30 minutes from the city centre, and at Dubai airport. It is the attraction of foreign business to its free-trade zones that has been one of Dubai's greatest economic achievements in the last decade.

Companies are enticed with the promise of full foreign ownership, full repatriation of capital and profits, no corporate tax for 15 years, no currency restrictions and no personal income tax for staff. The number of companies setting up business in the free trade zones increases by about 200 per year, with household names such as Daewoo, Heinz, Reebok and Sony enjoying the benefits (see Doing Business in the Facts for the Visitor chapter for more information).

Dubai's tourism industry has also exploded of late. The city's tolerance of western habits, profusion of hotels in different price ranges, long stretches of beach, warm winter weather, shopping incentives and desert activities have helped it become the leading tourist destination in the Gulf.

For Emiratis (or 'Nationals' as they are usually referred to in the local media), all this prosperity translates into the kind of benefits that much of the rest of the world only dreams of: free healthcare, free education, heavily subsidised utilities and, in some cases, free housing.

Dubai's per capita income is estimated to be about Dh58,800 per annum. This is far above the average wage of a professional expat and, when you consider the fact that many unskilled labourers from the Subcontinent are earning Dh500 to Dh1000 per month, you get an idea of the kind of salary and benefits that a National takes home.

Still, there is one hurdle in the economy that Dubai is seeking to overcome, albeit a small one. Dubai is highly dependent upon expat labour and, at the same time, its National citizens spend a great deal of money. The government has made some attempt to 'Emiratise' the economy by placing Nationals in the public workforce and imposing local employee quotas on private companies.

NONOIL – GDP BY SECTOR

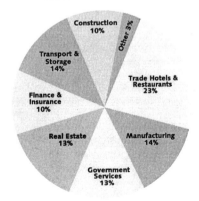

At the time of writing, Dubai's total GDP was Dh45.527 million, of which Dh38.047 million was nonoil derived.

However, encouraging people who have never had to work before is problematic. Many private companies are reluctant to hire Nationals, believing that it will result in a drop in profits and efficiency. There is no doubt that Dubai will be dependent on foreign labour and expertise for a long time to come, which means that much of the money generated in the workforce is leaving the country.

POPULATION & PEOPLE

The most recent statistics indicate that there are 772,500 people living in the Emirate of Dubai, a giant leap from 183,200 in 1975. These statistics apply to the whole of the Dubai emirate, though most of the population lives in the city of Dubai.

Only about 25% of the total population of Dubai (193,125 people) are Emiratis; the expatriate community makes up the rest of the population. The majority of expats (about 60%) are from India, Pakistan and the Philippines, supplying the city with cheap labour, although there are also a large number holding professional positions.

About 12% are from other Arab countries and western expats make up about 3% of the population. If you need proof of the fact that there are so many expat workers here, just look at the ratio of men to women in

POPULATION DISTRIBUTION

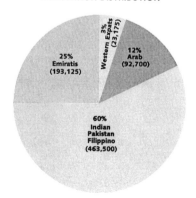

25% Emiratis (193,125)

3% Western Expats (23,175)

12% Arab (92,700)

60% Indian Pakistan Filippino (463,500)

Total Population: 772,500

The Expat Existence

From Tehran to Tripoli, every major Middle Eastern city has its community of expats. The experience is markedly different, however, for western and Asian expats in the UAE.

Some westerners are just here on short-term work contracts; others have entered into long-term relationships with their host country and may well stay here until the end of their working lives.

Just look at the benefits. For the 45,000 or so western expats living in the UAE, life is a fantasy world of no taxes and often no rent and a free air fare home once or twice a year.

A typical expat existence is one of continuously sunny weather, weekend camping and 4WD trips, beach resorts, pubs and restaurants. The ability to lead the sort of life that is just not possible back home seduces many people into staying long term.

But money is not the only draw card. There is also the opportunity to explore Arab culture and enjoy its hospitality and warmth. The crime rate is low and the streets are safe. Ask any western expat when they're going home for good and you'll find that most won't be able to give you a straight answer.

For the 1.5 million or so Asian expats living in the UAE, however, life is very different. Most Pakistanis, Indians, Sri Lankans, Bangladeshis and even some Chinese are employed as labourers. Working on building sites without proper safety precautions or digging roads in 45°C heat is hardly the easy life, but for most it's preferable to financial struggles and unemployment back home.

Even though their salaries are often one-tenth of those earned by western expats, these people make three or four times as much as they could at home. An Indian man is able to support an extended family back home on his pay packet alone.

Many Asian expats stay here for twenty years or more, only seeing their families for one month every two years.

Dubai. Of the 772,500 people in Dubai only 235,000 are women.

The Emiratis in Dubai stem mainly from the Bani Yas tribe who came from the isolated areas of Al-Ain and Liwa, both oases deep in the desert. There are also a large number of people with Iranian, Indian and Baluchi (from what is now a part of Pakistan and Afghanistan) ancestry. Whether or not these people gain UAE citizenship or not depends on how long they have been in the country (some sources claim 15 years is required).

EDUCATION

Universal education in Dubai has made great strides in the last 20 to 30 years. As recently as 1952, there were no schools in Dubai, and only a handful of *kuttab* where boys and girls learned the Quran by rote and some learned to read and write. A school building program began in the 1960s and by 1972 there were 16 boys' schools and 12 girls' schools. The teachers were recruited mainly from other Arab nations.

Primary education is now compulsory in Dubai and secondary education is available to all. It is estimated that there are around 78 government schools in Dubai, from kindergarten to secondary, with a total of 39,400 students, the slight majority of whom are girls. There are also 94 private schools with a total enrolment of around 75,000.

Since Dubai is a multi-ethnic society, there are a large number of schools that cater specifically to the different nationalities of expat families, offering curriculums from the UK, US and India.

Not long ago, Dubai residents had to go abroad, usually to the UK or Pakistan, with the help of government grants, to seek tertiary education. This changed in 1977 with the establishment of the UAE University in Al-Ain, about 1½ hours from Dubai. In 1988 a system of Higher Colleges of Technology was set up to offer more technically oriented courses. Curriculums are produced in consultation with potential employers such as banks, the hospitality industry and oil companies. In 1997 there were 1,088 men enrolled at tertiary colleges and 1,525 women.

All tertiary education is free. As a way of encouraging Nationals to contribute to the workforce, those who go on to tertiary education are given a very generous monthly salary simply for attending their course. The federal government is also willing to pay the cost of overseas study for UAE citizens.

ARTS
Song & Dance

Traditional songs and dances are often impossible to separate into two separate arts. It is the combination of the two that delivers a message or expresses an emotion. Traditional songs and dances are inspired by the environment – the sea, desert and mountains. Contact with other cultures through Dubai's trading history has brought many other influences. One of the most popular dances is the *liwa* which is performed to a rapid tempo and loud drum beat. It was most likely brought to the Gulf by East African slaves and it is traditionally sung in Swahili.

Another dance, the *ayyalah*, is a typical Bedouin dance, celebrating courage and strength. The ayyalah is performed throughout the Gulf, but the UAE has its own variation, which is performed to a simple drum beat. Anywhere between 25 and 200 men stand with their arms linked in two rows facing each other. They wave walking sticks or swords in front of them and sway back and forth, the two rows taking it in turn to sing. It is a war dance and the words expound the virtues of courage and bravery in battle. There is a display on video of this very dance in the Dubai Museum (see the Things to See & Do chapter).

Traditional song and dance displays are generally confined to special events and celebrations such as weddings, or heritage displays during the Dubai Summer Surprises or the Dubai Shopping Festival. It is unlikely that you will come across a spontaneous music or dance performance in Dubai.

Musical Instruments

The instruments used at musical celebrations are the same as those used in much of the rest of the Gulf. There is no instrument that is specific to the Dubai region.

The *tamboura*, a harp-like instrument, has five strings made of horse gut, which are stretched between a wooden base and a bow-shaped neck. The base is covered with camel skin and the strings are plucked with sheep horns. It has a deep and resonant sound that is a little like a bass violin.

A much less sophisticated instrument is the *manior*, a percussion instrument that is played with the body. It is a belt made of cotton and decorated with dried goats' hooves. It is wrapped around the player who keeps time with the beat of the tamboura while dancing.

The *mimzar* is a wooden instrument a little like a small oboe, but it delivers a higher pitched tone. The sound is haunting and undeniably Middle Eastern.

An unusual instrument and one that you'll often see at song and dance displays is the Arabian bagpipes, known as the *habban*. This is made from a goatskin sack that has two pipes attached. The sack retains its goat shape and the pipes resemble its front legs. One pipe is used to blow air into the sack and the other produces the sound. The habban sounds much the same as the Scottish bagpipes, but is shriller in tone.

The *tabl* is a drum, and has a number of different shapes. It can resemble a bongo drum that is placed on the floor, or a *jaser*, a drum with goatskin at both ends, which is slung around the neck and hit with sticks.

Literature

You will have trouble digging up many published Emirati authors in Dubai. The best known writer is perhaps US-educated Mohammed al-Murr. This may well be because two of his books have been translated into English.

One of these is *Dubai Tales*, a collection of 12 short stories exploring aspects of the traditional lives and values of the people of Dubai. The other is called *The Wink of the Mona Lisa*. Al-Murr's popularity could be attributed to the presentation of his characters: they all have great pride in their origins and tradition, which seems to strike a chord with readers in their search to find literature they can empathise with.

Painting

The encouragement of artists is still a relatively new concept in Dubai, though gallery owners agree that there has been an increase in patronage over the last five years. Patronage generally takes the form of commissions from government offices and hotels as well as from shaikhs and other wealthy Emiratis (see Art Galleries in the Things to See & Do chapter).

A few Emirati artists have gained well deserved attention from the international art community. Shaikha Hessah, the eldest child of Shaikh Maktoum, was trained by renowned Bangladeshi artist, Tina Ahmed.

Abdul Qader al-Rais is considered to be a torchbearer of the artistic movement in the Emirates. Abdul Rahim Salem, Chairman of the Emirates Fine Arts Society, is also a well known, successful artist who was born and bred in Dubai. His work is unusual in that he doesn't resort to the stereotypical Arabian themes that are so common in the work of other Dubai artists. His modern, striking paintings use colour boldly to evoke a very emotional reaction. Other Emirati artists are Azza al-Qasimi, Sawsan al-Qasimi (of the ruling family of Ras al-Khaimah), Safia Mohammed Khalfan and Khulood Mohammed Ali.

Nevertheless, most of the art you will see in the galleries and shops is by resident expatriates. This is due to the simple fact that they make up such a large percentage of the population. Still, artists who live and work in Dubai, whether Emirati or not, are considered local artists. Even though many of the well known artists are not Emiratis, it is nice to know that many of the themes adopted by them reflect the history and tradition of Dubai: family life, traditional pastimes, souq life, Bedouin heritage and seafaring.

Small exhibitions by local artists and school children are held almost every week in galleries, hotel lobbies, community centres, shopping centres and schools. You'll find details of these exhibitions in the *Gulf News* or *What's On* magazine.

[Continued on page 29]

ARCHITECTURE

Any visitor to Dubai will immediately be struck by its stunning architecture. The incongruous blend of traditional Arabian architecture with science fiction-like modern architectural constructions makes the city quite an amazing sight. A boat ride along the Creek will reveal most of the city's architectural treasures. Moving from the wind-tower houses in the Bastakia Quarter of Bur Dubai to the pointed dhow-like roof of the Dubai Creek Golf & Yacht Club, it's hard to believe you're in the same city.

These modern constructions do sit a little awkwardly with the traditional architecture of the city, but the contrast is representative of other clashes in Dubai – Islamic and western, traditional and modern. It is impossible to compare the traditional and modern architectural styles, simply because they are so different, although some contemporary architecture incorporates traditional elements.

Traditional Architecture

Dubai's traditional architecture was influenced by the demands of the environment, the teachings of Islam and the social structure of the town. There were four categories of buildings – domestic (residential houses), religious (mosques), defensive (forts and watchtowers) and commercial (souqs). Readily available materials, such as gypsum and coral from offshore reefs and from the banks of the Creek, were used. Shaikh Saeed al-Maktoum's House in Shindagha (Map 2) is a fine example of a construction using a mixture of coral and gypsum.

Limestone building blocks were also used and mud served to cement the stones together. However, mud constructions suffered badly in the heat and had a very limited lifespan, sometimes only a few years.

If you wander through the lanes surrounding the Dubai Souq and behind the Al-Ahmadiya School in Deira (Map 2; see the Things to See & Do chapter) you will notice that the alleyways are narrow and the buildings are in close proximity. Houses, souqs and mosques were built in this way to provide maximum shade so that inhabitants could move around the town in comfort, protected from the harsh sun.

There were two types of traditional house – the *masayf* was the summer house (incorporating a windtower) and the *mashait* was the winter house (incorporating a courtyard).

Top: Built in 1896, Sheikh Saeed's house is now a national monument housing an exhibition that traces the early days of the Emirate. Its facade comprises four stunning windtowers. (Photographer: Tony Wheeler)

Windtowers Called *barjeel* in Arabic, windtowers are the Gulf's unique form of nonelectrical air-conditioning. In Dubai, a handful still exist, some atop people's homes; others carefully preserved or reconstructed at museums.

Traditional windtowers rise 5 or 6m above a house. The tower is open on all four sides and catches even small breezes, which are channelled down around a central shaft and into the room below. In the process, the air speeds up and is cooled. The cooler air already in the

ARCHITECTURE

tower shaft pulls in, and subsequently cools, the hotter air outside through simple convection.

The towers work amazingly well. Sitting beneath a windtower when it is 40°C and humid, you will notice a distinct drop in temperature and a consistent breeze even when the air outside feels heavy and still.

The wealthy Persian merchants who settled in Dubai around the turn of the 20th century were the first to build a large number of windtowers in the city. You'll find them in the Bastakia Quarter in Bur Dubai (see Map 2). The merchants brought red clay from Iran, which they mixed with manure to make *saruj*. This was baked in a kiln and was used to build the foundations of the windtower house. Other materials used included coral rock and limestone (for the walls) and plaster (for decorative work). Chandel wood from East Africa, palm-frond matting, mud and straw were used to build the roofs.

Courtyards Traditional houses in Dubai were built around central courtyards. The courtyard, known as *al-housh* in Arabic, was considered the heart and lungs of a house. Today they still provide many homes with light, fresh air and the space for a garden. They are also a place for entertaining and somewhere for children to play; if a family owns livestock, this is where they usually wander.

All the rooms of the house surround the courtyard and all doors and windows open onto it, except those of the guest rooms, which open to the outside of the house. A verandah provides shade on one or more sides of the house and is usually the place where the women weave their mats or sew their clothes. The verandah also serves to keep sun out of the rooms at certain times of the day.

For a fine example of a courtyard house, visit the Heritage House (Map 2) in the Al-Ahmadiya district in Deira. The Bastakia Quarter is home to windtower houses that have been built around a central courtyard – the Majlis Gallery (Map 2) near the Al-Fahidi Roundabout is another prime example.

Barasti The term *barasti* describes both the traditional Arabian method of building a palm-leaf house and the completed house itself. Barasti houses consist of a skeleton of wooden poles made from the trunk of the date palm onto which palm leaves *(areesh)* are woven to form a strong structure through which air can still circulate.

They were extremely common throughout the Gulf in the centuries before the oil boom, though few examples of this type of house still survive today. Those that do are usually fishermen's shacks and storage buildings in rural and coastal areas of the UAE.

They were relatively easy to build and maintain since, unlike mudbrick houses you find in the oases around Al-Ain and Buraimi, they do not require water. The circulation of air through the palms also made barasti houses much cooler than mud-brick structures during the summer.

The courtyard in the Dubai Museum (Map 2) and the Heritage Village in Shindagha (Map 2) both have examples of barasti houses,

CHRIS MELLOR

LOU CALLAN

Top: The windtower, the Gulf's unique form of nonelectrical air-conditioning, enables cool air to be channelled down through the tower and into the house.

Bottom: The interior of Majlis Ghorfat Um-al-Sheef is decorated with cushions, rugs, a coffeepot, pottery and food platters. Built in 1955 and used by Shaikh Rashid bin Saeed al-Maktoum as an audience chamber, it has changed little over the past four decades.

Top: One of Dubai's 188 mosques; its central dome conforms to the Anatolian style.

Bottom Left: Al-Fahidi Fort, erected in 1787, is now home to the Dubai Museum.

Bottom Right: A detail of the original door to Al-Fahidi Fort.

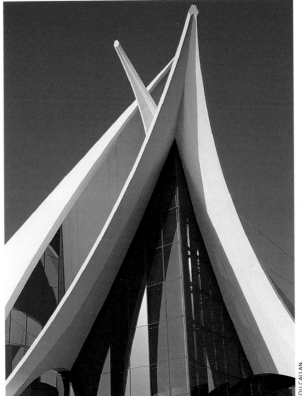

LOU CALLAN

TONY WHEELER

Top: The clubhouse of the Dubai Golf & Yacht Club mirrors the sails of a traditional dhow.

Bottom: The Jumeira Beach Hotel was designed to resemble a breaking wave.

CHRIS MELLOR

CHRIS MELLOR

TONY WHEELER

Top: The Clock Tower roundabout – a landmark in Rigga.

Middle: The modern metropolis: the Etisalat telecommunications building with its giant golfball on the roof (left); the gold-coloured, D-shaped National Bank of Dubai (middle); and the triangular-shaped Dubai Chamber of Commerce & Industry (right).

Bottom: Modern high-rise office buildings have transformed the desert into the commercial hub of the region.

which have been set up for the benefit of Emiratis as well as tourists. You can also see barasti constructions at the Majlis Ghorfat Um-al-Sheef just south-east of the Jumeira Beach Park (Map 1; see also the Things to See & Do chapter).

For a detailed description of how a barasti house is constructed see Geoffrey Bibby's book *Looking for Dilmun*.

Mosques Fundamentally simple structures, mosques are made up of a few basic elements. The most visible of these is the minaret, the tower from which the call to prayer is issued five times a day. Virtually every mosque in the world has a minaret; many have several.

Minarets can be plain or ornate. The first minarets were not built until the early 8th century, some 70 years after the Prophet's death. The idea for minarets may have originated with the bell towers that Muslim armies found attached to some of the churches they converted into mosques during the early years of Islam.

A mosque must also have a mihrab, a niche in the wall facing Mecca, indicating the *qibla*, the direction believers must face while praying. Like minarets, mihrabs can be simple or elaborate, and they are thought to have been introduced into Islamic architecture around the beginning of the 8th century.

The *minbar* (also pronounced 'mimbar') dates from the Prophet's lifetime. It is a pulpit chair, traditionally reached by three steps.

In addition, a mosque needs to have a water supply so that worshippers can perform the ablutions that are required before they begin praying.

There are currently 88 mosques in Deira, 61 in Bur Dubai and another 39 outside the central city. The neighbourhood mosques tend to be used for weekday prayers, with worshippers travelling further afield to the larger mosques for Friday prayers.

The Jumeira Mosque (Map 5) conforms to the Anatolian style, identified by a massive central dome. Some other mosques in Dubai are based on Iranian and Central Asian models, which have more domes covering different areas of the mosque.

Right: The Jumeira Mosque conforms to the 'Anatolian' style of design with its large central dome.

LOU CALLAN

One stunning example is the Iranian Mosque (Map 5) on Al-Wasl Rd. The multidomed Grand Mosque (Map 2) in Bur Dubai is a variation on the Anatolian style. Other mosques, such as the Bin Suroor Mosque (Map 2) in Shindagha, are small and box-like. Above all they serve the most basic of purposes – to provide a place for people to pray.

Modern Architecture

Dubai's relentless building boom has lured architects from the world over who want to be part of Dubai's metamorphosis into a modern metropolis. This has resulted in an eclectic influence in the design and architecture of the city. There is enough wealth in Dubai to fund the most ambitious of projects and, unlike in Abu Dhabi where all architecture must have Islamic features such as archways, there are no such restrictions on architects in Dubai. Only the normal provisos are enforced – a certain amount of ground coverage, sufficient public access and safety aspects, adequate parking amenities etc.

The intense heat and humidity, however, reduce the life expectancy of buildings in Dubai to only 20 to 25 years. Surprisingly, this is an issue that has not yet been addressed by the Dubai Municipality. The regulations followed up until now date to the early 1970s and completely ignore the heat factor.

About 90% of Dubai's architecture can be described as 'cosmopolitan' or 'international', and is made of concrete, steel and glass. These materials, more than any others, absorb the heat and transfer it to all parts of the construction, causing damage over a period of time. Recently, lightweight thermal blocks have been introduced. Though they are expensive, and therefore not widely used, they have great heat resistance. In addition, the final coating on buildings is usually light and contains reflective paint.

Most of the large-scale building projects in Dubai are carried out by foreign architecture firms, usually from Europe. Fortunately, these companies tend to take into account the heat and humidity and design and build accordingly.

Jumeira Beach Hotel Designed by UK-based architects WS Atkins & Partners, the Arabian Tower *(Burj al-Arab)* at the Jumeira Beach Hotel has become a major landmark in Dubai and its most recognisable structure. Completed in 1999, it was built on an artificially constructed island about 300m from the shore. The 60-floor, sail-shaped structure is 321m high, including the thin spire on top. The hotel has 300 suites, a casino and an underwater restaurant among other facilities. Two observation structures and a helipad extend from two sides at the top of the building.

The older, original hotel building is a long, S-shaped construction, intended to represent a wave with the Gulf as its backdrop. The glimmering facades of both buildings are achieved through the use of reflective glass and aluminium. The two structures combined – a huge sail hovering over a breaking wave – symbolise Dubai's maritime heritage.

National Bank of Dubai This shimmering golden building, overlooking Dubai Creek in Deira (Map 3), has become the quintessential symbol of Dubai. Designed by the Swedish firm, Carlos Ott & Norr Group International, and completed in 1997, it is best described as a long, thin D-shape, with the curved part facing the Creek. The bronze windows reflect the activity on the Creek and at sunset, when the light is just right, it is a beautiful sight.

Dubai Chamber of Commerce & Industry Next door to the National Bank of Dubai, this triangular building is blanketed in sheets of blue glass. From some angles the building takes on a one-dimensional appearance, like a great featureless monolith.

Dubai Creek & Yacht Golf Club When you cross over either bridge in Dubai you will no doubt notice the pointed white roof of the Dubai Creek Golf & Yacht Club (Map 1) set amid acres of lush green lawns and artificial, undulating hillocks. The idea behind this 1993 UK design by Brian Johnson (for Godwin, Austen and Johnson Architects) was to incorporate a traditional element into the design. From the outside, the white clubhouse mirrors the sails of a traditional Arab dhow. Inside, it's a temple of modern western comfort.

Left: The *Burj al-Arab* (Arabian Tower) at the Jumeira Beach Hotel, is built on an artificially constructed island 300m offshore.

Right: The shimmering golden coloured National Bank of Dubai building has become the quintessential symbol of Dubai.

LOU CALLAN

TONY WHEELER

Etisalat Building Recognisable by the giant, sparkling golf ball that perches above this building, the Etisalat headquarters is on the corner of Al-Maktoum Rd and Omar ibn al-Khattab Rd (Map 3). Designed by the Canadian firm Cansult Ltd and completed in 1990, the building's distinct ball now sits on top of Etisalat's other main buildings in each emirate, enabling Etisalat to be easily spotted wherever you go in the UAE. It represents the world encompassed by the power of global communications. At night the ball seems to sparkle as little lights come on all around it.

Emirates Training Building No, you're not about to get wiped out by an aircraft that's slightly off course. This building, designed by UK architect Brian Johnson (who also designed the Dubai Creek Golf & Yacht Club), is located on Al-Garhoud Rd at the Deira entrance to the bridge (Map 1) and is designed to look like the front end of an aeroplane. It's gimmicky, but eye-catching.

Port Rashid Customs Authority There are no prizes for speculating correctly on the concept behind this design. The Port Rashid Customs Authority (Map 2), on Al-Mina Rd (just south of Khalid bin al-Waleed Rd), looks like the hulls of two enormous dhows from a distance. The bows extend to sit like gargoyles on either side of the entrance to the building. The two hulls run down the side of the building and the offices sit between them. Construction began in 1999 and was still underway at the time of writing.

Left: The Etisalat telecommunications headquarters – identifiable by the giant golf ball on the roof.

Right: The triangular-shaped Dubai Chamber of Commerce & Industry building is covered in sheets of blue glass.

[Continued from page 22]

The Sharjah Art Museum (see the Excursions chapter), which is headed up by the painter Abdul Rahim Salem, exhibits some work by local artists although the bulk of its collection comes from overseas. There has been a concerted effort by the Sharjah Ministry of Culture to encourage local artists, both Emiratis and resident expatriates, to come together and practice their art at the Artists' Studio in Sharjah.

Crafts

On the whole, traditional crafts are confined to Dubai's museums and to exhibitions in hotel lobbies during the Dubai Summer Surprises or Dubai Shopping Festival. You will occasionally come across small amounts of local craft in the Dubai Souq in Bur Dubai.

Most of the pottery you will see is made outside Dubai in the mountainous areas of Ras al-Khaimah, Fujairah and Dibba where the sand is more suitable for making clay. Traditional pots of various shapes and sizes have different uses. A *khir* is used to preserve dates. Milk is stored in a *birnah* and a *hibb* keeps water cold. Pots are also used as cooking vessels.

For centuries the Bedouin have used date-palm fronds to weave various household items. The cone-shaped mat used to cover food is called a *surood* while the large, round floor mat on which food is placed is called a *semma*. A *jefeer* is a shopping basket and a *mehaffa* is a hand fan. You will also find some camel bags or cushion covers woven from camel hair as well as *talli* work. Talli is the interweaving of different coloured cotton threads with silver or gold threads to make decorative ankle, wrist and neck bands which are worn by women at special events such as weddings.

Arabic perfumes and incenses are still concocted in small workshops near the perfume souq in Deira. The most common type of Arabic perfume is *attar*, a heavily scented, oil-based fragrance. Another form is *bahoor* (incense) which comes in a compressed powder form. Then there is frank-incense (*luban* in Arabic). Traditionally used to perfume a room, incense was also used by men and women to keep their clothes smelling nice and to cover up the smell of sweat.

SOCIETY & CONDUCT
Traditional Culture

Although a tolerant and relaxed society, Dubai's cultural life is very firmly rooted in Islam (see Religion later in this chapter for more information). Day-to-day activities, relationships, diet and dress are dictated by religion as much as by Arabian traditions.

In Dubai there is very little of the traditional Arabic and Bedouin culture left for tourists to observe. The skeletons of this past life still exist in the form of the old buildings in Bur Dubai along the waterfront near the souq and in Deira around Al-Ahmadiya School (see Map 2). But, if you want an idea of traditional culture, you need to visit the Dubai Museum or venture out of Dubai to some of the villages around the east coast and to Al-Ain where life appears not to be too far removed from the way it was before federation.

Boat building is still practised, but only on a small scale. Date cultivation is still an important part of life, though it is no longer as necessary to survival as it once was. Pearling was once the livelihood of many coastal inhabitants, but you will have to visit the museum to learn about it now.

Dubai has been very active over the last few years in trying to revive and preserve many of the traditions that have diminished in the wake of modernity, wealth and the

---

The Nose Tickle

You may notice some Emirati men greeting each other by touching noses and making a clicking sound with their tongues while shaking hands. While this is a traditional Emirati greeting, you shouldn't try it yourself. It would be seen as very strange indeed if you attempted to greet an Emirati friend in this way.

Falconry

For this traditional Bedouin hunting method a falcon had to be caught and trained in time for the migration season of the houbara bustard. The houbara (now protected) was the preferred prey of the falconer because it was small enough to be caught by the falcon yet big enough to feed a small family. At the end of the migration season in spring, the falcon was let go and another would be caught in autumn to repeat the process. The Bedouin had many ways of catching a falcon, but the most amazing method was for a man to be buried in the sand with just his head and arm above the surface. His arm was then hidden within a bush that had a live pigeon tied to it. The fluttering pigeon would attract the falcon and, when the unsuspecting falcon was close enough, the buried man would throw a cloth over its head, immobilising it. It may sound primitive, but it was an effective method that has been passed down through generations of Bedouin.

Falconry is still practiced in the UAE, though now of course not so much out of necessity than as a social pastime, and as a way of continuing an ancient tradition. One place you're likely to see a spot of falconry is in Al-Ain in the late afternoon, at the west side of the base of Jebel Hafit.

Falconry is a traditional Bedouin hunting method.

influx of foreigners. The Heritage Village in Hatta (see the Excursions chapter) displays traditional village life, as does the Dubai Museum and the Heritage Village (Map 2) in Shindagha. Expensive restoration work is being carried out on traditional turn-of-the-century houses in Deira (Al-Ahmadiya District) and Bur Dubai (Bastakia Quarter). The aim of such work is not just to attract and entertain tourists, it is also designed to educate young Emiratis about their culture and heritage.

Festivals such as the Dubai Shopping Festival and Dubai Summer Surprises usually feature displays of traditional song and dance as well as food and crafts, although it seems that more and more of these events are being pushed aside in favour of such inane attractions as ice-cream eating competitions and giant sandwich-making contests.

Traditional lifestyle is being equally eroded by the latest trend in marriage: Nationals are increasingly marrying foreign women. In some cases this is because of the cost of a traditional wedding, plus the dowry that the groom must provide, has become a burden. It's cheaper and easier to marry a foreign wife. Sociologists in the UAE are adamant that this can only have a negative impact on Emirati children and the destruction of traditional culture.

The marriage fund, set up in 1994 by the federal government to facilitate marriages between UAE Nationals, grants Dh70,000 to each couple to pay for the exorbitant cost of the wedding and dowry. Mass weddings also take place regularly, allowing Nationals to save most of the grant for a down payment on a house and other living costs.

Traditional Dress

Almost all Emiratis wear traditional dress – there is rarely an exception. Men wear the 'I-don't-know-how-they-keep-it-so-clean' ankle-length, white dishdasha. The gutra is the white head cloth which is held on the head by a black coil called an agal. Sometimes men wear a red and white checked gutra although most often you'll find that they may be from elsewhere in the Gulf. Underneath the gutra men wear a lace skull-cap called a *taqia*; sometimes they will just wear the taqia on its own. On special occasions, shaikhs and other important men will wear a black or gold cloak, called an *abba*, over their dishdasha. You will see a picture in the newspaper almost every day of Shaikh Zayed or Shaikh Maktoum wearing their abbas for important diplomatic meetings.

Women wear a long, black cloak, called an *abaya*, which covers everything from head to foot. In addition, a black head cloth called the *shayla* is usually worn over the top to cover the face. In the more rural areas, women also wear the *burqa*, a stiff mask made of gold-coloured material that covers the eyebrows, nose and mouth. Sometimes, however, the burqa is just a simple piece of black chiffon tied around the head and covering the face from under the eyes down.

Underneath their abayas women wear whatever they want. Among the younger women in Dubai this may even be tight pants and tops; however, the traditional costume is a simple floral dress called a *kandoura*. Men also wear a kandoura that is like a short-sleeved kaftan. On special occasions women wear *sirwal* under their kandouras. These are loose trousers that come in tight from the knee down and are often decorated around the ankles with gold and coloured thread called talli.

Dos & Don'ts

- Though alcohol is legal in Dubai, you should never, ever drive while you're drunk. If you are caught doing so there will be, at the very least, a steep fine to pay and you may wind up spending a month or more in jail.
- It is impolite to photograph people without asking their permission. Avoid pointing your camera at police stations, airports and palaces.
- Even though Dubai is very used to the habits of a wide variety of nationalities and is particularly forgiving of westerners and their *faux pas*, etiquette is still very important. You will generate more respect for yourself if you remember a few basic rules.
- Always stand when someone enters the room. Upon entering a room yourself shake hands with everyone, touching your heart with the palm of the right hand after each handshake. This goes for both Arab men and women, though men finding themselves in the presence

of Arab women should not offer to shake hands unless the woman takes the lead by extending her hand first. Western women will occasionally find that a man may not extend his hand to shake theirs, or he will cover his hand with his dishdasha first and extend his fist. This is because some stricter Muslims will not touch a woman who is not part of their family.
- When two men meet it is considered polite for them to inquire after each other's families but *not* each other's wives.
- If you are in a frustrating situation, be patient, friendly and sensitive. Never lose your temper. A confrontational attitude doesn't go well with the Arab personality and loss of face is a sensitive issue. If you have a problem with someone, be firm, calm and persistent.
- You'll notice that people do not use the term 'thank you' as much as in the west. This is because one is expected to repay significant favours by actions – words alone are not enough. For a service that is paid for or expected, eg a bell-boy bringing luggage to a room, thanks are not considered necessary.
- Men should never appear bare-chested in public, except when at the beach or at a swimming pool. Emiratis in Dubai are used to seeing westerners in shorts and they are seen as something comical rather than offensive. If you do wear shorts they should be relatively long – all the way to the knee if possible – but don't wear them into someone's home.
- Women should wear loose-fitting clothing that is not revealing. Even in Dubai, where you see exposed midriffs, short skirts and tight pants, you should still consider the impression you are making. Bathing suits are OK for the beach, though women may want to cover up more at public beaches to avoid the ogling of men.
- It is common to attach forms of address to people's given names. Just as Arabs refer to each other as 'Mr Mohammed' or 'Mr Abdullah', they will refer to you as 'Mr John', 'Mr Stephen', 'Miss Simone' or 'Mrs Susan'. Often women will be referred to by their husband's name, for instance 'Mrs Tony'.
- The word 'shaikh' applies *only* to members of the ruling family. The rulers themselves carry the formal title of 'Emir' (literally, 'Prince'), but are usually referred to as 'shaikhs', as in 'Shaikh Mohammed bin Rashid al-Maktoum'. The feminine form of shaikh is 'shaikha'. It applies to all female members of the ruling family.

For information on business etiquette see Doing Business in the Facts for the Visitor chapter.

RELIGION

Though other religions are tolerated in Dubai, the most common religion in town is Islam. As with any religion embracing about one billion people, Islam has produced many sects, movements and offshoots.

Most of Dubai's Muslim population are Sunni Muslims subscribing to the Maliki or Hanbali schools of Islamic law. Many of the latter are Wahhabis, though UAE Wahhabis are not nearly as strict and puritanical as the Wahhabis of Saudi Arabia. There is also a smaller community of Shi'ite Muslims, descendants mainly from merchants and workers who crossed to the Trucial Coast from Persia in the late 19th or early 20th century.

Non-Muslims are not permitted to enter mosques in the UAE.

Islam

Muslims believe the religion preached by the Prophet Mohammed to be God's final revelation to humanity. For them the Quran (meaning 'the recitation' in Arabic) represents God's words revealed through the Prophet. It supplements and completes the earlier revelations around which the Christian and Jewish faiths were built, and corrects misinterpretations of those earlier revelations.

For example, Muslims believe that Jesus was a prophet second only to Mohammed in importance, but that his followers later introduced into Christianity the heretical idea that Jesus was the son of God. Adam, Abraham, Moses and a number of other Christian and Jewish holy men are regarded as prophets by Muslims. Mohammed, however, was the 'Seal of the Prophets' – the last one who has, or will, come.

The essence of Islam is the belief that there is only one God and that it is the people's duty to believe in and serve Him in the manner which He has laid out in the Quran. In Arabic, *Islam* means submission and a *Muslim* is one who submits to God's will.

In the first instance, one does this by observing five pillars which are the central tenets of the faith (see the boxed text 'The Five Pillars of Islam'). Beyond these five pillars there are many other duties incumbent on Muslims.

In the west the best known and least understood of these is jihad. This is usually translated into English as 'holy war', but literally means 'striving in the way of the faith'. Exactly what this means has been the subject of keen debate among Muslim scholars for the last 1400 years. Some scholars have tended to see jihad in spiritual, as opposed to martial, terms.

Muslims are forbidden to eat or drink anything containing pork or alcohol, and the meat (or blood) of any animal that died of natural causes (as opposed to having been slaughtered in the prescribed manner). Muslim women may not marry non-Muslim men, though Muslim men are permitted to marry Christian or Jewish women (but not, for example, Hindus or Buddhists).

Sunnis & Shi'ites

The schism that divided the Muslim world into two broad camps took place only a few years after the death of the Prophet. When Mohammed died in 632, he left no clear instructions either designating a successor or setting up a system by which subsequent leaders could be chosen. Some Muslims felt that leadership of the community should remain within the Prophet's family, and supported the claim of Ali bin Abi Taleb, Mohammed's cousin and son-in-law and one of the first converts to Islam, to become the caliph, or leader. But the rest of the community chose Abu Bakr, the Prophet's closest companion, as leader, and Ali was passed over in two subsequent leadership contests.

This split the Muslim community into two competing factions. Those who took Ali's side became known as the *shiat Ali*, or 'partisans of Ali'. Because Shi'ites have rarely held power over long periods of time, their doctrine came to emphasise the spiritual position of their leaders, the imams. Sunni belief, on the other hand, essentially holds that any Muslim who rules with justice and according to the Sharia'a (Islamic law) deserves the support of the Muslim community as a whole.

subterranean serenity: the Arabian Gulf is a perfect spot for scuba diving and the chance of a close encounter with a blue-spotted grouper (left) or a clown anemone fish (right).

LOU CALLAN

Urban Eden: the Dubai Creek Golf Club is home to the Dubai Creek Open on the Asian PGA Tour.

CHRIS MELLOR

The Dubai World Cup, the world's richest horse race, is held every March.

CHRISTINE OSBORNE

Sand-skiing on desert dunes has become the latest Arabian fad.

The Five Pillars of Islam

1. **Shahadah** (the profession of faith): To become a Muslim one need only state the Islamic creed, 'There is no God but God, and Mohammed is the messenger of God', with conviction.

2. **Salat** (Prayer): Muslims are required to pray five times every day: at dawn, noon, mid-afternoon, sunset and twilight. During prayers a Muslim must perform a series of prostrations while facing the Qaaba, the ancient shrine at the centre of the Grand Mosque in Mecca. Before a Muslim can pray, however, he or she must perform a series of ritual ablutions, and if no water is available for this purpose sand or soil may be substituted.

3. **Zakat** (charity or alms): Muslims must give a portion of their income to help the poor. How this has operated in practice has varied over the centuries: either it was seen as an individual duty or the state collected it as a form of income tax to be redistributed through mosques or religious charities.

4. **Sawm** (fasting): It was during the month of Ramadan that Mohammed received his first revelation in 610 AD. Muslims mark this event by fasting from sunrise until sunset throughout Ramadan. During the fast a Muslim may not take anything into his or her body. Food, drink, smoking and sex are banned. Young children, travellers and those whose health will not permit it are exempt from the fast, though those who are able to do so are supposed to make up the days they missed at a later time.

5. **Haj** (pilgrimage): All able Muslims are required to make the pilgrimage to Mecca at least once, if possible during a specific few days in the first and second weeks of the Muslim month of Dhul Hijja. Visiting Mecca and performing the prescribed rituals at any other time of the year is considered spiritually desirable. Such visits are referred to as *umrah*, or 'little pilgrimage'.

Wahhabism

Wahhabism takes its name from Mohammed bin Abdul Wahhab (1703-92), a preacher and judge who, after seeing an ever-increasing lack of respect for Islam among the Bedouin tribes of central Arabia, preached a return to Islam's origins and traditions as interpreted by the Hanbali school of Islamic jurisprudence. This meant strict adherence to the Quran and the Hadith (accounts of the Prophet's words and actions).

Wahhabism is a rather austere form of Islam. Wahhabis reject such concepts as sainthood and forbid the observance of holidays such as the Prophet's Birthday. Even the term Wahhabi makes strict followers of the sect uncomfortable because it appears to exalt Mohammed bin Abdul Wahhab over the Prophet. Strict Wahhabis prefer the term *muwahidin*, which translates as 'unitarian', because they profess only the unity of God.

Islamic Law

The Arabic word Sharia'a is usually translated as 'Islamic Law'. This is misleading. The Sharia'a is not a legal code in the western sense of the term. It refers to the general body of Islamic legal thought. Where the Quran does not provide guidance on a particular subject, Muslim scholars turn to the Sunna, a body of works recording the sayings and doings of the Prophet and, to a lesser extent, his companions as reported by a string of scholarly authorities.

The Quran and Sunna together make up the basis of Sharia'a. In some instances the Sharia'a is quite specific (eg inheritance law and punishments for certain offences). In many other cases it acts as a series of guidelines. Islam does not recognise a distinction between the secular and religious lives of believers. Thus, a scholar or judge can, with enough research through use of analogy, determine the proper 'Islamic' position on any problem.

There are many Sunna authorities and their reliability is determined by the school of Islamic jurisprudence to which one subscribes. There are four main Sunni and two principal Shi'ite schools of Islamic jurisprudence. The orthodox Sunni schools of jurisprudence are the Shafi'i, Hanbali, Hanafi and Maliki. All but the first of these schools are found widely in the Gulf, though Hanbali is the largest in Dubai. Hanbali Islam is generally regarded as the sternest of the four orthodox Sunni rites. The largest schools of Shi'ite jurisprudence are the Jafari and the Akhbari.

LANGUAGE

Arabic is the official language of Dubai while English is the language of business, though it competes with Urdu as the lingua franca. You will have little trouble making yourself understood, though when you venture out to the rural areas you will find that English is not as widespread. Knowing the Iranian language, Farsi, will help you get by. Urdu and Malayalam (the language of Kerala in India) can both be reasonably useful because of the large number of Pakistani and Indian expats. For some useful words in Arabic see the Language chapter.

Facts for the Visitor

ORIENTATION

Dubai is really two towns merged as one and divided by Dubai Creek: Deira is to the north of the Creek and Bur Dubai to the south. Both districts are home to Dubai's traditional architecture and souqs.

Although Deira and Bur Dubai are actually only small districts on either side of the Creek near its mouth, locals often use these terms to refer to entire areas north and south of the Creek.

Deira is the city centre, although new office buildings along Shaikh Zayed Rd on the south side of the Creek have created a second city centre. Activity in Deira focuses on Beniyas Rd, which runs along the Creek, Beniyas Square (which used to be called Al-Nasr Square and is still generally known by that name), Al-Maktoum Rd, Al-Maktoum Hospital Rd, and Naif Rd. The Deira souq, around which most of the cheap hotels are located, occupies most of the area west of Beniyas Square and south of Naif Rd.

On the Bur Dubai side, the older souq area runs from Al-Ghubaiba Rd (where the bus station is) to the Ruler's Office and inland as far as Khalid bin al-Waleed Rd.

There are four ways of crossing the Creek: Al-Shindagha Tunnel runs under the Creek at the western end, near its mouth (there is also a pedestrian tunnel here); Al-Maktoum Bridge, on the eastern edge of the centre, is the main traffic artery across the waterway; farther east, Al-Garhoud Bridge is used mostly by traffic trying to bypass the centre; and *abras*, small, flat-decked water-taxis crisscross the waterway throughout the day.

There are no street addresses in Dubai. People usually refer to the main roads by name but nobody knows the names of the smaller, numbered streets. You'll find that addresses are given as 'Green Emirates Building at the Falcon roundabout' or 'the white villa, next to the big tree, across from the Avari Hotel'. Of course, these instructions assume that you know the Falcon roundabout or the Avari Hotel. Don't worry if you don't know them because a taxi driver most likely will.

Many main streets are known by more familiar names and can therefore cause confusion. You should be aware of the following:

official name	other names
Al-Jumeira Rd	Jumeira Rd, Jumeira Beach Rd or Beach Rd
Al-Wasl Rd	Iranian Hospital Rd
Beniyas Square	Al-Nasr Square
Khalid bin al-Waleed Rd	Bank St (when referring to the section that runs from Za'abeel Rd to Trade Centre Rd)
Shaikh Zayed Rd	Abu Dhabi Rd

MAPS

Maps of Dubai are available from the bigger bookshops around town (see Bookshops in the Shopping chapter for location details). You should also be able to get all of the maps mentioned here in the bookshops at five star hotels.

Geoprojects publishes a map of Dubai which is reasonably good, but it doesn't include the names of all the minor streets. It is available from most bookshops and hotels for Dh50.

The maps in *Dubai Tourist and Business Guide* are also by Geoprojects and cost Dh50. They are very detailed and are probably the best maps available if you are negotiating your way around Dubai by car. However, at the time of writing, it was only available in Arabic.

The same maps appear in the enormous *Dubai Tourist Map*, at a cost of Dh60. It has a picture of the Dubai Creek Golf & Yacht Club on the front. There is also the *Dubai 3D Tourist Map* which is useful for locating landmarks such as hotels, souqs and banks around town. It costs Dh45.

When to Go

Month	Advantages	Disadvantages
January	The weather is a cool 24°C. It's Ramadan and hotels offer up to 70% off their normal rates, so luxury hotels become affordable for most budgets. You'll have the city to yourself – most tourists stay away in Ramadan. The breaking of the fast *(iftar)* each evening is a big event and the streets tend to come alive after dark. It's an exciting time to be here, though the restrictions can be a bane.	You can't eat, drink or smoke in public during daylight hours. Often the only place you can eat during the day is in your hotel room, although most hotels will serve breakfast and lunch in their restaurants. Shops are shut for the afternoon, even in the shopping centres, and they don't open until about 7 pm. Some tour companies reduce the number of tours on offer at this time of year and the tourist industry in general slows down during this sacred month.
February	This is probably the nicest month of the year weather-wise. The tour companies start up their day trips to the deserts and mountains again. Although many tourists come in February, it is not as busy as October and November.	There is the occasional rain shower although this can hardly be seen as a disadvantage as rain is such a treat in this part of the world.
March-April	The Dubai Shopping Festival is on (although any month is a good month to shop in Dubai). It's a shopping frenzy and shops supposedly lower their prices during the festival, but we have found that prices tend to be the same as any other time of the year. The advantage, however, is that each time you spend money in any of the shopping centres, you get raffle tickets that could win you cash, cars or shopping vouchers.	The hoards of shoppers can be a disincentive to travel to Dubai at this time of year. You'll need to book hotels ahead as they get very full and prices rise somewhat as proprietors look to cash in on the shopping season. The occasional dust storm sweeps into town and creates momentary havoc.

When to Go

Month	Advantages	Disadvantages
May	The tourist season is petering out and although it's hot (mid to high 30s), it's not too hot to walk around in the early mornings and evenings. The middle of the day is strictly for indoors, unless you are the sort of person who can lie on the beach in this heat. Hotels begin offering summer discounts (up to 70%) from mid to late May.	The heat will be too much for most people; you may find yourself restricted to indoor activities.
June	Cheap hotels	Too darn hot
July-August	The hotels are still remarkably cheap. Dubai Summer Surprises are held – a series of events and promotions, mainly to attract visitors to the shopping centres. (It's too hot to be anywhere else.) This is when you can see traditional dancing and music displays, handicrafts being made and exhibitions of local art works and crafts.	The heat and humidity is so extreme that you can only be outdoors for a few minutes at a time. Just walking along the street at night can be an exhausting and sweaty experience.
September	Most hotels have discounted summer rates until mid-September.	It's still too hot – about 39°C – though there is the occasional downpour that can entirely flood the roads.
October-November	The weather is tropical and lovely and it's the perfect time for a beach holiday. Tour companies are well and truly back into the swing of things by now and there are countless activities on offer.	Hotels put their prices up in early November because of the Dubai Air Show, which attracts people from all over the world – though one wonders why.
December	Delicious, wonderful winter. Warm days and cool evenings.	None to speak of.

FACTS FOR THE VISITOR

FACTS FOR THE VISITOR

RESPONSIBLE TOURISM

Although tourism in Dubai has not reached the heights it has in other Middle Eastern cities, it does have an impact on the environment. There are a number of things you can do to be a more responsible tourist. A British organisation called Tourism Concern (☎ 020-7753 3330), Stapleton House, 177-281 Holloway Rd, London N7 8NN, has come up with some guidelines for travellers who wish to minimise the impact on the countries they visit. They have a Web site at www.gn.apc.org/tourismconcern. We have adapted some of their suggestions for visitors to Dubai:

- Preserve natural resources. Try not to waste water. Switch off lights and air-con when you go out, though in midsummer you will need to leave the air-con on.
- Ask before taking photographs of people, especially women. Don't worry if you don't speak Arabic. A smile and gesture will be understood and appreciated.
- Remember that the UAE is a Muslim country and even though Dubai is the most international and cosmopolitan city of the Gulf, revealing clothes will still cause offence to most people.
- Similarly, public displays of affection between members of the opposite sex are inappropriate.
- Learning something about Dubai's history and culture helps prevent misunderstandings and frustrations.

You must also be aware of environmental issues. The invention of the jet ski has to be seen as an environmental step backwards. Before you hire a jet ski remember that they pollute the water, make an awful noise and are just plain dangerous when there are swimmers and other watercraft around.

Desert safaris in a 4WD make for a popular day excursion for visitors, but they are not environmentally sound activities. Expats are just as guilty of 'dune-bashing' the environment as tourists are, as the sport is increasingly becoming a popular weekend pastime. The government has set out a number of guidelines, aimed at the tour companies for whom these activities are the main source of income. If you are taking part in any desert activities you should take note of these guidelines:

- To minimise your impact on the land, stick to the tracks and avoid damaging the all-too-rare vegetation that is such an important part of the fragile desert ecosystem.
- Driving in wadis (seasonal river beds) should be avoided if possible to ensure that they are not polluted with oil and grease. They are sometimes important sources of irrigation and drinking water.
- When diving or snorkelling, avoid touching or removing any marine life, especially coral.
- If you plan to camp out, remember to take your own wood – don't pull limbs from trees or uproot shrubs. Plants may look dead but usually they are not.

TOURIST OFFICES
Local Tourist Offices

The Department of Tourism and Commerce Marketing (DTCM) is the official tourism board of the Dubai Government (☎ 223 0000). It is also the sole regulating, planning and licensing authority for the tourist industry in Dubai. It has three Welcome Bureaus you can call for information or for help in booking hotels, tours and car hire: at the airport arrivals area (☎ 224 5252), in Beniyas Square in Deira (Map 2; ☎ 228 5000) and about 40km out of town on Shaikh Zayed Rd on the way to Abu Dhabi (☎ 846 827). All they'll give you are a few glossy pamphlets and some fairly useless maps. The one at the airport is open 24 hours and the other two are open from 7 am to 2 pm and from 4 to 11 pm daily. You can generally get better information, however, from tour operators and some of the larger hotels.

Dubai National Travel & Tourist Authority (known as 'Danata') is the quasi-official travel agency in Dubai; it has the monopoly on travel services at wholesale level. The head office (Map 3; ☎ 295 1111) is at the Airline Centre on Al-Maktoum Rd, Deira (for information on organised tours arranged outside the UAE see the Getting There & Away chapter; for tours arranged in Dubai see the Getting Around chapter).

Tourist Offices Abroad

The DTCM has a number of branches overseas that are vigorously promoting Dubai as an upmarket tourist destination. These branches go by the name of the Dubai

Commerce & Tourism Promotion Board and contact details are:

Australia & New Zealand
(☎ 02-9267 7871, fax 9283 1202)
Level 7, 210 Clarence St, Sydney 2000
CIS & Baltic States
(☎ 95-745 8700, fax 745 8706)
Krasina St, 14, Bldg 2, 1st Floor, 123056 Moscow
East Africa
(☎ 2-246 909, fax 219 787)
Jubilee Insurance Exchange, Kaunda St, PO Box 30702, Nairobi, Kenya
France
(☎ 01-44 95 85 00, fax 01-45 63 13 14)
15 bis Rue de Marignan, 75008 Paris
Germany
(☎ 69-710 0020, fax 710 0234)
Bockenheimer Landstrasse 23, D-60325, Frankfurt/Main
Hong Kong
(☎ 852-802 9002, fax 827 2511)
Suite 1203-4 Shui On Centre, 6-8 Harbour Rd, Hong Kong
India
(☎ 22-283 3497, fax 283 3510)
51 Bajaj Bhavan, 5th Floor, Nariman Point, Mumbai 400 021
Italy
(☎ 2-7202 2466, fax 7202 0162)
Piazza Bertarelle 1, 20122 Milan
Japan
(☎ 3-3379 9311, fax 3379 9313)
One-Win Yoyogi Bldg, 4th Floor, 3-35-10 Yoyogi Shibuya-ku, Tokyo 151
Scandinavia
(☎ 8-411 1135, fax 411 1138)
Skeppsbron 22, SE-111 30 Stockholm
South Africa
(☎ 11-784 6708, fax 784 6442)
5th Floor, Sandton City Office Towers, Sandton City, Johannesburg 2000
UK & Ireland
(☎ 20-7839 0580, fax 7839 0582)
34 Buckingham Palace Rd, London SW1W ORE
USA
(☎ 215-751 9750, fax 751 9551)
8 Penn Centre, Philadelphia, PA 19103
(☎ 310-752 4488, fax 752 4444)
901 Wilshire Blvd, Santa Monica, CA 90401

Note that if you are dialling from within these countries you may have to dial 0 before the city code.

DOCUMENTS
Visas

To visit Dubai your passport must have at least two months validity left from your date of arrival.

Citizens of other Gulf Cooperative Council (GCC) countries and British nationals with the right of abode in the UK do not need visas to enter the UAE. GCC nationals can stay pretty much as long as they want. For others a transit or tourist visa must be arranged through a sponsor. This can be a hotel, a company or a resident of the UAE. Most hotels will charge a fee for arranging a visa (see the Hotel-Sponsored Visas section later in this chapter). If you are flying on Emirates or Gulf Air they can arrange a single-entry visa for Dh150. Emirates can also arrange a visa and accommodation at a four star hotel for US$55 per day. Good value if you're stopping over for a couple of days; not so for economical stays.

A standard, single-entry visa is valid for two months, costs Dh110 and must be used within two months of the date of issue. The most common way to enter Dubai is on a 14-day transit visa which costs Dh120. This cannot be extended or renewed, but it is processed more quickly. If your visa has been arranged by a friend through their company, this is probably what you will get.

Wusta

This translates loosely as 'influence high up'. Never underestimate the power of wusta. It is a very desirable thing to have. It can be especially useful when you're trying to get through tedious and protracted administrative procedures, such as registering a car. A little wusta at the Traffic Police is very handy indeed.

Most westerners get a little outraged at the thought of a select few receiving favours and special treatment because of powerful contacts. While wusta is an accepted part of life in Dubai, in the west it's given other names: 'favouritism', 'bias', 'nepotism' and often just plain 'luck'.

Visas for Other Middle Eastern Countries

You may want to apply for a visa for further travel in the Middle East while you are in Dubai. Remember that it is not possible to get visas to some countries in the region from consulates in Dubai. You may have to arrange them before you leave home. Also, if you are a resident in Dubai the requirements are sometimes different to those that apply if you are here on a tourist visa.

Bahrain Transit visas and one week tourist visas can be purchased on arrival at the airport. Prices differ for almost every nationality.

Egypt The procedure is the same for both tourists and GCC residents. You'll need your passport and one photo. Fees vary and visas take a few days to process: for most nationalities it costs Dh65, for British passport holders it costs Dh235.

Iran Tourist visa holders will not be able to obtain an Iranian visa from the consulate. You will have to go through a travel agency that will organise your trip and sponsor your visa. The one recommended by the Iranian consulate is Al-Firdoos Travel (☎ 666 422), 5th floor, office No 516, Gate 8, Hamarain Centre, Abu Baker al-Siddiq Rd, Rigga. You'll need a photocopy of your passport and two photos. GCC residents can go to the consulate with their passport, one photo and Dh185 to obtain a one month tourist visa. Allow a few days for processing.

Kuwait If you are in Dubai on a tourist visa you cannot organise a visa through the Kuwaiti consulate. You will have to organise it before you leave from the embassy in your home country. GCC residents will need a sponsorship letter from their employer, two photos, original passport plus one photocopy and an invitation from a company or hotel in Kuwait. Fees vary and visas take two days to process. It's free for some nationalities, Dh70 for US passport holders.

Oman You will need two photos, original passport plus one photocopy and, if you are a GCC resident, a sponsorship letter from your company. Resident spouses without a company sponsorship who wish to travel alone will also need a letter of no objection from their partner. Fees vary and visas take two to three days to process: Dh70 for Australians, Americans and New Zealanders; Dh200 for Brits. GCC residents who have been in the country for at least one year and have six months validity left on their residence visa can purchase visas at major border posts or on arrival at the airport in Muscat. Be sure to have two photos and a copy of your passport ready.

Qatar The consulate in Dubai does not issue visas to people on a tourist visa (nor does the embassy in Abu Dhabi). This must be arranged before you leave home. As for GCC residents, only those holding certain professions can get a visa on arrival. Others will need to go through a sponsor. Call airport immigration in Doha on ☎ 00974-351550 (ext 490) for further information.

Turkey Multi-entry visas, valid for three months, can be obtained at the airport on arrival in Istanbul. These cost UK£10 or US$15 (these currencies must be used). You can also get one from the Turkish consulate in Dubai for Dh110 (two passport photos required). GCC residents will also need a sponsorship letter from their employer in Dubai. Spouses without a company sponsorship who wish to travel alone will also need a letter of no objection from their partner. Allow one week for processing.

Multi-entry visas are available for British, US, Canadian and German passport holders from the UAE embassy in their home country. These are valid for two years and cost, on average, Dh400.

The authorities in the Immigration Department say they will issue an on-the-spot two week visa to foreigners (which in practice excludes Asian passport holders) with certain professions (management-type jobs usually) holding a GCC residence permit who turn up at airports and at land border crossings. If you are receiving a visa through a sponsor, make sure you have a faxed copy of your visa before your flight to Dubai or you may find that the airline will not allow you to board. The original visa is almost always deposited at the airport for you to pick up on arrival. If this is the case, go to the desk in the arrivals area and pick up a form which you then take to passport control. If you are entering the country on a transit visa you will leave passport control carrying a copy of this form. Don't lose it, as you have to give it back on the way out.

You can also pick up visas at the port in Sharjah if you are arriving by boat from Iran.

According to the Immigration Department, if your passport shows any evidence of travel to Israel you will be denied entry to the UAE. A few travellers have informed us, however, that there is no longer a problem with Israeli stamps in passports, although the embassy has not officially declared this as such.

At the time of writing, a combined single tourist visa for both UAE and Oman was soon to be introduced. At first this would be for GCC residents alone, but would eventually be extended to include people travelling on tourist visas.

Hotel-Sponsored Visas To get a visa this way, phone or fax one of the big hotels and ask them to sponsor you. The hotel will usually require you to stay up to three nights and will charge you anywhere from Dh180 to Dh300 for the service – though you should not really pay any more than Dh180. Once you have the visa, however, you are free to go anywhere in the country or to move to a

cheaper hotel. Be sure to get the hotel to fax you back a copy of the visa when it is ready or the airline may not let you travel.

Processing the visa can take anywhere from two days to three weeks. Generally, the biggest and most expensive hotels in Dubai are the fastest while smaller hotels take longer. While there are a lot of cheap hotels which claim to sponsor visas, many of them provide rather questionable service and we advise that you receive a hotel-sponsored visa from a reputable hotel.

Visa Extensions Transit visas cannot be extended. Tourist visas can be extended for one month, but it is expensive at Dh500 and there is a lot of fiddling about with paperwork. People have been known to stay in Dubai for a year or more simply by flying out to Bahrain, Doha or Kish (an island off the Iranian coast) every month and picking up a new visa on their return at a total cost of about Dh450.

For visas to other Middle Eastern countries see the boxed text 'Visas for Other Middle Eastern Countries'.

Other Documents
International Student Cards and Seniors' Cards are not recognised in the UAE and having one will not grant you discounts at hotels or tourist sites.

Photocopies
All important documents (passport data page and visa page, credit cards, travel insurance policy, air/bus/train tickets, driving licence etc) should be photocopied before you leave home. Leave one copy with someone at home and keep another with you, separate from the originals.

It's also a good idea to store details of your travel documents in Lonely Planet's free online Travel Vault in case you lose the photocopies or can't be bothered with them. Your password-protected Travel Vault is accessible online anywhere in the world – create it at www.ekno.lonelyplanet.com.

If you need to make photocopies while in Dubai, there are hundreds of small 'Typing & Photocopy' shops as well as photography shops around Bur Dubai and Deira which charge 10-25 fils a copy. If you have some more complex photocopying to do there's a 24-hour Kinko's copying store opposite the Bur Juman Centre on Khalid bin al-Waleed Rd near the corner of Trade Centre Rd.

EMBASSIES & CONSULATES

It's important to realise what your own embassy can and can't do to help you if you get into trouble.

Generally speaking, it won't be much help in emergencies if the trouble you're in is remotely your own fault. Remember that you are bound by the laws of the UAE. Your embassy will not be sympathetic if you end up in jail after committing a crime locally, even if such actions are legal in your own country.

In genuine emergencies you might get some assistance, but only if other channels have been exhausted. For example, if you need to get home urgently, a free ticket home is exceedingly unlikely – the embassy would expect you to have insurance. If you have all your money and documents stolen, it might assist with getting a new passport, but a loan for onward travel is out of the question.

Some embassies used to keep travellers' letters and stock home newspapers, but the mail holding service has usually been stopped and newspapers tend to be out of date.

UAE Embassies Abroad

Australia
    (☎ 02-6286 8802, fax 6286 8804)
    36 Culgoa Circuit, O'Malley ACT 2606
Bahrain
    (☎ 723 737, fax 727 343)
    House No 221, Road 4007 – Complex 340, Manama
France
    (☎ 01-45 53 94 04, fax 01-47 55 61 04)
    3, Rue de Lota, 75116 Paris
Egypt
    (☎ 02-360 9722, fax 570 0844)
    4 Ibn Seena Street, Giza, Cairo
Germany
    (☎ 228-267 070, fax 267 0714)
    Erste Fahrgasse, D-54113, Bonn
India
    (☎ 22-687 2822, fax 687 3272)
    EP 12 Chandra Gupta Marg, Chanakyapuri, New Delhi 11002

Iran
    (☎ 021-295 027, fax 878 9084)
    Wali Asr Street, Shaheed Waheed Dastakaardi St No 355, Tehran
Kuwait
    (☎ 252 1427, fax 252 6382)
    Al-Istiqlal Street, Qaseema 7, Al-Assaffa, PO Box 1828, Kuwait 13019
Oman
    (☎ 600 302, fax 602 584)
    Al-Khuwair, PO Box 551 code 111, Muscat
Qatar
    (☎ 885 111, fax 822 837)
    22 Al-Markhiyah Street, Khalifa Northern Town, PO Box 3099, Doha
Saudi Arabia
    (☎ 1-482 6803, fax 482 7504)
    Abu Bakr al-Karkhi Zone, Amr bin Omayad Street, PO Box 94385, Riyadh 11693
UK
    (☎ 020-7581 1281/4113)
    30 Princes Gate, London SW1
USA
    (☎ 202-338 6500, fax 337 7029)
    3000 K Street, NW, Suite 600, Washington DC 20007

Consulates in Dubai

Most countries have diplomatic representation in the UAE. Dubai is home to the consulates; the embassies are located in Abu Dhabi and are listed in the front pages of the Dubai phone book.

Australia
    (Map 1; ☎ 331 3444, fax 331 4812)
    6th Floor, World Trade Centre, Shaikh Zayed Rd, Za'abeel; open 8 am to 3.30 pm Sunday to Wednesday, 8 am to 2.45 pm on Thursday
Canada
    (Map 4; ☎ 521 717, fax 397 7722)
    7th Floor, United Bank Bldg, Khalid bin al-Waleed Rd, Bur Dubai; open 8 am to 12.30 pm Sunday to Thursday
Egypt
    (Map 4; ☎ 397 1122, fax 397 1033)
    Khalid bin al-Waleed Rd (opposite the Strand Cinema), Bur Dubai; open 9 am to 12 pm Saturday to Wednesday
France
    (Map 3; ☎ 223 2442, fax 227 0887)
    10th Floor, Arbift Tower, Beniyas Rd (between the Chamber of Commerce & Industry Bldg and the Etisalat office); open 8.30 am to 1 pm Saturday to Wednesday

Germany
(Map 2; ☎ 397 2333, fax 397 2225)
6th Floor, Sharaf Bldg, Al-Mankhool Rd, near the Ramada Hotel; open 9 am to 12 pm Saturday to Wednesday
India
(Map 4; ☎ 397 2000, fax 397 0453)
Khalid bin al-Waleed Rd (opposite the Strand Cinema), Bur Dubai; open 8 am to 12.30 pm Monday to Thursday
Iran
(Map 4; ☎ 397 1150, fax 397 2069)
Khalid bin al-Waleed Rd (opposite the Strand Cinema), Bur Dubai; open 8 am to 12 pm Saturday to Thursday
Italy
(Map 1; ☎ 331 4167, fax 331 7469)
18th Floor, World Trade Centre, Shaikh Zayed Rd, Za'abeel; open 9 to 11 am and 2 to 3 pm Saturday to Wednesday
Jordan
(Map 4; ☎ 397 7500, fax 524 675)
Khalid bin al-Waleed Rd (opposite the Strand Cinema), Bur Dubai; open 8 am to 11 am Saturday to Thursday
Kuwait
(Map 3; ☎ 228 4111, fax 223 2024)
Beniyas Rd (opposite the Sheraton Dubai), Deira; open 8.30 am to 12 pm Saturday to Thursday
Netherlands
(Map 2; ☎ 528 700, fax 397 0502)
1st Floor, ABN-Amro Bank Bldg, Khalid bin al-Waleed Rd, Bur Dubai; open 9 am to 3 pm Saturday to Wednesday
Oman
(Map 4; ☎ 397 5000, fax 397 0666)
Khalid bin al-Waleed Rd (opposite the Strand Cinema), Bur Dubai; open 7.30 am to 2.30 pm Saturday to Wednesday
Qatar
(Map 4; ☎ 398 2888, fax 398 3555)
Trade Centre Rd (behind Department of Health & Medical Services Bldg), Mankhool; open 8 to 11.30 am Saturday to Wednesday
Saudi Arabia
(Map 1; ☎ 663 383, fax 662 524)
28 St (behind Al-Ittihad Rd), Hor al-Anz; open 8 am to 11 am Saturday to Wednesday
Turkey
(Map 1; ☎ 331 4788, fax 331 7317)
11th Floor, World Trade Centre, Shaikh Zayed Rd, Za'abeel; open 9 am to 12 pm Saturday to Thursday
UK
(Map 2; ☎ 397 1070, fax 397 2153)
Al-Seef Rd (near the Dhow Restaurant), Bur Dubai; open 8 am to 1 pm Saturday to Wednesday
USA
(Map 1; ☎ 331 3115, fax 331 4043)
21st Floor, World Trade Centre, Shaikh Zayed Rd, Za'abeel; open 8.30 am to 5 pm Saturday to Wednesday

CUSTOMS

Arriving in Dubai is a real treat. It has a reputation for fast passport and customs control, and it's not unusual to get from the aeroplane to the street in 12 minutes – a feat rarely matched anywhere.

The duty-free allowances for tobacco are huge: 2000 cigarettes, 400 cigars or 2kg of loose tobacco (this is *not* a country cracking down on smoking). Non-Muslims are allowed to import 2L of wine and 2L of spirits. Note that if you are entering through Sharjah, where alcohol is prohibited, you won't be able to bring any in. You are generally not allowed to bring in alcohol if you cross into the UAE by land. No customs duties are applied to personal belongings. If you bring videos into Dubai, or even if they are sent to you by mail, it's likely they will be confiscated for about a month while they are inspected for any offensive content.

MONEY
Currency

The UAE dirham (Dh) is divided into 100 fils. Notes come in denominations of Dh5, 10, 20, 50, 100, 200, 500 and 1000. There are Dh1, 50 fils, 25 fils, 10 fils and 5 fils coins (although the latter two are rarely used today). A few years ago the government issued new coins, which are smaller than the old ones. Both types remain legal tender, but you should look at your change closely as the new Dh1 coins are only slightly smaller than the old 50 fil coins. You may hear the currency occasionally referred to as rupees, especially by elderly people. When Britain controlled India, the rupee was the official currency in what is now the UAE and from 1948 until independence in 1971, a currency known as the 'Gulf Rupee' was legal tender throughout the area.

Exchange Rates

The UAE dirham is fully convertible and is pegged to the US dollar. Exchange rates, at the time of writing, were as follows:

country	unit		dirhams
Australia	A$1	=	2.36
Canada	C$1	=	2.45
euro	€1	=	4.07
France	FF10	=	6.20
Germany	DM1	=	2.08
Japan	Y1	=	0.03
New Zealand	NZ$1	=	1.98
Oman	OR1	=	9.54
Saudi Arabia	SR1	=	0.97
UK	UK£1	=	6.03
USA	US$1	=	3.68

Exchanging Money

The first thing to be said about money in Dubai is that you should not exchange it at the airport, where the rates are terrible. Once in the city, there is no shortage of banks and exchange houses. In central Deira, especially along Sikkat al-Khail St, and around Beniyas Square, every other building seems to contain a bank or a moneychanger. In Bur Dubai there are a lot of moneychangers (though most of them only take cash and not travellers cheques) around the abra dock. Thomas Cook al-Rostami has a number of branches around the city: on Shaikh Zayed Rd, south of the Crowne Plaza Hotel; on Al-Fahidi Rd in Bur Dubai; and on Road 14 in Deira, near Al-Khaleej Hotel.

If you are changing more than US$250 it might pay to do a little shopping around. Moneychangers sometimes have better rates than banks, and some do not even charge a commission. The problem with moneychangers is that some of them either will not take travellers cheques or will take only one type. Some places will only exchange travellers cheques if you can produce your original purchase receipt. If you don't have the receipt try asking for the manager. Currencies of neighbouring countries are all recognised and easily changed with the exception of the Yemeni rial.

If you need an ATM in central Deira look for Emirates Bank International. It has a branch on Beniyas Rd (near Al-Khaleej Palace Hotel), another on Al-Maktoum Rd (near the Metropolitan Palace Hotel) and another on Al-Souq St in Bur Dubai. Its ATMs are tied into the Electron, Cirrus, Switch and Global Access systems. ATMs at branches of the British Bank of the Middle East are linked to the Global Access system. You'll find one on Beniyas Square and another in Bur Dubai, opposite Al-Falah St. The highest concentration of international banks is along Khalid bin al-Waleed Rd in Bur Dubai, east of Mankhool Rd.

All major credit cards are accepted. If you use American Express (AmEx), however, you will be hit with a 5% merchant fee.

AmEx (☎ 336 5000, fax 336 6006) is represented in Dubai by Kanoo Travel. The office is on the 1st Floor of the Hermitage Building, next to the main post office on Za'abeel Rd in Karama. It's open daily, except Friday, from 8.30 am to 1 pm and from 3 to 6.30 pm. It won't cash travellers cheques but will hold mail for AmEx clients. Address mail to: c/o American Express, Client's Mail, PO Box 290, Dubai, UAE.

Security

Large amounts of cash are often carried around by Nationals, so you shouldn't be too worried about doing the same. Crime is relatively low in Dubai, but you should exercise the same caution with your personal belongings as you would anywhere. Take care in the souqs, as pickpockets have been known to operate here.

Costs

Dubai is not a low-budget city such as Cairo or Bangkok, but it is possible to keep costs under control. Decent hotels can be found for Dh100 to Dh150 in Dubai, but they tend to be more expensive elsewhere. Eating well for Dh10 to Dh15 is rarely a problem, though alcohol will add considerably to your bill. Taxis around the centre will cost from Dh5 to Dh12, and admission to museums and other tourist sites is either very cheap or free.

Plan on spending Dh150 to Dh200 per day for budget travel. If you stay in the youth hostel you might be able to keep your budget down to half that. For mid-range to top-end travel you'll spend from Dh300 (if you eat cheaply) to whatever your pocket allows.

Tipping & Bargaining

Tips are not generally expected since a service charge is added to your bill (this goes to the restaurant, not the waiter, however). If you want to leave a tip, 10% is sufficient.

Bargaining in souqs can be exhausting. Hang in there, be firm and be prepared to spend some time at it. Prices probably won't come down by more than about 20%, but if you are at a souq in the country, you'll find that prices will come down by about 50%. Even in shopping centres in Dubai you can ask for a discount or for their 'best price'. Most hotels will offer a discount if you ask for it, but the prices of meals and taxis are always fixed.

Taxes & Refunds

Almost all hotel and restaurant bills will have 10% tacked on for service and another 10% for municipality tax. If a price is quoted 'net', this means that it includes tax and service.

POST & COMMUNICATIONS
Post Offices

The main post office (Map 4) is on the Bur Dubai side of the Creek, on Za'abeel Rd, near 25A Rd in Karama. It is open Saturday to Wednesday from 8 am to 11.30 pm, Thursday from 8 am to 10 pm and Friday from 8 am to noon. It has a philatelic bureau.

The Deira post office (Map 2), on Al-Sabkha Rd near the intersection with Beniyas Rd, is open Saturday to Wednesday from 8 am to midnight, and Thursday from 8 am to 1 pm and 4 to 8 pm. Al-Musalla post office (Map 2) at Al-Fahidi roundabout in Bur Dubai, the Satwa post office on Al-Satwa Rd and Al-Rigga post office (Map 3) opposite the Royalton Plaza hotel (near the Clock Tower roundabout) are open Saturday to Thursday from 8 am to 1pm and 4 to 7 pm.

There are also a number of fax and postal agencies dotted along the small streets around Deira Souq and Dubai Souq.

Postal Rates

Letters up to 20g cost Dh3 to Europe and most African countries; Dh3.50 to USA, Australia and the Far East; Dh2.50 to the Indian Subcontinent; Dh1.50 to Arab countries; and Dh1 within the Gulf. Double these rates for letters weighing 20g to 50g. For letters weighing 50g to 100g, rates to these destinations are Dh13/11/9/6/4.

Postcard rates are Dh2 to Europe, the USA, Australia and Asia; Dh1 to Arab countries; and 75 fils to the Gulf.

Parcels weighing between 500g and 1kg cost Dh68 to the USA, Australia and the Far East; Dh45 to Europe and Africa; Dh36 to the Indian Subcontinent; Dh34 to other Arab countries; and Dh23 within the Gulf. For parcels weighing between 1kg and 2kg, the rates to the these destinations are Dh130/85/68/64/45.

Rates for surface mail are roughly half those for air mail.

Sending Mail

Mail generally takes about a week to 10 days to Europe or the USA and eight to 15 days to Australia. There does not seem to be any way of tracing packages that have gone missing, however. I have reeived a surly brush off whenever I've tried to find out the fate of a missing parcel.

Mumtaz Speed Post is available, but it is very expensive (Dh100 to send a letter to Australia). If you need to send something in a hurry it will cost you half as much to use a courier company, and they will come and collect the package from you. We recommend Kanoo Rapid Transport (☎ 474 845, PO Box 290, Dubai) or FedEx (☎ 800 4050, PO Box 9239, Dubai).

Receiving Mail

Poste restante facilities are not available in Dubai. The American Express office will hold mail for AmEx clients (see Exchanging Money earlier in this chapter for the AmEx office address). If you are staying at a five star hotel, the reception desk will usually hold letters and small packages for two or three days prior to your arrival. Be sure to mark these 'Guest in Hotel' and, to be sure, 'Hold for Arrival'.

Telephone

The UAE has an efficient telecommunications system. The state telecommunications monopoly is Etisalat, recognisable by the giant, sparkling golf ball on top of its HQ building on the corner of Beniyas and Omar ibn al-Khattab Rds (Map 3). It is open 24 hours a day. There is another office on Al-Mankhool Rd, near the corner of Khalid bin al-Waleed Rd (Map 2).

If you need to make a call from the airport, there are telephones at the far end of the baggage-claim area where local calls (ie within Dubai) can be made free of charge. Some of the lounges at the gates in the departures area also have phones from which you can make free local calls. Coin phones have almost completely been taken over by card phones. Phone cards are available in denominations of Dh30 from grocery stores, supermarkets, petrol stations and street vendors.

To phone out from the UAE, dial '00', followed by the country code. If you want to call the UAE, the country code is 971. The area code for Dubai is 04, though if you are calling from outside the UAE you just dial 4. The following is a list of area codes in the UAE:

Abu Dhabi	☎ 02
Ajman	☎ 06
Al-Ain	☎ 03
Dibba	☎ 09
Fujairah	☎ 09
Hatta	☎ 085
Khor Fakkan	☎ 09
Ras al-Khaimah	☎ 07
Sharjah	☎ 06
Umm al-Qaiwain	☎ 06

Mobile numbers begin with 050 in the UAE. Often people will give their seven digit mobile number without mentioning this prefix. There are Home Country Direct services to 43 countries. Dialling these codes connects you directly to an operator in the country being called. A list of access codes to these countries is in the Etisalat Services section of the phonebook.

Useful Numbers The following are some useful telephone numbers:

ambulance	☎ 998
directory information (Arabic)	☎ 181
directory information (English)	☎ 180
emergency	☎ 997
fire department	☎ 998
operator	☎ 100
police	☎ 999
talking clock	☎ 140

Call Charges The following are some direct-dial rates per minute from the UAE:

to	peak (Dh)	off-peak (Dh)
Australia	4.62	2.54
Canada	4.62	2.54
France	4.62	3.21
Germany	5.45	4.50
Hong Kong	5.81	5.29
India	6.43	4.50
Italy	4.62	3.21
Japan	6.21	5.45
USA	4.62	3.00
UK	4.62	3.21

Telephone Troubles?

At the time of writing, phone numbers in Dubai, and around the UAE, were in the process of changing from six digits to seven digits. Even though most numbers will have changed by May 2000, you will still be able to call the old number for some months and get a recorded message telling you the new number. There are no set rules as to how numbers will change, but many numbers repeat the first digit at the beginning (eg 200 becomes 2200). If you require assistance or further information regarding these changes, call the Etisalat helpline on ☎ 222 0444.

❀❀❀❀❀❀❀❀❀❀❀❀❀❀❀❀❀❀❀❀

FACTS FOR THE VISITOR

Mobile Madness

This little accessory that fits so nicely inside the pocket of a dishdasha has to be the gadget of the century in Dubai. You can't go anywhere without hearing annoying electronic renditions of the William Tell Overture or Beethoven's Ninth. Emiratis just love to talk on the phone. They love it so much in fact that most of them have more than one mobile, sometimes as many as four. The dexterity with which these guys can juggle three simultaneous conversations on three different phones is astounding.

There is a complete list of rates in the 'green pages' at the back of the Dubai phonebook. The off-peak rates apply from 9 pm to 7 am every day and all day on Fridays and public holidays.

Fax, Telex & Telegraph

Most Etisalat offices are also equipped to send and receive fax, telex and telegraph messages. They may ask for your local address and contact number before they'll send a fax, and though the service is fairly good, it is expensive at Dh10 per page to most international destinations. Most typing and photocopying shops also have faxes you can use. You'll find the highest concentration of these just north of the Clock Tower roundabout on Abu Baker al-Siddiq Rd.

Email & Internet Access

Etisalat is the sole provider of Internet in Dubai. Private Internet is quite cheap at Dh20 per month for rental and Dh2 per hour for usage. As you would expect, the Internet is heavily censored in the UAE. This can occasionally be frustrating because many sites that are not the least bit pornographic in nature (eg 'The History of Sextants'), can be inaccessible. Most five star hotels offer Internet access to their guests, though sometimes this is only available to

executive guests who are paying a premium for their rooms.

The Internet Cafe (Map 5; ☎ 453 390) on Al-Dhiyafa Rd in Jumeira charges Dh15 per hour and is open Saturday to Thursday from 10 am to 3 am and on Friday from 2 pm to 3 am. For the same cost you can use the Internet at the British Council Library (Map 1) from Saturday to Wednesday, 10 am to 1 pm and from 5 to 8pm. Meraj Typing Centre (Map 2) opposite the Swiss Plaza Hotel in Bur Dubai offers Internet access for Dh10 per hour. Public libraries will soon have public Internet access.

INTERNET RESOURCES

For a brief run down on visas, accommodation, restaurants and entertainment in Dubai, go to the Web site www.dubai.com. There is also business information, including comprehensive economic statistics (although these don't seem to have been updated for a number of years).

A relatively new Web site is www.godubai.com, which is a large site with lists of travel agencies, airlines, libraries and links to other sites. It also has information on the Emirates Environmental Group, as well as promotions and giveaways.

Through the Middle East Institute of Japan, at www.meij.or.jp, you can get to a huge list of links to sites on Dubai and the UAE that cover government departments, newspapers and other publications, phone directories, universities and businesses. Another Web site, www.waiviata.com.au/Dubai/DubGen/dubattra.htm details major tourist sites, shopping centres and offers information on local customs. Elsewhere, www.uaeforever.com breaks up information by emirates allowing you to select the page on Dubai. It has comprehensive lists of travel agents in the city as well as things to see and do. It also includes lists of government departments and embassies. For the latest travel information, check www.lonelyplanet.com.au.

BOOKS

Books in Dubai are neither abundant, nor cheap. The reason given for the high prices are that consumers in Dubai expect the latest material to be on the shelves as soon as possible, which means that books must be air-freighted in. This doesn't explain why books have the same exorbitant price tag a year later, however. We suggest you bring your own reading material (see the Shopping chapter later in this book).

Most books are published in different editions by different publishers in different countries. As a result, a book might be a hardcover rarity in one country while it's readily available in paperback in another. Your local bookshop or library is best placed to advise you on the availability of the following recommendations.

Lonely Planet

Lonely Planet's *Middle East* includes a chapter on the UAE, incorporating Dubai.

For those seeking more in-depth coverage, a new Lonely Planet title, *Oman & the UAE,* focuses solely on these two Gulf States as opposed to the region as a whole, and will be on the shelves from July 2000.

Guidebooks

Dubai Explorer, from Explorer Publishing, has information on just about everything there is to see and do in this city, from paragliding to Mexican restaurants, and lists of all kinds of clubs and societies. It's particularly useful for expats and costs Dh50.

For those who have 4WDs, *Off Road in the Emirates I* and *II* by Dariush Zandi are a must, though directions given to sites can be vague and confusing. They are published by the UAE-based Motivate Publishing and are widely available for Dh55. *The Off-Roaders' Manual* by Jehanbaz Ali Khan, also from Motivate, covers the practicalities of a 4WD trek on all kinds of terrain, including deserts, oases and rocky mountains such as you'll come across in the UAE.

UAE: A Meed Practical Guide is the most comprehensive business guide to the country. It gives a good background to the finance and trade of the country and includes a practical guide to living in the Emirates. It features a section on Dubai,

which has particularly useful lists of organisations, departments and ministries.

Don't They Know it's Friday by Jeremy Williams is a guide to social and business etiquette, written by an expat who has lived and worked all over the Gulf and now runs courses for westerners doing business with Arabs. It's very interesting and straightforward and should be compulsory reading for those intending to live and work in the Gulf.

Eating Out in the Emirates is a spiral-bound publication that features a section on dining out in Dubai, although you are probably better off with the *Dubai Explorer* for this sort of information.

History & Society

Father of Dubai: Shaikh Rashid Bin Saeed al Maktoum by Graeme Wilson is a tribute to the acknowledged founder of modern Dubai. *The Merchants* by Michael Field gives a brief sketch of the rise of Dubai as a trading centre, although you may find it difficult to find.

Jonathan Raban's *Arabia Through the Looking Glass* has a lengthy section on Dubai and is well worth reading. Translated from the Arabic is *Dubai Tales* by Muhammed al-Murr, one of the UAE's best known writers. His short stories provide an intimate view of the lives and values of the people of Dubai.

General

Dubai Life & Times: Through the Lens of Noor Ali Rashid is a pictorial history of Dubai over the last four decades by a man who was the Royal Photographer during most of this time. The photographs are absolutely stunning and very candid.

Dubai – A Pictorial Tour is a collection of pictures by various photographers depicting the modern aspects of Dubai as well as the traditional. *Dubai – An Arabian Album* by Ronald Codrai is a collection of mid-20th century photos of Dubai.

NEWSPAPERS & MAGAZINES

Gulf News, *Khaleej Times* and *Gulf Today*, all published in Dubai, are the three English-language newspapers. They cost Dh2 and carry pretty much the same international news, though *Gulf News* is probably the best of the bunch. Local news consists largely of 'business' stories, which are little more than advertisements masquerading as news. Like most countries in the Gulf, you're rarely told what decisions have been made by political bodies in the country. They also tend to have fairly comprehensive coverage of the Indian and Pakistani political and entertainment scenes. The Arabic dailies are *Al-Bayan* (published in Dubai), *Al-Khaleej* and *Al-Ittihad* (both published in Abu Dhabi). Foreign newspapers are available in larger bookshops and hotels as well as Spinney's and Choitram's supermarkets.

What's On is a monthly magazine catering mostly to the expat community. It's a pretty good source of information about what's new at the hotels, restaurants, bars, clubs and discos. The magazine costs Dh12, though you will often find it free in five star hotels.

RADIO & TV

The Dubai radio station, Dubai FM, is at 92 FM. Channel 4 FM is on 104.8. Both are English-language and both feature DJs playing mainstream chart music along side occasional speciality music programs featuring classical or country & western. The newest radio station, Emirates FM, broadcasts all over the UAE. It is at 99.3 FM and carries much of the same music and style as the others. QBS, at 97.5 FM and 102.6 FM, features radio plays in English, jazz specials and world music shows.

Channel 33 shows an English-language movie and one or two American sitcoms most days of the week as well as news in English. It can be picked up on 33 UHF Dubai TV, the Arabic channel, features religious and educational programs as well as the occasional variety show or drama serial from Egypt or Lebanon. It can be picked up on 2 and 10 VHF or 30, 38 or 41 UHF.

Most hotels, even the smaller ones, have satellite TV. This usually consists of the standard package of four channels from Hong Kong-based Star TV: a music video channel, a sports channel, a movie channel and the BBC World Service. There may also be one or two Indian or Pakistani services (Zee TV/PTV) and sometimes one or more of the Arabic satellite services (MBC, Dubai Satellite Channel, Nilesat, ART).

The newest TV station in Dubai is the Dubai Business Channel, which covers business around the world with a particular focus on business in Asia and the Middle East. It broadcasts continuously from 6 pm until 2 pm the next day.

VIDEO SYSTEMS

Video tapes bought here are for use with the PAL system, which is prevalent in most of Western Europe and Australia. Note that they are incompatible with the North America NTSC system and France's SECAM system. They can be played on multisystem VCRs, which are available from electronics shops in Dubai (see the Shopping chapter).

PHOTOGRAPHY
Film & Processing

Getting colour prints developed is never a problem – 20-minute services are advertised by photo developers on nearly every street in the city. These places will also take four passport photos for Dh10. It costs Dh9 for a 24 exposure print film, Dh10 for a 36 exposure print film. Developing charges are Dh5, plus Dh1 for each photo, and you'll usually get a replacement film and a photo album thrown in. The best place to get slides and B&W film developed is Prolab (Map 1; ☎ 669 766) on Abu Baker al-Siddiq Rd. It costs Dh24 for a 36 exposure slide film and Dh33 for developing/mounting. Prolab offers same-day service and is one of the few places where you can buy slide film, though some shops in larger hotels may sell it, too.

When taking photographs during the day in Dubai you should use a UV filter on your lens, since the glare is very strong (you could also try reducing your aperture by around 1 f-stop).

Restrictions

Do not photograph anything even vaguely military. This includes airports, police stations (or police officers), palaces, the

Diwan Building, the Dubai Courts, consulates and government ministries. It's discourteous to photograph people without their permission; and never photograph women.

TIME
Dubai is four hours ahead of GMT. The time does not change during the summer. When it's noon in Dubai, the time elsewhere is:

city	time
Paris, Rome	9 am
London	8 am
New York	3 am
Los Angeles	midnight
Perth, Hong Kong	4 pm
Sydney	6 pm
Auckland	8 pm

ELECTRICITY
The electric voltage is 220V AC. British-style three pin wall sockets are used, even though most appliances are sold with two pin plugs. Adaptors are available in small grocery stores and supermarkets and cost Dh5.

WEIGHTS & MEASURES
The UAE uses the metric system (see the conversion chart at the back of this book if you are not familiar with it).

LAUNDRY
There are no laundrettes in Dubai, but small laundries can be found in many spots around central Deira and in Bur Dubai. On average you will be charged Dh2 for T-shirts, Dh5 for pants, Dh1 for underwear, Dh10 for dresses and Dh7 for blouses and skirts. You can also have clothes ironed for Dh1 to Dh2 per item. Turnaround time at these places is usually 24 hours.

Dry-cleaning services are also available around the city and from most mid-range and top-end hotels. In Deira try Tide Dry Cleaners & Laundry (Map 2; ☎ 227 7796) on the north side of Beniyas Square, or Golden Laundry (Map 2) on Naif Rd. In

Bur Dubai there's Al-Warda al-Ahmar Laundry (Map 2) on Al-Esbij St near the corner with Khalid bin al-Waleed St. In Satwa try Adnan Ali Laundry (Map 5; ☎ 398 5055) on 6B St, just off Al-Dhiyafa Rd. Prices are Dh2.50 for shirts and T-shirts, Dh3.50 for trousers, Dh13 for dresses and Dh1 to Dh2.50 for socks and underwear.

TOILETS
The best advice is to go when you can. The very few public toilets on the streets are usually only for men. Public toilets in shopping centres, museums, restaurants and hotels are western style and are generally well-maintained. Outside Dubai you'll have to contend with 'hole in the ground' loos at the back of restaurants or petrol stations.

LEFT LUGGAGE
Dubai Airport has a left luggage office (☎ 224 5555) in the arrivals hall, which charges Dh15 per item per day (24 hours). If you are staying at a mid-range or top-end hotel you will be able to leave your luggage at reception for up to a day.

HEALTH
The standard of healthcare is quite high throughout the UAE. Western medicines are widely available at pharmacies. Emergency medical care is free at government hospitals (see Hospitals under Medical Services later in this chapter). Some travel insurance would be very much in order though to cover you for nonurgent care. Should you get sick, consult either the hotel doctor (if you are in a big hotel) or go to a private hospital or clinic. Expats are covered by a health card entitling them to free care at government hospitals and clinics.

Immunisations
There are no vaccination requirements for entry to Dubai. An International Health Certificate is required only from travellers arriving from yellow fever infected areas such as parts of Africa and South America.

As a general rule, and especially before you travel anywhere, it's a good idea to make sure you are up to date with 'routine' vaccinations such as tetanus, diphtheria and polio (boosters are required every 10 years). Discuss your requirements with your doctor, but other vaccinations you should consider before coming to Dubai are: hepatitis A, which is a common food and water-borne disease; hepatitis B, which is transmitted through sexual activity and blood products; and meningococcal meningitis. Other vaccinations for a longer term stay could include typhoid, tuberculosis and rabies.

Plan ahead for vaccinations: some of them require more than one injection, while some vaccinations should not be given together. Note that some vaccinations should not be given during pregnancy or to people with allergies – discuss this with your doctor. You should seek medical advice at least six weeks before travel.

Malaria Medication

Malaria does not exist in Dubai, though malarial mosquitos are a possibility in the mountainous areas outside the city where there are water holes. Check requirements before you leave home, but to be on the safe side you should take appropriate precautions. Antimalarial drugs do not prevent you from being infected, they kill the malaria parasites during a stage in their development and significantly reduce the risk of becoming very ill or dying. Expert advice on medication should be sought, as there are many factors to consider, including the area to be visited, the risk of exposure to malaria-carrying mosquitoes, the side effects of medication, your medical history and whether you are a child, adult or pregnant woman.

Further Information

If you are looking for more detailed information, *Staying Healthy in Asia, Africa & Latin America*, by Dirk Schroeder (Moon Publications), or *Travellers' Health* by Dr Richard Dawood (Oxford University Press) are both good guides. There are also a number of excellent travel health sites on the Internet. From the Lonely Planet home page there are links at www.lonelyplanet .com/weblinks/wlprep.htm#heal to the

Medical Kit Check List

Following is a list of items you should consider including in your medical kit – consult your pharmacist for brands available in your country.

- ☐ **Aspirin or paracetamol (acetaminophen in the USA)** – for pain or fever
- ☐ **Antihistamine** – for allergies, eg, hay fever; to ease the itch from insect bites or stings; and to prevent motion sickness
- ☐ **Cold and flu tablets, throat lozenges and nasal decongestant**
- ☐ **Multivitamins** – consider for long trips, when dietary vitamin intake may be inadequate
- ☐ **Antibiotics** – consider including these if you're travelling well off the beaten track; see your doctor, as they must be prescribed, and carry the prescription with you
- ☐ **Loperamide or diphenoxylate** –'blockers' for diarrhoea
- ☐ **Prochlorperazine or metaclopramide** – for nausea and vomiting
- ☐ **Rehydration mixture** – to prevent dehydration, which may occur, for example, during bouts of diarrhoea; particularly important when travelling with children
- ☐ **Insect repellent, sunscreen, lip balm and eye drops**
- ☐ **Calamine lotion, sting relief spray or aloe vera** – to ease irritation from sunburn and insect bites or stings
- ☐ **Antifungal cream or powder** – for fungal skin infections and thrush
- ☐ **Antiseptic (such as povidone-iodine)** – for cuts and grazes
- ☐ **Bandages, Band-Aids (plasters) and other wound dressings**
- ☐ **Water purification tablets or iodine**
- ☐ **Scissors, tweezers and a thermometer** – note that mercury thermometers are prohibited by airlines
- ☐ **Syringes and needles** – in case you need injections in a country with medical hygiene problems; ask your doctor for a note explaining why you have them

World Health Organization and the US Centers for Disease Control & Prevention.

Other Preparations

Make sure you're healthy before you start travelling. If you are going on a long trip go to the dentist and optician. Take a spare pair of glasses plus a prescription (if applicable). If you require a particular medication take an adequate supply, as it may not be available locally. Take part of the packaging showing the generic name rather than the brand, which will make replacements easier to locate. It's a good idea to have a legible prescription or letter from your doctor to show that you legally use the medication to avoid any problems.

Jet Lag

Jet lag is experienced when a person travels by air across more than three time zones (each time zone usually represents a one-hour time difference). It occurs because many of the functions of the human body (such as temperature, pulse rate and emptying of the bladder and bowels) are regulated by internal 24-hour cycles. When we travel long distances rapidly, our bodies take time to adjust to the 'new time' of our destination, and we may experience fatigue, disorientation, insomnia, anxiety, impaired concentration and loss of appetite. These effects will usually be gone within three days of arrival, but to minimise the impact of jet lag:

- Rest for a couple of days prior to departure.
- Try to select flight schedules that minimise sleep deprivation; arriving late in the day means you can go to sleep soon after you arrive. For very long flights, try to organise a stopover.
- Avoid excessive eating (which bloats the stomach) and alcohol (which causes dehydration) during the flight. Instead, drink plenty of non-carbonated, nonalcoholic drinks such as fruit juice or water.
- Avoid smoking.
- Make yourself comfortable by wearing loose-fitting clothes and perhaps bringing an eye mask and ear plugs to help you sleep.
- Try to sleep at the appropriate time for the time zone you are travelling to.

Food & Water

The tap water in Dubai is OK to drink but, as it comes from desalination plants, it tastes pretty awful. Most residents stick to bottled water, which is readily available from shops and from vending machines all over the city.

In general, the standard of hygiene in restaurants, even the smaller ones, is quite good. Take note of the cleanliness of a place when you walk in. If it's clean and devoid of flies, then the kitchen and the food is likely to be clean as well. The only food you should avoid is shwarmas from street stands. The skewered meat that sits on these grills out in the open attracts flies and dirt. They are not very hygienic and the Health Department is making moves to get rid of them. You can still get shwarmas from cafes where the meat is cooked indoors. Also, if you are eating at some of the smaller Arab-Indo and Pakistani restaurants, you may want to avoid raw salads. If you are buying food from Shindagha market or the meat, fish, fruit and vegetable market in Deira you should get there early. It's just common sense to buy food as fresh as possible. If it's been sitting out for hours it will become affected by the heat and the flies. Avoid buying meat from these markets. The risk of disease is too high. It's better to buy packaged meat from Europe, Australia or Saudi Arabia available from supermarkets.

Cuts & Scratches

Wash well and treat any cut with an antiseptic such as povidone-iodine. Where possible avoid bandages, which can keep wounds wet. Coral cuts are notoriously slow to heal and if they are not adequately cleaned, small pieces of coral can become embedded in the wound.

Heat-Related Problems

You can get sunburnt surprisingly quickly in Dubai, even if it's cloudy. If you are at the beach, you are more susceptible to sunburn due to the reflection from the water. Use sunscreen, a hat and a barrier cream for your nose and lips. Calamine lotion is good for mild sunburn. The glare in Dubai is very strong. Protect your eyes with good quality sunglasses, particularly if you are going to be near water or sand.

Prickly heat is an itchy rash caused by excessive perspiration trapped under the skin. It usually strikes people who have just arrived in a hot climate. Keeping cool, bathing often, drying the skin and using a mild talcum or prickly heat powder or resorting to air-con may help.

Warm, moist conditions also encourage fungal skin infections. To help prevent these, wear loose clothing, wash frequently, and dry yourself carefully. If you do get an infection, an antifungal cream or powder may help, and try to expose the infected area to sunlight as much as possible.

Dehydration and salt deficiency, caused by diarrhoea, profuse sweating or just not drinking enough fluids, can cause heat exhaustion. Take time to acclimatise to high temperatures, drink sufficient liquids and do not do anything too physically demanding.

Salt deficiency is characterised by fatigue, lethargy, headaches, giddiness and muscle cramps; adding extra salt to your food may help.

Medical Problems & Treatment

Dubai has a good standard of hygiene, advanced healthcare and efficient hospitals.

Everyday Health

Normal body temperature is up to 37°C (98.6°F); more than 2°C (4°F) higher indicates a high fever. The normal adult pulse rate is 60 to 100 per minute (children 80 to 100, babies 100 to 140). As a general rule the pulse increases about 20 beats per minute for each 1°C (2°F) rise in fever.

Respiration (breathing) rate is also an indicator of illness. Count the number of breaths per minute: between 12 and 20 is normal for adults and older children (up to 30 for younger children, 40 for babies). People with a high fever or serious respiratory illness breathe more quickly than normal. More than 40 shallow breaths a minute may indicate pneumonia.

The heat can really take it out of you though and there are a few things you should know to keep yourself healthy during your stay.

Diarrhoea Simple things like a change of water, food or climate can all cause a mild bout of diarrhoea, but a few rushed toilet trips with no other symptoms is not indicative of a major problem. Dehydration is the main danger with any type of diarrhoea, particularly in children or the elderly. Under all circumstances, fluid replacement (at least equal to the volume being lost) is the most important thing to ensure. Weak black tea, with a little sugar, soda water or soft drinks allowed to go flat and diluted 50% with clean water are all good. With severe diarrhoea, a rehydrating solution is preferable to replace minerals and salts lost. Commercially available oral rehydration salts (ORS) are very useful; add them to boiled or bottled water.

In an emergency you can make up a solution of six teaspoons of sugar and a half teaspoon of salt to a litre of boiled or bottled water. You need to drink at least the same volume of fluid that you are losing in bowel movements and vomiting. Urine is the best guide to the adequacy of replacement – if you have small amounts of concentrated urine, you need to drink more. Keep drinking small amounts often. Stick to a bland diet as you recover. Gut-paralysing drugs such as Lomotil or Imodium can be used to bring relief from the symptoms, although they do not actually cure the problem. Only use these drugs if you do not have access to toilets (if, for example, you must travel). For children under 12 years, Lomotil and Imodium are not recommended. Do not use these drugs if the person has a high fever or is severely dehydrated.

In certain situations antibiotics may be required: diarrhoea with blood or mucus (dysentery), any diarrhoea with fever, profuse watery diarrhoea, persistent diarrhoea not improving after 48 hours and severe diarrhoea. These suggest a more serious cause of diarrhoea and in these situations gut-paralysing drugs should be avoided.

In these situations, a stool test may be necessary to diagnose what bug is causing your diarrhoea, so you should seek medical help urgently.

Hepatitis Hepatitis is a general term for inflammation of the liver. It is a common disease worldwide. There are several different viruses that cause hepatitis, and they differ in the way that they are transmitted. The symptoms are similar in all forms of the illness, and include fever, chills, headache, fatigue, feelings of weakness and aches and pains, followed by loss of appetite, nausea, vomiting, abdominal pain, dark urine, light-coloured faeces, jaundiced (yellow) skin and yellowing of the whites of the eyes. People who have had hepatitis should avoid alcohol for some time after the illness, as the liver needs time to recover.

Hepatitis A is transmitted by contaminated food and drinking water. You should seek medical advice, but there is not much you can do apart from resting, drinking lots of fluids, eating lightly and avoiding fatty foods. **Hepatitis E** is transmitted in the same way as hepatitis A; it can be particularly serious in pregnant women.

There are almost 300 million chronic carriers of **hepatitis B** in the world. It is spread through contact with infected blood, blood products or body fluids (for example, through sexual contact, unsterilised needles, or contact with blood via broken skin). Other risk situations include being shaved, tattooed or body pierced with contaminated equipment. The symptoms of hepatitis B may be more severe than type A and the disease can lead to long-term problems such as chronic liver damage, liver cancer or a long-term carrier state. **Hepatitis C** and **D** are spread in the same way as hepatitis B and can also lead to long-term complications.

There are vaccines against hepatitis A and B, but there are currently no vaccines against the other types of hepatitis. Following the basic rules about food and water (hepatitis A and E) and avoiding risk situations (hepatitis B, C and D) are important preventative measures.

HIV & AIDS Infection with the Human Immunodeficiency Virus (HIV) may lead to Acquired Immune Deficiency Syndrome (AIDS), which is a fatal disease. Any exposure to blood, blood products or body fluids may put the individual at risk. The disease is often transmitted through sexual contact or dirty needles – vaccinations, acupuncture, tattooing and body piercing can be potentially as dangerous as intravenous drug use. Fear of HIV infection should never preclude treatment for serious medical conditions.

Sexually Transmitted Diseases Gonorrhoea, herpes and syphilis are among these diseases; sores, blisters or rashes around the genitals and discharges or pain when urinating are common symptoms. In some STDs, such as wart virus or chlamydia, symptoms may be less marked or not observed at all, especially in women. Chlamydia infection can cause infertility in men and women before any symptoms have been noticed. Syphilis symptoms eventually disappear completely, but the disease continues and can cause severe problems in later years. While abstinence from sexual contact is the only 100% effective prevention, using condoms is also effective. Gonorrhoea and syphilis are treated with antibiotics. The different sexually transmitted diseases each require specific antibiotics.

Women's Health
Gynaecological Problems Antibiotic use, synthetic underwear, sweating and contraceptive pills can lead to fungal vaginal infections, especially when travelling in hot climates. Fungal infections are characterised by a rash, itch and discharge. Nystatin, miconazole or clotrimazole pessaries or vaginal cream are the usual treatment, but they can also be treated with a vinegar or lemon-juice douche or with yoghurt. Maintaining good personal hygiene and wearing loose-fitting clothes and cotton underwear may help prevent these infections.

STDs are another cause of vaginal problems. Seek medical attention, and remember that male sexual partners must also be treated.

Pregnancy It is not advisable to travel to some places while pregnant as some vaccinations normally used to prevent serious diseases are not advisable during pregnancy (eg yellow fever). In addition, some diseases are much more serious for the mother (and may increase the risk of a stillborn child) in pregnancy (eg malaria).

Pregnant women should avoid all unnecessary medication, but vaccinations and malarial prophylactics should still be taken where needed. Additional care should be taken to prevent illness and particular attention should be paid to diet and nutrition. Alcohol and nicotine, for example, should be avoided.

Medical Services
Hospitals The following government hospitals have emergency departments:

Al-Maktoum Hospital
(Map 3; ☎ 221 211) Al-Maktoum Hospital Rd, Rigga; near the corner of Omar ibn al-Khattab St
Al-Wasl Hospital
(Map 1; ☎ 324 1111) Oud Metha Rd, Bur Dubai; south of Al-Qataiyat Rd
New Dubai Hospital
(Map 1; ☎ 229 171) Abu Baker al-Siddiq Rd, Deira; near the corner of Al-Khaleej Rd
Rashid Hospital
(Map 1; ☎ 337 4000) off Oud Metha Rd, Bur Dubai; near Al-Maktoum Bridge

Doctors & Dentists If you need nonurgent care through a multispecialist private clinic you should ask your consulate for the latest list of recommended doctors and dentists. Some are listed here in case you need to find one and your consulate is closed:

Al-Zahra Private Medical Centre
(Map 1; ☎ 331 5000) Shaikh Zayed Rd, about 200m south of the Crowne Plaza Hotel
Dubai London Clinic
(Map 1; ☎ 446 663) Al-Wasl Rd, Jumeira. The clinic also has an emergency section.
General Medical Centre
(Map 5; ☎ 495 959) 1st Floor, Magrudy's Shopping Centre, Al-Jumeira Rd. The clinic also has an emergency section.
Manchester Clinic
(Map 5; ☎ 440 300) Al-Jumeira Rd, just north of McDonald's

Pharmacies You'll have trouble avoiding pharmacies. They are on just about every street in Dubai. See the *Gulf News* for a list of pharmacies that are open 24 hours on that day. If you can't get to a newspaper and you need to get to a pharmacy urgently, call ☎ 223 2232 for details.

Emergency
For an ambulance and police call ☎ 999; for fire emergencies call ☎ 997.

WOMEN TRAVELLERS
Attitudes Towards Women
In general, Dubai is one of the best places in the Middle East for women travellers. Checking into hotels is not usually a problem, though unaccompanied women might want to think twice about taking a room in some of the budget hotels in Deira. They are renowned for accommodating prostitutes from the CIS and Africa and you run the risk of being mistaken for one (as this author has a couple of times).

Even though things might be better in Dubai than in other parts of the Gulf it does not mean that all of the usual problems that accompany travel in the Middle East will not arise here as well: unwanted male attention, long, lewd stares and being beeped at by men in passing cars. Always remember to retain your self-confidence and sense of humour.

Safety Precautions
You'll find that Dubai, as opposed to other places in the region, is a very liberal place and people here are used to western women and their ways. It's once you're out of Dubai that you might encounter a different attitude. Apply common sense – don't wear tight and revealing clothes that are just going to make your life difficult. Sit in the back seat of taxis and avoid making chitchat. You'll find that you'll often be asked to take the front seat in buses or be asked to sit next to other women. This is so you can avoid the embarrassment of men's stares.

In banks, Etisalat offices, post offices and libraries there are usually separate sections

Women in Dubai

The young, modern Emirati woman, with her lime-green platform shoes, confidently strolling through a Dubai shopping centre while chatting on her mobile phone, is an enormous contrast to the older Emirati woman, completely covered from head to toe, selling handicrafts in a country souq.

The modernisation of Dubai has dragged many women with it. Attitudes towards the traditional role of women are gradually shifting, and women now have a strong presence in public life.

Although there are no published statistics for Dubai alone, the number of Emirati women in the workforce, in both private and government sectors, has increased enormously over the past two decades. In the civil service, women now account for over 40% of employees. Apart from the traditionally female-dominated professions (such as teaching and nursing), Emirati women can be found in the media, military, travel and tourism industry and police force.

It may surprise you to hear that female students outnumber male students in universities by three to one. This means that more women than men are demanding and obtaining a variety of jobs at graduate level. In 1995, the government made a great effort to encourage people seeking work to register with the Ministry of the Interior. Of those who registered, 61% were women.

This doesn't mean that the traditional role of women in UAE society has been abandoned. Traditional handicrafts, such as weaving, are still practiced and encouraged. The role of women as carers, mothers and nurturers is still very much in place, and the family is still considered the most important unit in UAE society. The task at hand for the Emirati woman is to strike a comfortable balance between these two roles.

❀❀❀❀❀❀❀❀❀❀❀❀❀❀❀❀❀❀

or windows for women – great when there's a queue. In the small Arab-Indo restaurants you will often be ushered into the 'family room'. You don't have to sit here but the room is there to save you from being stared at by some of the locals.

It is refreshing to know that something positive is being done about harassment of women. Under the directive of Shaikh Mohammed, the Crown Prince of Dubai, any man found harassing women in public is arrested and has his picture published on page two of the *Gulf News*. Very embarrassing!

Organisations

The following organisations may be of use to women travellers:

American Women's Association
  (☎ pager 9115 5823) This is a 300-member strong social and philanthropic club that meets once a month for breakfast. Sporting activities and outings are also arranged. You must have a US passport to become a member; you can become an associate member if your spouse has a US passport.
Business Women's Group
  (☎ 345 2282, fax 345 2123) With over 200 members, this is a networking support group for women in the UAE who are in senior management or who own their own companies. It meets on the second Monday of each month and is open to all nationalities.
Dubai & Sharjah Women's Guild
  (☎ 394 5331) This is a social group of predominantly western women who meet twice a month to hear a guest speaker or to go on an excursion in or out of Dubai. It's also a fundraising organisation that donates to various local and overseas charities.
German Women's Club
  (☎/fax 490 432) This is a club for German women in Dubai. Much like the American Women's Association it provides social events and support to members. It seems to be primarily aimed at the nonworking wives of German expats.

GAY & LESBIAN TRAVELLERS

Officially, homosexuality is illegal in the UAE and can incur a jail sentence. Unofficially, prosecution is unlikely to happen if you are reasonably discrete. We have had a number of letters from gay travellers who have had no trouble travelling in the UAE and have met other gays quite easily. The only trouble is likely to come from homophobic westerners. Men walking hand in hand is quite common in the UAE and not seen as indicative of sexual orientation as it often is in the west. Women walking hand in hand is not so common.

The Hard Rock Cafe, on Shaikh Zayed Rd, has achieved a reputation as being a gay hang-out but not exclusively so, as has Jules Bar (Map 1) at Le Meridien.

DISABLED TRAVELLERS

At the time of writing there were no official associations or societies for the disabled although a pressure group in Dubai was calling for an Association for Disabled Persons. The group's aims are to develop a disabled-friendly environment and transport system, promote tourism for the disabled and ensure a wide range of rehabilitation services.

There are 12 hotels in Dubai with rooms equipped for disabled guests. Unfortunately for the budget traveller they are all five star – the Crowne Plaza, Hilton, Hyatt Regency, Jumeira Beach Hotel, JW Marriott, Oasis Beach Hotel, Renaissance Hotel and Ritz Carlton (see the Places to Stay chapter for contact details). All the major shopping centres have wheelchair access, but ramps in car parks and into most buildings in the city are few and far between. There are a number of disabled car parks, but often these are taken up by completely insensitive, nondisabled drivers.

Dubai Transport (☎ 331 3131) has a number of taxis that can take wheelchairs. The newly renovated airport has facilities for the disabled including low check-in counters but things get more difficult once you are out of the airport. Dubai Museum has ramps; however, other tourist attractions are difficult for disabled visitors to get around on their own.

The first point of contact for travellers should be North Tours in Bur Dubai (☎ 737 474). It is run by a man who is disabled himself so he understands the needs of the disabled traveller. North Tours can arrange cruises, desert safaris, mountain tours, what-

ever you like. It can also book hotels that have facilities for disabled guests and it can sponsor visas. Desert Rangers (☎ 453 091) also caters tours for disabled travellers.

SENIOR TRAVELLERS

For a country that traditionally respects its elders, it is surprising to learn that there are no discounts available to senior travellers for such things as admission fees and public transport. One good thing is that all hotels have elevators, even the cheapest ones, so you won't have to contend with endless flights of stairs.

DUBAI FOR CHILDREN

As in most Gulf cities, families are well looked after in Dubai and there are plenty of activities for children. All the parks mentioned in this book have kids' playgrounds and there are plenty of grassy stretches where they can expend energy (see the Things to See & Do chapter). All the shopping centres have nurseries or play areas for little kids though most of the time you won't be able to leave them unattended.

Magic Planet at City Centre (Map 1) has various rides, amusements and play areas aimed primarily at kids under 12. It also has a minigolf course and numerous video games that usually attract much larger kids. It's open from 10 am to 11 pm Saturday to Thursday and 1 to 11 pm on Friday. Individual rides cost Dh2.50 or Dh40 for unlimited rides with six video game tokens thrown in. You can catch buses No 3 and 6 to get there.

Encounter Zone in the Wafi Shopping Centre (Map 1) is a techno-adventure playground for kids of all ages. It is divided into 'Galactica', which has amusements and rides for teenagers and adults, and 'Lunarland', which is a play area for kids under 10. It's open from 10 am to midnight every day. Individual rides cost Dh4.50 or you can pay Dh40 to go on everything. Younger children can be left under the supervision of employees at Lunarland for Dh40 for half a day. Routes No 14, 16 and 44 go past the Wafi Shopping Centre.

By far the most appealing place for older kids is the Wild Wadi Waterpark 14km south of Jumeira. Entry is Dh95/75 for adults/children and Dh65/50 if you go between 3 and 7 pm, and the rides are some of the most exciting in the world (see Activities in the Things to See & Do chapter for more information).

Wonderland (Map 1) in Dubai, next to Al-Boom Tourist Village, is divided into SplashLand (which has been completely overshadowed by the Wild Wadi Waterpark), an amusement park with various rides and video-game parlour. SplashLand is open from 10 am to 4 pm and the amusement park is open from 4 to 11 pm Monday to Saturday. Wonderland is closed on Sunday, and Wednesday is for ladies and children only. Entry is Dh10 (Dh20 on Friday) then you have to pay for rides individually. A family pass costing Dh175 gives two adults and two children unlimited rides. Bus No 44 will take you there.

If you are planning to take a day or overnight trip from Dubai there are plenty of places to take the kids. Aquapark Dreamland in Umm al-Qaiwain claims to be the largest water park in the Gulf. It has all kinds of wet rides plus a go-kart track, a video-game parlour and a number of swimming pools, kiosks and restaurants. It's open from 10 am to 7 pm every day. Admission costs Dh30/20 for adults/children, which gives you unlimited use of the rides. If you're catching public transport, you'll need to pay for a minibus to Ras al-Khaimah (Dh20) as the water park is 10km out of Umm al-Qaiwain on the road to Ras al-Khaimah. Alternatively, an engaged taxi will cost you Dh50.

One place guaranteed to keep children and adults fascinated for a couple of hours is the Sharjah Science Museum. There is also Hili Fun City & Ice Rink in Al-Ain (see the Excursions chapter for details).

North Star Expeditions (☎ 332 8702, PO Box 31753, Dubai) specialises in educational and adventure trips around the UAE for children.

The best time of year for kids is during special events such as the Dubai Shopping Festival and Dubai Summer Surprises. Everyday there are activities for children at one shopping centre or another. You have to wonder at the intelligence behind such events as burger eating competitions though.

USEFUL ORGANISATIONS

The following is a list of organisations that might be of interest to those living and working in Dubai:

Dubai Natural History Group
(☎ 313 324, PO Box 9234, Dubai) This group was formed by people with a common interest in Dubai's flora, fauna, geology and archaeology. Lectures and discussions are held on the first Sunday of every month and anyone is welcome to attend. Topics range from bird-watching to Bedouin. Regular field trips are organised for members and nonmembers.
The British Community Assistance Fund
(☎ 337 1413, PO Box 51299, Dubai) This is a voluntary organisation which provides help to British citizens in Dubai and the northern Emirates who find themselves in distress. It offers legal, financial and medical assistance and can help with repatriation and counselling.

LIBRARIES

If you forget to bring books with you, or have a special interest, the following libraries may be of use:

Archie's Library (Map 4; ☎ 396 7924) In the Pyramid building, behind the Ministry of Health, Trade Centre Rd, Karama. It has a huge collection of books in English – fiction and nonfiction – as well as children's books and magazines. You can read books on site for a small charge, but you have to be a member to take books home. This costs Dh75 per year plus a Dh100 deposit. It's open from 10 am to 2 pm and 5 to 10 pm every day except Friday morning.
British Council (Map 1; ☎ 337 1540) Just south of Al-Maktoum Bridge. It has a reference library for students of its courses so the collection's emphasis is on business studies and English literature. It also has educational videos and reference CD-ROMs. You must become a member to use the library. This will cost you Dh200 per year. Internet access is also available. The library is open Saturday to Wednesday from 10 am to 1pm and 5 to 8 pm.
Dubai Lending Library (Map 5; ☎ 446 480) At the Dubai International Arts Centre in Jumeira.

It has 12,000 books covering adult fiction, children's, biographies and reference. You must be a member to take books out, which is Dh80 per year if you want to take out five books at a time or Dh50 if you want to take out two. The library is open Saturday to Thursday from 10 am to midday and from 4 to 6 pm.

Juma al-Majid Cultural & Heritage Centre (☎ 624 999) Just off Salah al-Din Rd in the Hor al-Anz district. This is a nonprofit reference library and research institute. They have a large collection of books, periodicals and journals in English on the history, politics and culture of the UAE and other Gulf countries. They also have titles in French, German, Russian and other languages. You cannot take books home, but you are welcome to use the reading room. The library is open Saturday to Wednesday from 8 am to 1 pm and 4 to 7.30 pm. On Thursday it's open from 8 am to 1 pm.

Public Library (Map 2; ☎ 226 2788) At the western end of Beniyas Rd, in the Al-Ras district of Deira. Everyone is welcome to browse the collection and use the reading rooms. The English collection covers mainly the social sciences. Even though there are some works on the Gulf, the main focus of the collection is international. You can only take books home if you are a member, which means you must have a residence visa and pay Dh150 deposit for one year. The library is open from 7.30 am to 1.30 pm and 3 to 8.30 pm everyday except Friday.

US Consulate (Map 1; ☎ 331 4043) On the 21st floor of the World Trade Centre in Za'abeel. It has a commerce library comprising mainly trade directories, reference books, periodicals, journals, databases and CD-ROMs. It is open from 9 am to 1 pm Saturday to Wednesday.

CULTURAL CENTRES

Dubai has become such a multi-ethnic melting pot, that cultural centres have sprung up all over town.

Alliance Francaise (Map 1; ☎ 335 8712 Oud Metha Rd, Za'abeel). Promotes French culture and teach French. Events such as concerts, lectures and ballets are occasionally organised.

Australian & New Zealand Association (☎ 511 579, PO Box 28691, Dubai). A social society for Australian and New Zealand expats in Dubai. The group organises activities, events, social gatherings and produces a newsletter.

British Council (Map 1; ☎ 337 0109) Just south of Al-Maktoum Bridge, near the Dubai Courts building. Conducts English and Arabic classes

as well as courses in computer studies and business. There is also a reference library with videos and CD-ROMS providing information on studying in Britain.

Dubai Irish Society (☎ 394 1053, PO Box 37208, Dubai) Primarily a social group for Irish expats and has about 500 members. In addition to a couple of social events each month, they also organise sporting events and, of course, the ever popular St Patrick's Day Ball. The society can also give support or advice for any Irish people who find themselves in any trouble or distress.

Shaikh Mohammed Centre for Cultural Understanding (☎ 447 755, fax 497 787, PO Box 21210, Dubai) Set up to help break down cultural barriers between Nationals and foreigners. It seeks to teach visitors more about Arab and Islamic culture. The centre arranges cultural tours and outings, such as a visit to Jumeira Mosque or a meal in an Arab home, but bookings are essential.

DANGERS & ANNOYANCES

On the whole, Dubai is a very safe city, but you should exercise the same sort of caution with your personal safety as you would anywhere.

There is one real danger in Dubai, and that is bad driving. We have received a number of letters from travellers reiterating this sentiment. Be wary of drivers, whether you're behind the wheel or on foot. Don't expect them to drive carefully, sensibly or courteously.

Finally, we don't recommend that you swim, water-ski or jet-ski in the Creek. The tides in the Gulf are not strong enough to flush the Creek out on a regular basis so it is not a clean waterway, despite what the tourist authorities might tell you.

LEGAL MATTERS

If you are found with illegal drugs you are likely to cop a jail sentence and deportation. Those attempting to bring in very large amounts could receive the death sentence, though a stiff jail sentence is more likely. Jail sentences for being involved in drugs just by association are also likely. That means that even if you are in the same room where there are drugs, but are not partaking, you could be in as much trouble as those who are. Theft and writing bad cheques are also taken pretty seriously and usually involve jail and deportation.

If you are arrested you have the right to a phone call, which you should make as soon as possible (ie before you are detained in a police cell or prison pending investigation, where making contact with anyone could be difficult). Call your embassy or consulate first. If there is an accident, it's a case of guilty until proven innocent. This means that if you are in a car accident, you may be held under police guard until an investigation reveals whose fault the accident was. If you are in hospital this can mean being chained to a bed.

There was a high profile case in early 1999 in which a British tourist was released on bail for two months pending trial after she was injured in a jet-ski accident in which a Russian tourist was killed. She had her passport confiscated and had to be present at court to prove that the accident was not her fault. If it was found that she had caused the Russian's death by driving recklessly she would have received a jail sentence and would have had to pay Dh160,000 in blood money to the victim's family. Luckily for her she was acquitted. This case received a lot of bad press in the UK, a major source of tourists for Dubai.

BUSINESS HOURS

The weekend here is Thursday and Friday. Government offices start work at 7.30 am and finish at 1 or 1.30 pm from Saturday to Wednesday. Some are also open on Thursday mornings, but this will gradually be phased out with the reduction of the working week from 5½ days to 5 days. Businesses are open Saturday to Wednesday from 8 or 9 am until 1 or 1.30 pm and reopen in the afternoon from 4 to 7 or 8 pm. Some businesses, especially those run by western staff, are open from 8 am to 5 pm, and their weekend may be Friday and Saturday instead of Thursday and Friday.

Shops open from 8 am to 1 pm and from 4.30 or 5 pm to 8 or 9 pm everyday except Friday morning. Most shopping centres are open from 10 am to 10 pm or midnight every day except Friday when they open at around 2 pm. Souqs start up early, usually from around 7 am until midday, and from 5 to 7 or 8 pm everyday except Friday morning.

PUBLIC HOLIDAYS

See the Table of Islamic Holidays for a list of those observed in Dubai. *Lailat al-Mi'raj* is the celebration of the Ascension of Prophet Mohammed. *Eid al-Fitr* is a three day celebration that occurs after Ramadan and *Eid al-Adha* is a four day celebration that occurs after the main pilgrimage to Mecca *(haj)*. Secular holidays are New Year's Day (1 January) and National Day (2 December). The death of a minister, a member of the royal family or the head of state of another Arab Country is usually marked by a three day holiday. These extraordinary holidays are announced in the newspaper on the day they occur. Note that if a public holiday falls on a weekend, the holiday is usually taken at the beginning of the next working week.

The Islamic calendar begins in the year 622 AD, the year that Prophet Mohammed fled Mecca for the city of Medina. It is called the *Hejira* calendar (hejira meaning 'flight') and is 11 days shorter than the Gregorian (western) calendar, which means that Islamic holidays fall 11 days earlier each year. This is not a fixed rule, however, as the exact dates of Islamic holidays depend upon the sighting of the moon at a particular stage in its cycle. This is why Islamic holidays are not announced until a day or two before they occur.

Ramadan

This is the month during which Muslims fast from dawn until dusk. Bars and pubs are closed throughout the month and restaurants do not serve alcohol. Those with a liquor licence can still buy alcohol for consumption at home. Everyone, regardless of their religion, is required to observe the fast in public. That not only means no eating and drinking but no smoking as well. Although it is unlikely you will be arrested for breaking these rules, as you would be in Saudi Arabia, you may be stopped by the police and told to get rid of your sandwich or put your cigarette out.

Table of Islamic Holidays

Hejira Year	New Year	Prophet's Birthday	Ramadan Begins	Eid al-Fitr	Eid al-Adha	Lailat al-Mi'raj
1420	17.04.99	25.06.99	08.12.99	07.01.00	17.03.00	04.11.99
1421	06.04.00	14.06.00	27.11.00	27.12.00	06.03.01	24.10.00
1422	26.03.01	03.06.01	16.11.01	16.12.01	23.02.02	13.10.01
1423	15.03.02	23.05.02	05.11.02	05.12.02	12.02.03	02.10.02
1424	04.03.03	12.05.03	25.10.03	24.11.03	01.02.04	21.09.03

Some hotels will still serve breakfast and lunch to guests, but most of the time eating during the day means room service or self-catering. Non-Muslims offered coffee or tea when meeting a Muslim during the daytime in Ramadan should initially refuse politely. If your host insists, and repeats the offer several times, you should accept so long as it does not look as though your doing so is going to anger anyone else in the room who may be fasting.

SPECIAL EVENTS

Dubai hosts two main tourist-oriented events during the year. One is the Dubai Shopping Festival (DSF), which is fiercely promoted to the extent of having the festival logo painted on the Emirates fleet of 747s. It runs from late March to late April and shopping centres bust themselves to bring in the spenders. Every time you make a purchase you get raffle tickets that can win you cash, cars and shopping vouchers. Shopping centres hold entertainment for kids and displays of traditional culture.

Dubai Summer Surprises is designed, along with cheap hotel rates, to attract tourism and dollars to Dubai during the tourist slump. The 'surprises' include such things as food and cooking exhibitions, technology displays, events for children, ice sculpting and traditional culture displays such as henna painting and art shows. Most events are held at the shopping centres and big hotels. Some shops, though not all, offer big discounts on their merchandise and

every Dh100 you spend entitles you to a raffle ticket. There are daily draws of Dh10,000 worth of shopping vouchers, weekly draws of a car and the end of festival draw of Dh1 million.

Emirates will arrange your visa at no extra charge if you visit during these events, and the Dubai Municipality offers free medical care if required for the duration of your stay.

DOING BUSINESS

Business comes first in Dubai. If you need proof of this then consider the fact that, in 1998, Dubai's prisoners were given access to phones, faxes, conference rooms and secretaries to enable them to keep their business going while they served their sentence!

Foreign investors have been pouring into Dubai over the last two decades, making it the major business hub in the GCC. The reason for this is predominantly Dubai's relaxed business policies: no tax on profits or income (direct taxation goes against the traditions of the UAE and it is highly unlikely that it will be introduced in the future), no foreign exchange controls and 100% repatriation of capital and profits. There are no import duties on food, building materials, unworked silver and gold, agricultural products, medical products and anything destined for the Jebel Ali Free Zone (see below). Other products attract a 4% duty. Dubai is well positioned between the major markets of Europe and Asia and has excellent airport, port, storage and shipping facilities. The major areas of investment are mining, construction, banking and finance, trade and manufacturing.

Trade laws are such that only UAE or other GCC Nationals can own the lion's share of commercial companies. The most a foreign investor can hold is 49%. Foreign companies and individuals are not permitted to own real estate in Dubai. All property must be rented or leased.

To set up a bank account in Dubai you'll need to have a residence visa and a sponsorship letter from your employer, plus your original passport and a photocopy.

Jebel Ali Free Zone

The Jebel Ali Free Zone was set up in 1985 to provide incentives to foreign investors. The legal status here is quite different to the rest of Dubai as companies enjoy the benefits of being 'offshore'. It is most suited to companies intending to use Dubai as a manufacturing or distribution base where most of their turnover is outside the UAE. The added incentives of the free zone are: 100% foreign ownership; exemption from export and import duties; a guarantee of no corporate taxes for 15 years, which is then renewable for another 15 years; and abundant energy and administrative support from the Jebel Ali Free Zone Authority.

Useful Organisations & Government Departments

American Business Council
  (☎ 331 4735, fax 431 4227)
  PO Box 9281, Dubai
Department of Economic Development
  (☎ 229 922, fax 225 577)
  PO Box 13223, Dubai
Dubai Chamber of Commerce & Industry
  (☎ 228 0000, fax 221 1646)
  PO Box 1457, Dubai
Dubai International Airport Free Zone Authority
  (☎ 206 6333, fax 224 5740)
  PO Box 2525, Dubai
Jebel Ali Free Zone Authority
  (☎ 815 000, fax 816 093)
  PO Box 17000, Jebel Ali

Publications

If you intend to set up a business and live in Dubai you should get *UAE – A Meed Practical & Business Guide*. It spells out the requirements of obtaining trade licences, discusses trade laws, has thorough profiles of the major industries and provides listings of trade organisations and useful government departments. It is available from the major bookshops and costs Dh60. The Dubai Chamber of Commerce & Industry on Beniyas Rd sells a number of publications cheaper than the bookshops. *Dubai 99 – The City of Opportunities* has information on setting up a business in Dubai, trade laws and useful organisations; it costs Dh80 and is updated every year. The *Dubai Industrial Directory* has alphabetical listings of companies by industry and information on setting up a business. It costs Dh35. The *Dubai Commercial Directory* is the same sort of thing, but concentrates on listings of commercial companies; it costs Dh60.

Business Facilities & Services

Dubai's hotels are very much geared towards the business traveller and almost all of the mid-range and top-end hotels mentioned in this book have business centres where guests can use computers, faxes, Internet and hire secretarial services. Meraj Typing Centre (Map 2; ☎ 556 617, fax 593 500) opposite the Swiss Plaza Hotel in Bur Dubai offers a typing and translation service, as well as Internet access for Dh10 per hour. There are similar places on Abu Baker al-Siddiq Rd, just north of the Clock Tower roundabout, although they don't offer Internet access.

All the five star hotels listed in this book have conference and exhibition facilities. The Dubai World Trade Centre (Map 1; ☎ 322 1000, fax 331 8034) is the largest venue and its exhibition hall can take up to 4500 people. The Dubai Chamber of Commerce & Industry (Map 3; ☎ 228 0000, fax 221 1646), Dubai Creek Golf & Yacht Club (Map 1; ☎ 295 6000, fax 295 6044) and Dubai Golf & Racing Club (☎ 336 3666, fax 336 3717) also offer substantial facilities for receptions and conferences.

For all the information you could possibly need on business laws, trade licences, business organisations and statistics, go to the website www.dubaicity.com.

Mobile Phones

If you want to use your mobile phone while in Dubai you can buy a prepaid SIM card from Etisalat. It costs Dh300 and is valid for two months or when the credit runs out, whichever comes first. Just pay more money if you want to increase the credit available. You can hire mobiles from car-rental companies at the airport arrivals area.

Business Etiquette

The biggest business blunder you can make is to offend prospective clients, employers and colleagues. That is why you should keep the following things in mind when you are doing business with the Emiratis (also refer to the Dos and Don'ts section in the Facts about Dubai chapter).

- Many Gulf Arabs prefer to begin meetings with small talk. In such situations you may cause offence if you try to move directly to business. This tradition for chitchat becomes more pronounced in rural areas and when dealing with older people.
- Remember that 'timing' and not 'time' is important. If someone fails to appear for a meeting, try not to take offence. This simply means that something more important has come up.
- According to Jeremy Williams, who has written a book on the subject of business etiquette (see Books earlier in this chapter), 95% of time spent on business activity in the Gulf will be taken up with waiting, the other 5% will involve intense work to meet extremely demanding deadlines.
- Never cause someone to lose face in a public situation. If someone has made a mistake it's best to take them aside, explain the situation and take the blame yourself as much as possible.
- Meeting agendas are considered too static for most people, who will prefer to discuss things as the mood takes them rather than stick to a rigid list of topics.
- Gulf Arabs do not make harsh divisions between business and pleasure. Meetings may occur over dinner or coffee or after hours, so be prepared to talk business at any time of the day.

- Don't telephone an Arab colleague for a business chat during siesta time, between about 2 and 5 pm. And remember, Friday is a day of prayer and rest.

WORK

You can pre-arrange work in the UAE, but if you enter the country on a tourist visa and then find work, you will have to leave the country for one day and re-enter under your employer's sponsorship. Unfortunately, you will have to go right out of the Gulf States and then return.

If you have arranged work in Dubai you will enter the country on a tourist visa sponsored by your employer while your residence visa is processed. This process involves a blood test and lots of paperwork. Those on a residence visa who are sponsored by a spouse who is in turn sponsored by an employer, are not officially permitted to work. This rule is often broken, and it is possible to find work in the public or private sector. If you are in this situation, remember that your spouse, and not the company you work for, is your sponsor. One effect of this is that you may only be able to apply for a tourist visa to another Arabian Peninsula country with a consent letter from your spouse. In some cases you will need to be accompanied by your spouse who has company sponsorship. Similarly, if you want to apply for a driving licence you will also need a consent letter from your spouse.

If you obtain your residence visa through an employer and then quit because you've found something better, you may find yourself under a six month ban from working in the UAE. This rule is designed to stop people from job hopping.

If you are employed in Dubai and have any work related problems you can call the Ministry of Labour Helpline for advice on ☎ 0904 0044.

Getting There & Away

AIR

You can fly direct to Dubai from most destinations in the world. Dubai's long-standing reputation as the travel hub of the Gulf was built on a combination of easy landing rights for transiting aircraft and a large, cheap duty-free centre at the airport.

For general airport information call ☎ 224 5555.

The national carrier is Emirates, which flies to 45 destinations in the Middle East, Europe, Australia, Africa and the Subcontinent. The secondary carrier is the regional airline, Gulf Air. It flies to many of the same destinations as Emirates, although all flights go via Bahrain. Both airlines have a perfect safety record.

For all the talk of free markets, air fares out of the UAE are just as strictly regulated as anywhere. There are no bucket shops.

Remember when you are buying air tickets that direct routes are going to be more expensive than nondirect routes. This means that flying Emirates or British Airways between London and Dubai for instance, is going to be more expensive than flying Gulf Air via Bahrain or Qatar Airways via Doha. Sometimes, however, connecting flights can be more trouble than they're worth and you should be sure of how long you will have to wait at an airport before you buy that cheaper ticket.

High season for air travel varies from airline to airline. Generally, it is from late May or early June to the end of August, and from the beginning of December to the end of January. Low season is generally any other time. Regardless, special fares are offered throughout the year by different airlines and travel agents, so make sure you shop around.

Departure Tax

Dubai international airport has no airport departure tax, although it has been suggested that a tax may be introduced in the future.

The USA & Canada

The *New York Times*, the *LA Times*, the *Chicago Tribune* and the *San Francisco Examiner* all produce weekly travel sections in which you'll find any number of travel agents' ads. Council Travel and STA Travel have offices in major cities nationwide. The magazine *Travel Unlimited* (PO Box 1058, Allston, MA 02134) publishes details of the cheapest air fares and courier possibilities from the USA to destinations all over the world. Coming from the US, you'll pay just over US$2100 return on KLM, Lufthansa Airlines or United Airlines (via London). From New York on Northwest Airlines (via Amsterdam), American (via London) or Lufthansa Airlines, it costs US$1690 return.

The only carrier flying nonstop from Dubai to New York is Malaysia Airlines. It costs Dh4380, though there are usually special offers. All other flights go via Europe and fares cost between Dh4500 and

Top: Wooden trading dhows moored in Dubai Creek await their cargo.
Middle: Stunning views of Deira's modern skyline from across the Creek in Bur Dubai.
Bottom: Abras crisscross the Creek all day ferrying passengers between Deira and Bur Dubai.

Savour the sights and smells of Dubai's many souqs, a truly Arabian experience where bargaining over prices is still considered an acceptable form of negotiation.

Dh5000. The cheapest tickets to New York at the time of writing were with Kuwait Airways for Dh3280 and Czech Airlines (via Prague) for Dh3500. To west-coast USA or Vancouver it costs Dh3950 with Cathay Pacific Airways (via Hong Kong), Singapore Airlines (via Singapore) or EVA Airways (via Taipei).

In Canada, Travel CUTS has offices in all major cities. The Toronto *Globe & Mail* and the *Vancouver Sun* carry travel agents' ads. The magazine *Great Expeditions* (PO Box 8000-411, Abbotsford BC V2S 6H1) is also useful. The best deal from Vancouver direct to Dubai is on Canadian Airlines International, British Airways (BA) or Air Canada for US$2300 return. One-way tickets on all these flights are generally about US$500 cheaper. There are no direct flights from Dubai to Canada.

Australia & New Zealand
STA Travel and Flight Centres International are major dealers in cheap air fares. The *Age* in Melbourne and the *Sydney Morning Herald* have travel sections that feature special deals, as does the *New Zealand Herald* in Auckland. From Melbourne or Sydney you'll pay from A$1649 to A$1849. Fares from Auckland are NZ$2527 to NZ$2775.

A return air fare from Dubai to Melbourne (via Singapore) costs Dh3800 to Dh4200 on Emirates, depending on the season. Singapore Airlines and Malaysia Airlines are usually a cheaper alternative to Australia or New Zealand. Prices vary, depending on the season, between Dh3600 and Dh4100.

Asia & the Subcontinent
Hong Kong is the discount-airline-ticket capital of the region. Its bucket shops are at least as unreliable as those of other cities. Ask the advice of other travellers before buying a ticket. STA Travel, which is reliable, has branches in Hong Kong, Tokyo, Singapore, Bangkok and Kuala Lumpur.

There are daily flights from Dubai to major Asian travel hubs. A return flight to Bangkok on Thai Airways costs Dh2000. The best return fare to Singapore is with Royal Brunei Airlines for Dh2000. To Hong Kong it costs Dh2550 return on Cathay Pacific Airways.

Dubai probably has the best air links to Pakistan and India of any city in the world. The cheapest return ticket to Karachi is Dh650 with Kenya Airways. With Pakistan International Airlines (PIA) it costs Dh1070 return; a one-way fare is Dh590. Lahore is more expensive at Dh1580/940 for return/one-way tickets.

There is not much difference between the cost of tickets to/from India between one airline and another. An average fare to Mumbai and New Delhi is Dh1535 return; a one-way fare is Dh940.

The UK & Continental Europe
Trailfinders in west London produces a lavishly-illustrated brochure which includes air fare details. STA Travel (☎ 020-7361 6262) has branches in the UK. Also try Bridge the World (☎ 020-7911 0900). Look in the Sunday papers and *Exchange & Mart* for ads. Free magazines are widely available in London – start by looking outside railway stations. If you have access to the Internet look up Flightbookers.com for some good deals.

Most British travel agents are registered with the Association of British Travel Agents (ABTA). If you have paid for your flight through an ABTA-registered agent which then goes out of business, ABTA will guarantee a refund or an alternative. Unregistered bucket shops are riskier, but also sometimes cheaper.

The Globetrotters Club (BCM Roving, London WC1N 3XX) publishes a newsletter called *Globe*, which covers obscure destinations and can help in finding travelling companions.

From London you will pay around UK£265 on Turkish Airlines via Istanbul and Qatar Airways via Doha. The cheapest nonstop flight at the time of writing was with Royal Brunei Airlines for UK£390. If you're lucky enough to strike a BA special offer you'll pay about the same. Emirates charges about UK£465 return.

There are daily services from Dubai to most major European hubs. Return fares to

Air Travel Glossary

Baggage Allowance This will be written on your ticket and usually includes one 20kg item to go in the hold, plus one item of hand luggage.

Bucket Shops These are unbonded travel agencies specialising in discounted airline tickets.

Bumped Just because you have a confirmed seat doesn't mean you're going to get on the plane (see Overbooking).

Cancellation Penalties If you have to cancel or change a discounted ticket, there are often heavy penalties involved; insurance can sometimes be taken out against these penalties. Some airlines impose penalties on regular tickets as well, particularly against 'no-show' passengers.

Check-In Airlines ask you to check in a certain time ahead of the flight departure (usually one to two hours on international flights). If you fail to check in on time and the flight is overbooked, the airline can cancel your booking and give your seat to somebody else.

Confirmation Having a ticket written out with the flight and date you want doesn't mean you have a seat until the agent has checked with the airline that your status is 'OK' or confirmed. Meanwhile you could just be 'on request'.

Courier Fares Businesses often need to send urgent documents or freight securely and quickly. Courier companies hire people to accompany the package through customs and, in return, offer a discount ticket which is sometimes a phenomenal bargain. In effect, what the companies do is ship their freight as your luggage on regular commercial flights. This is a legitimate operation, but there are two shortcomings – the short turnaround time of the ticket (usually not longer than a month) and the limitation on your luggage allowance. You may have to surrender all your allowance and take only carry-on luggage.

Full Fares Airlines traditionally offer 1st class (coded F), business class (coded J) and economy class (coded Y) tickets. These days there are so many promotional and discounted fares available that few passengers pay full economy fare.

ITX An ITX, or 'independent inclusive tour excursion', is often available on tickets to popular holiday destinations. Officially it's a package deal combined with hotel accommodation, but many agents will sell you one of these for the flight only and give you phoney hotel vouchers in the unlikely event that you're challenged at the airport.

Lost Tickets If you lose your airline ticket an airline will usually treat it like a travellers cheque and, after inquiries, issue you with another one. Legally, however, an airline is entitled to treat it like cash and if you lose it then it's gone forever. Take good care of your tickets.

MCO An MCO, or 'miscellaneous charge order', is a voucher that looks like an airline ticket but carries no destination or date. It can be exchanged through any International Association of Travel Agents (IATA) airline for a ticket on a specific flight. It's a useful alternative to an onward ticket in those countries that demand one, and is more flexible than an ordinary ticket if you're unsure of your route.

No-Shows No-shows are passengers who fail to show up for their flight. Full-fare passengers who fail to turn up are sometimes entitled to travel on a later flight. The rest are penalised (see Cancellation Penalties).

On Request This is an unconfirmed booking for a flight.

Air Travel Glossary

Onward Tickets An entry requirement for many countries is that you have a ticket out of the country. If you're unsure of your next move, the easiest solution is to buy the cheapest onward ticket to a neighbouring country or a ticket from a reliable airline which can later be refunded if you do not use it.

Open Jaw Tickets These are return tickets where you fly out to one place but return from another. If available, this can save you backtracking to your arrival point.

Overbooking Airlines hate to fly empty seats and since every flight has some passengers who fail to show up, airlines often book more passengers than they have seats. Usually excess passengers make up for the no-shows, but occasionally somebody gets 'bumped' onto the next available flight. Guess who it is most likely to be? The passengers who check in late.

Point-to-Point Tickets These are discount tickets that can be bought on some routes in return for passengers waiving their rights to a stopover.

Promotional Fares These are officially discounted fares, available from travel agencies or direct from the airline.

Reconfirmation If you don't reconfirm your flight at least 72 hours prior to departure, the airline may delete your name from the passenger list. Ring to find out if your airline requires reconfirmation.

Restrictions Discounted tickets often have various restrictions on them – such as needing to be paid for in advance and incurring a penalty to be altered. Others are restrictions on the minimum and maximum period you must be away, such as a minimum of 14 days or a maximum of one year.

Round-the-World Tickets RTW tickets give you a limited period (usually a year) in which to circumnavigate the globe. You can go anywhere the carrying airlines go, as long as you don't backtrack. The number of stopovers or total number of separate flights is decided before you set off and they usually cost a bit more than a basic return flight.

Stand-by This is a discounted ticket where you only fly if there is a seat free at the last moment. Stand-by fares are usually available only on domestic routes.

Transferred Tickets Airline tickets cannot be transferred from one person to another. Travellers sometimes try to sell the return half of their ticket, but officials can ask you to prove that you are the person named on the ticket. This is less likely to happen on domestic flights, but on an international flight tickets are compared with passports.

Travel Agencies Travel agencies vary widely and you should choose one that suits your needs. Some simply handle tours, while full-service agencies handle everything from tours and tickets to car rental and hotel bookings. If all you want is a ticket at the lowest possible price, then go to an agency specialising in discounted fares.

Travel Periods Ticket prices vary with the time of year. There is a low (off-peak) season and a high (peak) season, and often a low-shoulder season and a high-shoulder season as well. Usually the fare depends on your outward flight – if you depart in the high season and return in the low season, you pay the high-season fare.

Paris, London or Frankfurt range from Dh3300 to Dh3680. During the summer and Christmas seasons, when many expats return home, airlines lock horns and fares to/from London can be as low as Dh2000 return. At other times the cheapest return fare to London may be with Cyprus Airways via Larnaca for Dh2100. A return ticket to Athens costs Dh2000 with Olympic Airways; a one-way fare is Dh1300.

Middle East & Africa
There are daily services to most Middle East capitals. The best direct fares available at the time of writing were:

destination	one way (Dh)	return (Dh)
Amman	830	1560
Bahrain	640	490
Beirut	1220	1810
Cairo	1010	1550
Damascus	1350	1800
Doha	470	360
Jeddah	1250	1620
Kuwait	910	1190
Muscat	700	520
Riyadh	630	880
San'a	1235	1660
Tehran	700	1240

From Africa, a return air fare to Johannesburg costs Dh3630 with Emirates. Kenya Airways flies direct to Nairobi for Dh1570 return, which is cheaper than Gulf Air's fare of Dh1700 return or Dh1250 one way. Gulf Air also flies to Khartoum for Dh2000 return and Dar es Salaam for Dh1950 return.

Travel Agencies
The highest concentration of travel agencies is along Al-Maktoum Rd in Deira (Map 3), between the Clock Tower roundabout and Omar ibn al-Khattab St. Below are four agencies that we recommend:

Al-Ghaith & Al-Moosa Travel Agency
(☎ 221 1164, fax 223 3054)
Al-Maktoum Rd, Deira; just west of the Clock Tower roundabout

Al-Rais Travels
(☎ 557 700, fax 532 411)
Al-Rais Centre, Al-Mankhool Rd, Mankhool
MMI Travel Centre
(☎ 209 5000, fax 229 1928)
Al-Khor St, Al-Ras, Deira
The Travel Market
(☎ 664 455, fax 685 168)
Corner of Al-Murraqqabat Rd and Abu Baker al-Siddiq Rd, Deira

Airline Offices
The following is a selection of carriers that fly to and from Dubai. Some of them also have desks at the Airline Centre (Map 3) on Al-Maktoum Rd in Deira.

Air France
(☎ 667 775, fax 629 877)
Al-Maktoum Rd, Deira; just east of Al-Khaleej Palace Hotel
Air India
(☎ 227 6787, fax 227 1293)
Al-Maktoum Rd, Deira; just west of the Clock Tower roundabout
Air New Zealand
(☎ 209 5522, fax 229 1923)
MMI Centre, Al-Khor St, Al-Ras, Deira
Alitalia
(☎ 228 4656, fax 223 6148)
Nasser Air Travel & Shipping Agency, Al-Maktoum Rd, Deira; near the Khaleej Palace Hotel
British Airways
(☎ 307 5555, fax 334 7403)
Airline Centre, Al-Maktoum Rd, Deira
Cathay Pacific Airways
(☎ 228 3126, fax 227 9954)
11th Floor, Pearl Bldg, 18 St, Deira; near Beniyas Square
EgyptAir
(☎ 224 8555, fax 227 3300)
Al-Maktoum Rd, Deira; just west of the Clock Tower roundabout
Emirates
(☎ 295 3333, fax 295 1410)
Airline Centre on Al-Maktoum Rd, Deira; other offices on Naif Rd; near Al-Karnak Hotel in the Deira Souq and on Shaikh Zayed Rd (near Interchange No 2)
Gulf Air
(☎ 713 111, fax 736 465)
Salah al-Din Rd, Rigga
KLM-Royal Dutch Airlines
(☎ 224 4747, fax 224 4452)
Dubai airport; above Emirates departures

Lufthansa Airlines
(☎ 343 2121, fax 343 1687)
2nd Floor, 4th Bldg on Shaikh Zayed Rd
Malaysia Airlines
(☎ 397 0250, fax 397 1286)
1st Floor, National Bank of Umm al-Qaiwain
Bldg, Khalid bin al-Waleed Rd, Bur Dubai
Middle East Airlines (MEA)
(☎ 203 3761, fax 295 4422)
Airline Centre, Al-Maktoum Rd, Deira
Olympic Airways
(☎ 221 4761, fax 221 1016)
Nasser Air Travel & Shipping Agency, Al-Maktoum Rd, Deira; near Al-Khaleej Palace Hotel
Qatar Airways
(☎ 221 4448, fax 221 5561)
Doha Centre, Al-Maktoum Rd, Deira; opposite Al-Khaleej Palace Hotel
Royal Brunei Airlines
(☎ 514 111, fax 519 332)
3rd Floor, Rais Hassan Saadi Bldg next to Panorama Hotel, Al-Mankhool Rd, Mankhool
Singapore Airlines (SIA)
(☎ 223 2300, fax 221 8357)
3rd Floor, Pearl Bldg, St 18, Deira; near Beniyas Square
Swissair
(☎ 228 3151, fax 221 6037)
1st Floor, Dubai Tower Bldg, Beniyas Square

BUS
Other Parts of the UAE
The only intercity route within Dubai that really matters is the one to Hatta (Route No 16; 1¼ hours; Dh10). It leaves from the Deira bus station (Map 2), near the Gold Souq, and also stops at Al-Ghubaiba bus station (Map 2) in Bur Dubai and a number of other places on the way out of town. Buses depart every hour from 6.10 am to 9 pm. From Hatta they begin at 6 am and finish at 9 pm.

To get to any other cities in the Emirates you have to take a Dubai Transport minibus. They have replaced the long-distance taxis that used to be the only means of transport between the seven Emirates. These taxis still operate within greater Dubai, and into Dubai from other parts of the country, but they rarely take passengers out of the Emirate, leaving the minibus as the only option to get elsewhere in the UAE.

Minibuses run from Dubai to all major cities in the other Emirates. They leave every 15 or 20 minutes depending on when they fill up. They are very clean and efficient and fixed prices save you the hassle of bargaining for a seat in a shared taxi. Minibuses leave Deira from the minibus and taxi station near the intersection of Omar ibn al-Khattab and Al-Rigga Rds (Map 3). Minibuses for Abu Dhabi and Al-Ain leave from the bus station on Al-Ghubaiba Rd (Map 2) in Bur Dubai. Get your tickets from the ticket windows at each station. Prices per person are:

Abu Dhabi	Dh30
Ajman	Dh7
Al-Ain	Dh30
Fujairah	Dh25
Ras al-Khaimah	Dh20
Sharjah	Dh5
Umm al-Qaiwain	Dh10

To get to Khor Fakkan and Dibba on the east coast, you will need to get a minibus to Fujairah, then a local service taxi from there.

Oman
There are two buses per day to Muscat, Oman. These depart at 7.30 am and 5.30 pm from the parking lot of the Airline Centre on Al-Maktoum Rd, Deira. The trip takes 5½ hours and costs Dh75/140 one way/return, or Dh48/96 for children. Tickets are available at the Airline Centre or from the bus driver. For more information, call ☎ 203 3799.

From Muscat they leave at 7.30 am and 4.30 pm from the Ruwi bus station. The fare is OR9 (Dh90) one way, OR16 (Dh160) return.

If you have an Omani tourist visa in your passport, getting from Dubai to Muscat by land involves nothing more than purchasing a bus ticket. Coming the other way, however, is another story. There is no UAE border post on the road used by the bus. That means that there is no place to pick up a visa, or get a stamp on your passport. If you cross the border this way – even if you already have a valid UAE visa in your passport – it is considered that you are in transit, allowing you to remain in the country for only 48 hours. After this period you will be fined Dh100 per day when you do try to leave, or when you get caught.

Jordan, Syria & Lebanon

There are a few bus companies with services to Lebanon and Syria, via Saudi Arabia and Jordan, although most are located in Abu Dhabi so you will have to make your way there first. Bus companies will arrange the Saudi transit visa only; it's up to you to organise the visa to your destination country.

With Balawi Bus Services (☎ 710 539), however, you can get to Jordan from Dubai and back again for only Dh350/200 for adults/children, including the cost of the Saudi transit visa. Buses run once a week on Thursday from the roundabout on Al-Khaleej Road (just north of the Hyatt Regency Hotel); the trip takes 38 hours.

To get to Syria and Lebanon you will have to arrange tickets through Alfajan (☎ 02-729 944) in Abu Dhabi. This means sending your passport details off before the trip so they can arrange your transit visa. You will need to call them for details about this process. Buses to Syria leave twice a week and return tickets cost Dh400/200 for adults/children. Buses to Lebanon leave once a week and cost Dh500/250. The trips to both countries take nearly 48 hours.

Egypt

Balawi Bus Services runs to Egypt each Wednesday. Return tickets cost Dh850/450 for adults/children. Again, buses leave from the roundabout on Al-Khaleej Road (just north of the Hyatt Regency Hotel); the trip takes three days all up so it's a bit of a trek. Unless money is a real concern, you might be better off catching a plane for only a couple of hundred dirhams more.

CAR
Other Parts of the UAE

There are no border or customs controls between the Emirates and you can freely drive into Dubai from other parts of the country with either your own UAE-registered car or a hire car.

Just remember that cars rented in Dubai do not cover accidents in Omani territory. If you are driving to Hatta from Dubai you will pass through 20km or so of Omani territory. Also, if you are driving around Al-Ain and wish to pop over to the Omani town of Buraimi (which you can do without an Omani visa) you will not be covered.

Oman

It's possible to drive your own car from Dubai to Muscat and vice versa. The trip takes nearly four hours and you do not need a *carnet de passage* or any other documentation. If you have a rental car you will not be permitted to drive it over the border.

TAXI

Long-distance taxis can take you to any other emirate on a shared or 'engaged' basis (which means you will have to pay for all of the seats in it – generally five times the shared cost). If you do take an engaged taxi you should settle the price before you leave. Most taxi drivers will charge a fare per head for your luggage if it is larger than a backpack. Taxis for Abu Dhabi, Al-Ain and Hatta leave from Al-Ghubaiba bus station in Bur Dubai. Taxis for all other destinations leave from the taxi and minibus station on Omar ibn al-Khattab Rd in Deira. The following is a list of approximate fares to destinations within the Emirates for both shared and engaged taxis:

destination	shared (Dh)	engaged (Dh)
Abu Dhabi	30	150
Al-Ain	30	150
Fujairah	25	125
Hatta	20	100
Ras al-Khaimah	20	100
Sharjah	5	25
Umm al-Qaiwain	10	50

There is a Dh20 tax to pay at UAE border posts if you leave the country by land.

BOAT

There are passenger services between Sharjah (only 10 minutes drive from Dubai) and the port of Bandar-é Abbas in Iran. The trip takes 12 hours and costs Dh160 one way. You can take a hydrofoil for Dh215/205 for first/economy class, which takes four hours. For more details contact Oasis Freight Co (☎ 06-596 325) in Sharjah. If you are taking this ferry, make sure that the hotel organising your visa deposits it at Sharjah port.

There is a passenger and car ferry between Jebel Ali, 30km south of the city centre, and Umm Qasr Port in Iraq every Saturday. Passengers taking their cars from Dubai to Iraq must return on the ferry with their cars. Bookings are handled by Al-Majid Travel Agency (☎ 221 1176) on Al-Maktoum Rd in Deira. One-way/return fares are Dh830/1280 in economy and Dh1065/1640 in first class, including meals and port taxes. GCC residents can get a visa on arrival in Iraq for US$100, but they must submit a blood test. The trip takes one and a half days.

If you leave the UAE by boat, there's a Dh20 port tax.

ORGANISED TOURS

Several major tour companies offer package holidays to Dubai. The programs are either 'sea & sun' holidays or a combination of 'sea & sun' with a desert safari sightseeing trip outside of Dubai. These companies tend to accommodate their clients at the beach hotels on the outskirts of Dubai or at Jebel Ali Hotel. The facilities are wonderful, but you may end up wishing that you were closer to town.

From the USA

African Travel (☎ 1-800-421-8907; email ati@africantravelinc.com) runs five-day packages to Dubai from New York during the Shopping Festival (March/April) each year for around US$2600. Global Destinations (☎ 757-490 3466, fax 490 3468; email global@visi.net) was also offering a 10-day trip to Dubai from New York for US$2725 per person.

From Australia

Contact Abercrombie & Kent (☎ 03-9699 9766) or Destination Dubai (☎ 03-9576 0952) for information on upmarket packages to Dubai.

From the UK & Europe

Flightbookers.com was offering a great deal at the time of writing – a return flight from London and five nights in a five star hotel for UK£359. Danata (☎ 020-7932 9900), the Dubai government travel agency, is also based in London. During the 1999 Dubai Shopping Festival (March-April) a return flight and three nights' accommodation cost UK£299. You can also book an upmarket tour with Abercrombie & Kent (☎ 020-7773 9600). British Airways Holidays (☎ 020-7773 9600). British Airways Holidays (☎ 0870-722 628) arranges packages to Dubai as does Arabian Odyssey (☎ 01242-224 482) and Kuoni (☎ 020-7499 8636).

In Norway, Home Tour A/S (☎ 22 11 32 60, fax 22 11 32 66) in Oslo offers a one-week package to Dubai.

Getting Around

THE AIRPORT

Dubai international airport has recently undergone a US$540 million expansion project in an attempt to ensure that Dubai retains its position as the regional travel hub of the Gulf. An estimated 12 million passengers are expected to pass through the expanded airport in its first year of operation. New facilities include a spa, swimming pool, business and conference rooms, restaurants, a five star hotel, improved road access, increased check-in counters and, of course, an expanded duty-free shopping complex.

TO/FROM THE AIRPORT

From the Deira bus station (Map 2), bus Nos 4, 11, 15 and 44 go to the airport about every half hour for Dh1. Only the beige-coloured Dubai Transport taxis are allowed to pick up passengers outside the arrivals area. They charge Dh30 to any point in the city centre (both Deira and Bur Dubai). A ride from the Deira Souq area to the airport with a (metered) Dubai Transport taxi costs Dh12; from Bur Dubai it will cost about Dh17.

BUS

Local buses operate out of the main stations in both Deira and Bur Dubai. The Deira bus station is off Al-Khor St, near the gold souq. The Bur Dubai bus station, Dubai's main bus station, is on Al-Ghubaiba Rd. Note that in the official timetables the two stations appear as 'Gold Souq Bus Stn' and 'Al-Ghubaiba Bus Stn' respectively. Numbers and routes are posted on the buses in English as well as Arabic. Fares are Dh1 to Dh3.50 depending on the distance travelled.

For Dh20 you can buy a Smart Card from both bus stations. This actually gives you Dh22 worth of travel. Each time you use the card the fare is automatically deducted from the credit. You can also purchase monthly bus passes, known as *taufeer*, at both stations. There are two versions: the Dh75 pass

Duty-Free Frenzy

For around 15 years, Dubai international airport has been known as one of the best duty-free zones in the world, and has picked up awards for it from various travel magazines. This is predominantly to do with the sheer volume of items for sale, as well as very competitive prices compared to other airport duty-free complexes, such as Singapore.

Arriving, departing and transit passengers are all welcome to shop in the duty-free complex. Most shops are open 24-hours as flights tend to arrive or depart in the small hours of the morning.

Dubai airport's recent multimillion dollar expansion program promises to expand the duty-free complex to four times its original size by March 2000. If people are not lured by perfumes, watches, clothes, souvenirs and rugs, then the chance of winning US$1million in cash will surely make them stop here. With a limited number of tickets available (5000) at Dh1000 each, the chances are high. But not as good as buying one of 1000 tickets for Dh500 to win a luxury car. This last raffle has yielded 800 luxury cars in the last 10 years.

While most are lured by the vast volume of wares, others have alternative agendas. In 1988 Iranian travellers allegedly bought 1.5 million bananas in the airport's duty-free store. Bananas were said to be virtually unobtainable in Iran back then.

gets you unlimited travel for a month on one or the other side of the Creek; the Dh120 pass gets you unlimited travel all over the city. Neither pass can be used on the intercity buses within the Dubai Emirate (ie for trips to Jebel Ali, Hatta etc). You'll need two passport photos to purchase one of these passes.

Dubai by Bus

Dubai	Route No
Al-Dhiyafa Rd, Satwa	06, 07, 09
Al-Mankhool Rd, Mankhool	09
Khalid bin al-Waleed Rd, Bur Dubai	03, 05, 09, 16, 19, 44, 61, 90
Khalid bin al-Waleed Rd, Mankhool	03, 05, 16, 44, 61, 90
Trade Centre Rd, Karama	05, 06, 44, 61, 90

Deira	Route No
Abu Baker al-Siddiq Rd	03, 06, 19, 20,
Al-Maktoum Rd	04, 05, 11, 14, 15
Al-Rigga Rd	20
Beniyas Rd	04, 05, 08, 11, 14, 15, 19, 20, 22
Beniyas Square	02, 06, 17, 18
Clock Tower roundabout	03, 04, 05, 06, 11, 14, 15, 20,
Salah al-Din Rd	03, 06, 13, 19

Things to See	Route No
Al-Ahmadiya School & Heritage House	08, 19, 20
Bastakia Quarter	19
Dubai International Arts Centre	08, 20
Dubai Museum	19
Dubai Zoo	08, 20
Heritage & Diving Villages; Shaikh Saeed al-Maktoum House	08, 16, 19, 20
Majlis Gallery	19

Souqs & Shopping Centres	Route No
Al-Ghurair Centre	05, 06, 13, 19, 20
Bur Dubai Souq	03, 05, 07, 08, 09, 12, 16, 19, 20, 44, 61, 90
Bur Juman Shopping Centre	03, 05, 16, 44, 61, 90
Deira City Centre	03, 04, 06, 11, 15
Gold Souq	02, 04, 05, 06, 08, 11, 13, 14, 15, 16, 17, 18, 19, 20
Karama Centre	05, 06, 44, 08,
Markaz al-Jumeira	20
Wafi Shopping Centre & Wafi Pyramids	14, 16, 44

Parks	Route No
Al-Mamzar Beach Park	22
Al-Safa Park	12
Creekside Park	05, 06, 03, 14, 44
Jumeira Beach Park	08, 20

Other	Route No
Al-Maktoum Hospital	02, 06, 13, 17, 18
Aviation Club & Irish Village	44
Consulate Area	04, 11, 15, 44
DNATA	03, 05, 06, 16
Dubai Chamber of Commerce	04, 05, 08, 11, 14, 15, 19, 20, 22
Dubai Creek Golf & Yacht Club	03, 06
Dubai Hospital	17, 18
Dubai international airport	04, 11, 15, 44
Dubai Police HQ	02, 03, 13, 17
Emirates Golf Club	90
Etisalat (main branch)	04, 05, 08, 11, 14, 15, 19, 20, 22
Jebel Ali Free Zone	90
Jumeira Beach Hotel	08, 20
Public Library	04, 05, 08, 11, 14, 15, 19, 20, 22
Rashid Hospital	03, 05, 06, 14, 16, 44
World Trade Centre	06, 61, 90, 98

GETTING AROUND

A free schedule and route map can be picked up from both bus stations. Note that most buses both start and finish their days a bit later on Friday. You can count on there being no Friday service from about 11.30 am until about 1.30 pm (except routes 16 and 90) while noon prayers, the most important of the week, are underway. For information on public buses you can call the 24-hour Dubai Municipality hotline on ☎ 861 616.

There are no trains in Dubai, or the rest of the UAE, and there are no plans for a railway system in the future.

CAR

If you are planning on taking a day or overnight excursion from Dubai, hiring a car is the best and cheapest way to do it. If you decide to hire a car to get around the city, remember that traffic congestion in Dubai can be a real problem at peak hours, which occur three times a day: between 7 and 9 am, 1 and 2 pm and most of the evening from 6 pm onwards.

It is compulsory to wear seatbelts in the front and it is illegal to use a hand-held mobile phone while driving. As you can well imagine, Dubai is not short on petrol stations. Petrol is sold by the imperial gallon (an imperial gallon is just over 4.5 litres). Regular petrol costs Dh3.65 per gallon and premium is Dh3.95.

It is not possible to hire motorcycles in Dubai.

Rental

As seems to be the case with most things in Dubai, you must have a credit card to be able to hire a car. There are few exceptions to this. If you do find a car-rental company that will take a cash deposit instead, you will probably have to leave your passport with them as security. This could be difficult, as most hotels require you to leave your passport in their safe for the duration of your stay. Some agencies insist on a credit card deposit as well as your passport. Find another agency if this is the case. You do not have to leave your passport with them. A photocopy of it is sufficient. The reason for

Dangerous Drivers

If you're going to drive in Dubai, be warned. Most drivers seem oblivious to other cars around them, and courtesy on the road simply does not exist. Although it's not as bad as in other parts of the UAE, people tend to cut in front of you, turn without indicating, race each other and take up three parking spaces or double park right next to your car. They have a tendency to wander across lanes at roundabouts and try to turn out of them from inside lanes. Eternal vigilance is necessary to avoid fender-benders. Drivers sitting behind you at a red traffic light also tend to have a very annoying habit of beeping you impatiently the minute the light goes green. Also, be very careful crossing the road. Not all drivers seem to understand the purpose of a pedestrian crossing and will not slow down, let alone stop, unless there are lights.

The UAE has one of the highest incidents of road deaths per capita in the world. Speeding and reckless driving is the major cause. The worst thing about all this is that there doesn't seem to be enough incentive not to drive badly. Although speeding fines are meted out, it doesn't stop most of the population from driving way too fast. Causing a death through an accident requires the payment of blood money to the victim's family. Although this is a large sum (about Dh160,000), Nationals are insured against it. This often means that the only punishment for causing death or injury through reckless driving is an increased insurance premium. Licences are not even cancelled.

all this security is to protect themselves against people who run up traffic violations and then leave town without paying them.

Most foreign driving licences are accepted in Dubai so long as you are either a citizen or a resident of the country that issued the licence. Some companies insist on an international licence, however, so you might want to get one of these before you leave home.

If you are a resident of Dubai, you will need to get a permanent UAE licence. For most western nationalities this means just swapping your own driving licence for a UAE one. For others it is necessary to sit a test.

At large international agencies, small cars start at about Dh120 per day with another Dh20 for Collision Damage Waiver (CDW) insurance. Avis offers a 25% discount on hire for three days or 30% for one week. The larger agencies do not charge an excess in the case of an accident that is your fault if you have taken out CDW. Always call the police if you are involved in an accident (see boxed text 'Accident Alert').

At the smaller agencies, you should be able to negotiate a net rate of around Dh100 per day, including CDW insurance. With

---

Accident Alert

All accidents, no matter how small, must be reported to the traffic police. In Bur Dubai call ☎ 450 111 and in Deira call ☎ 660 555. Unless your car is causing a traffic jam, do NOT move it until the traffic police get there. For insurance claim purposes you must have a police report and if you move your car, the police may not be able to issue a complete report. Outside Dubai you should leave your car exactly where it is, no matter how bad an obstruction it is causing, and call the police immediately. If you are driving a hire car and you have a crash, your insurance may not cover any damage unless a police report is written. One reader tells of such an experience:

I hired a car from Avis. I backed into a post in the hotel car park and I even had to call the police for that! If I had not done so, Avis would not have paid for the damage, even though I had taken out full insurance.

Caroline Williams

✿✿✿✿✿✿✿✿✿✿✿✿✿✿✿✿✿✿

---

these agencies, no matter what they tell you, you may still be liable for the first Dh1000 to Dh1500 of damage in the event of an accident that is your fault, even if you have CDW. Sometimes this excess is only Dh200 if you have paid CDW. Ask questions and read the small print on the contract carefully.

The first 100 or 150km per day are usually free with additional kilometres costing 40 or 50 fils each. If you rent a car for more than three days you will usually be given unlimited mileage.

Most agencies have free pick-up and delivery within Dubai, either to/from a hotel or the airport. They also offer a chauffeur service, but you'll pay around Dh150 per eight hours for this privilege. If you are just moving around Dubai for the day it is much cheaper to use taxis.

Although smaller agencies are generally cheaper than the larger chain companies, it's worth considering the convenience of being able to contact the local office of a reliable company if you are driving out of Dubai and something goes wrong. It's also worth ensuring complete insurance cover (zero liability).

The highest concentrations of smaller, local car rental companies are on Abu Baker al-Siddiq Rd (Map 3), just north of the Clock Tower roundabout, and on Omar ibn al-Khattab St (Map 3), just north of the Claridge Hotel. They are also found opposite the taxi and minibus station on Omar ibn al-Khattab St in Deira and on the Bur Dubai side of the creek on Trade Centre Rd (Map 4), just north of Al-Adhid Rd.

Arab Link
 (☎ 684 637, fax 689 559)
 Abu Baker al-Siddiq Rd, Deira
Avis
 (☎ 295 7121, fax 295 6807)
 Al-Maktoum Rd, Deira
 (☎ 224 5219, fax 224 4150)
 Airport arrivals hall (24 hours)
 (☎ 331 3731, fax 331 7394)
 World Trade Centre, Za'abeel roundabout, Za'abeel
Budget
 (☎ 823 030) Al-Maktoum Rd just before Cargo Village; Airport Arrivals hall (24 hours)

Europcar
   (☎ 520 033) Desks at the Hilton, Inter-Continental, Al-Bustan Rotana and Hyatt Regency hotels
Hertz
   (☎ 824 422) Al-Maktoum Rd, just before Cargo Village; Airport arrivals hall (24 hours)
Patriot Rent-A-Car
   (☎ 221 4440, fax 227 3386)
   Abu Baker al-Siddiq Rd, Deira
   (☎ 224 4244) Airport arrivals hall
White Falcon
   (☎ 295 8000, fax 295 8008)
   Al-Maktoum Rd; at the Clock Tower roundabout

Road Rules

Drive on the right in Dubai. The speed limit is 60km/h in town with a maximum of 80km/h, and 100km/h on the highways with a maximum of 120km/h. If you are caught speeding, you will be fined, but in some cases you will simply be sent a bill by the police. For this reason, many car rental companies require customers to sign a statement acknowledging that they are aware of this and authorising the rental company to charge their credit card for any tickets that turn up after they have left town. There are also speed cameras on the major highways.

The traffic situation in Dubai has improved immensely since the government started forcing people to pay for the priviledge of parking in the centre. For years the flow of traffic through the city had been clogged, in no small part by triple-parked cars in Beniyas Square. On the square, and in other parts of the centre, there is now a strictly enforced four-hour limit on parking. Tickets must be purchased from one of the numerous ticket-dispensing machines. Rates are Dh2 for the first hour, Dh5 for up to two hours, Dh8 for up to three hours and Dh11 for up to four hours. Place the ticket on top of your dashboard. Parking rates apply from 8 am to 1 pm and from 4 to 9 pm Saturday through Thursday. Parking in the centre is free on Friday and holidays.

TAXI

The starting fare in Dubai Transport taxis is Dh3. This goes up to Dh3.50 after 10 pm.

There are also private taxis which come in all sizes and colours and do not have meters. This presents you with a choice: negotiate the fare in advance (and perhaps pay too much) or get in, tell the driver your destination, pay him what you think is an appropriate fare once you get there and hope that it is accepted without an argument.

Should you go for the latter option, expect to pay a little less than the metered taxis (ie about Dh5 for trips around the centre of Dubai that do not involve crossing the Creek). Crossing the Creek immediately runs the standard fare up to about Dh8 or Dh9. For a trip from the Clock Tower roundabout to Satwa you should pay Dh12; a trip to Jumeira will cost about Dh15. Drivers will expect a 50% premium after midnight.

However, expired licenses for private taxis without meters are not being renewed so, eventually, all taxis will all be operated by Dubai Transport. They will all have meters and English-speaking drivers dressed in uniforms.

You can also call Dubai Transport (☎ 331 3131) to send a taxi to pick you up. These cars are very comfortable and clean, the drivers are helpful and friendly and the fares are reasonable. Expensive, fixed-price cabs also operate from some of the bigger hotels. If you ask someone to call a taxi for you, be sure you know who they are calling. One service in Dubai uses Jaguars – and charges accordingly. Here are some private taxi companies that can be booked in advance:

Emirates Rent-A-Car
   (☎ 691 555, fax 666 054)
Emirates Taxis
   (☎ 515 515, fax 515 551)
Golden Taxis
   (☎ 396 5444, fax 334 8529)
Limousine Dubai
   (☎ 627 333, fax 697 388)

If you are on a budget, shared local taxis run from the Dubai bus station on Al-Ghubaiba Rd to Jumeira, Karama and Satwa for Dh1 to

Dh2 per passenger or Dh7 to Jebel Ali. These are mostly seven passenger Peugeots and are really only a good bet if you are at the bus station anyway, one going in your direction is nearly full and you can't wait until the next regular bus to your destination departs.

ABRA
Scores of abras constantly cross the Creek from early morning until around midnight. On the Deira side of the Creek, the dock is at the intersection of Al-Sabkha and Beniyas Rds. On the Bur Dubai side, the dock is at the west end of the souq. Abras, like service taxis, leave when full, but it never takes more than a few minutes for one of them to fill up. The fare of 50 fils is collected once you are out on the water.

BICYCLE
You can't hire bicycles in Dubai and we don't recommend that you cycle here. With an abundance of bad drivers who are not accustomed to sharing the road with cyclists, there's a high chance that you will be knocked down. Even on the highways out of the city, it's not a good idea. It has been done though, so if you want to bring your bike to tour Dubai remember its always hot and humid here: drink plenty of water. And always yield to car drivers. Don't think they're going to watch out for you.

Also, bear in mind that bikes used in the region tend to be old-fashioned versions used by labourers. Getting any repairs done on a modern mountain bike is likely to be difficult if not impossible, so take plenty of spare parts and come prepared to be your own mechanic.

WALKING
The older parts of Dubai, with their souqs, fascinating architecture and museums, can be covered on foot as long as it's not too hot. A walk along the Creek to see the dhows is a pleasant way to spend half a morning. The rest of Dubai is very spread out though, and getting from a shopping centre to a beach, for instance, is impossible by foot. See the Things to See & Do chapter for two walking tours that take in the best sights on both sides of the Creek.

HITCHING
Hitching is never entirely safe in any country in the world, and we don't recommend it. Travellers who decide to hitch should understand that they are taking a small but potentially serious risk. People who do choose to hitch will be safer if they travel in pairs and let someone know where they are planning to go. It is common to see people trying to hitch a ride on the outskirts of Dubai. Almost without exception the hitchers are locals or Pakistani or Indian expats. Tourists may find it difficult to get a ride: people tend to be a bit mystified by westerners trying to hitch a ride, especially if they're female.

ORGANISED TOURS
There are literally hundreds of different tours you can take, both inside and outside of Dubai itself. Basically, the tours are all pretty similar, but even though prices don't vary much it's still worth shopping around. Most companies can arrange individually tailored tours so if you want to go bird-watching or mountain biking, or even get married in the desert Bedouin-style, it can be arranged. These specialist tours can be very pricey though.

For a complete list of tour operators in Dubai, see *What's On* magazine or the 'Tourist Guide' section at the beginning of the phone book. Brochures for tour companies can also be picked up from the reception desks of most hotels. When you book a tour with one of these companies you will usually be picked up from your hotel. Some of them require a deposit which is nonrefundable if there is less than 24 hours' notice of cancellation.

Arabian Adventures (☎ 343 9999, 331 4696, next to the Metropolitan Hotel (Map 1), Interchange No 2, Sheikh Zayed Rd offers half-day tours of Dubai daily for Dh110 per person. This takes you to the Jumeira Mosque, the Bastakia Quarter and the Dubai Museum. It then takes in an abra ride across the Creek and a visit to the Gold Souq and Spice Souq.

Net Tours Net Tours & Travel (☎ 666 555/668 661, Al-Ittihad Rd, Deira) has a similar day tour which also includes a visit to one or two shopping malls for Dh90 per person. Considering how cheap taxis and abras are, and given that most of these sites are free and can easily be covered on foot, it is beyond me why anyone would want to pay this sort of money for an organised tour of them.

If it's within your budget you might want to take a 45 minute Fly By Dubai tour with Desert Air Tours (☎ 299 4411) on a Cessna 207 for Dh 250 per person. Alternatively, you can charter the plane for Dh1900 per hour.

Bird-watching tours for small groups can be arranged through Colin Richardson, who heads the Emirates Bird Records Committee and is author of *Birds of the United Arab Emirates* and the *Shell Bird-Watching Guide to the UAE*. A half-day tour of Dubai Creek Golf Course & Khor Dubai Wildlife Sanctuary costs Dh190 per person. Tours to other hot spots around the UAE can also be arranged (for more information call Colin on ☎ 472 277 or mobile 050-650 3398).

For tours out of Dubai, see Organised Tours in the Excursions chapter. For tours involving activities such as desert safaris and sand-skiing, see Activities in the Things to See & Do chapter.

Things to See & Do

WALKING TOURS (MAP 2)

If you only have one day, and you don't want to spend it shopping, then a walking tour around the older parts of Bur Dubai and Deira should be the first thing on your list. These areas lend themselves well to walking tours as they are quite small and the attractions worth seeing are all fairly close together. The rest of Dubai, that is the modern sprawl, does not have as many sights and they are all spread out anyway, making a walking tour impossible.

The following are two walking tours – one takes in the sights of Bur Dubai and the other the sights of Deira. Both tours can be done within half a day, broken up with an *abra* ride and a refreshment. If you are in Dubai when it is warm, you might want to do one walking tour in the early morning and the other in the early evening.

Most things to see on these walking tours are discussed more fully later in this chapter, so just flick ahead a few pages for more information.

There are no official guided walking tours of Dubai, but a brochure called *Dubai Town Walk* (Dh5) maps out one tour on each side of the Creek. These tours differ from the walking tours in this book in that they are slightly shorter and do not feature some of the heritage sights that have been opened more recently.

Walk 1: Bur Dubai

Begin this walking tour at the **Dubai Museum** on Al-Fahidi Street. Before you enter the museum you might like to make a small diversion to an interesting backstreet of the Dubai Souq. Walk north from the museum's entrance on 76A St for a closer look at the multidomed **Grand Mosque**. When you visit the Shaikh Saeed al-Maktoum House, later on this walk (see also later in this chapter), you will be able to see old photos of Dubai showing the original Grand Mosque.

Walk past the mosque on its right-hand side for about 20m, go under an old

Dubai Highlights

The following is a list of our favourite things to see and do in Dubai.

The Souqs of Deira

No one should miss out on a wander through the Spice Souq, the Covered Souq or the Gold Souq in Deira. They are bustling with smells, sights and sounds and, if there is a Dubai trademark, experiencing one of the souqs is it (see page 87).

Dubai Museum

A great introduction to the culture of the Emirates and the history of Dubai. There is a reconstruction of a souq; displays on ecology, pearling and fishing; traditional arts and crafts; and an audiovisual presentation depicting the city's development (see page 82).

Abra Ride on the Creek

For only 50 fils you can jump on an abra at any time of the day and evening. It's the best way to view the city – with its incongruous mixture of old and new architecture (see page 81).

Sheesha at the Fatafeet Cafe

This is the best place to sit and admire Dubai's stunning skyline and enjoy a puff of apple-flavoured tobacco and cup of Arabic coffee. The best time to be here is just before sunset so you can see the golden reflection of the Creek on the magnificent National Bank of Dubai building on the other side of the water (see page 116).

Jumeira Beach

Smear on the sun block and enjoy a quick visit to this public beach to cool off in the crystal clear waters of the Arabian Gulf (see page 90).

❁❁❁❁❁❁❁❁❁❁❁❁❁❁❁❁❁❁

archway then turn left into a side street. Along here you will notice vendors selling baskets of fruit. You may also notice lots of shoes at the bottom of some stairs. This is not a back entrance to the mosque, it's the way up to the **Hindu Temple**. The baskets of fruit are sold as offerings to the Hindu gods. From here continue along this side street then turn right and you will be in the Dubai Souq, surrounded by dozens of colourful fabric stores. It is better now to make your way back to the Dubai Museum, unless you want a shortened walking tour.

Opposite the museum's entrance, and slightly to the north-east, you will see a large white building. This is the Diwan office, but you'll get a better view of it a little later in the tour. After you have spent an hour or two inside the museum you will come out on Al-Fahidi St. Turn left and continue along this street until you get to the next roundabout. This is Al-Fahidi roundabout; Al-Musalla post office should be across the road on your right.

You are now standing on the edge of the **Bastakia Quarter**, which features a number of old windtower houses (see the special section 'Architecture' in the Facts about Dubai chapter), which were once the homes of wealthy Dubai merchants. On your left you will see a white building, this is the **Majlis Gallery** (see Art Galleries later in this chapter for more information) and it is housed within a restored windtower house. Walk inside to see this typical Gulf construction, featuring a courtyard with a number of rooms coming off it.

Wend your way northwards through the small streets that wrap around the windtower houses towards the **Creek**. Once you reach the Creek, turn left and walk along the front of the Creek past the impressive **Diwan** (Ruler's Office) with its traditional windtowers, modern sculptures and black cast-iron fence. The Diwan is the highest administrative body of the Dubai government. It is also Shaikh Maktoum's office and so it is often referred to as the Ruler's Office. Look over to the other side of the Creek and you'll notice some other windtowers. These form part of the Deira Old

Souq, which you can explore on the next walking tour.

Once past the Diwan you will come to an open area on the Creek waterfront. You won't be able to walk any farther here (unless you want a swim) so turn left into the **Dubai Souq**. Before you pass through the wooden pillars of the souq entrance look to your right and notice the restored **waterfront houses**. There is no access to these places yet, but one of them, the **Bait al-Wakeel**, has been designated as a maritime museum and will be open sometime in 2000.

Once you have wandered through the souq, which sells mainly materials from Asia, you will come out at its western entrance. The **abra dock** will be ahead of you and to your right. Walk past the abras and continue along the waterfront to the **Shindagha Tower** set behind low stone walls. This watchtower was built in 1910 and differs from most watchtowers in the Emirates as it is square in shape. It protected the old town at the mouth of the Creek during the heyday of Dubai's merchant-trading era.

The rest of the walking tour takes you farther along this peaceful stretch of waterfront towards the mouth of the Creek. The next attraction is the **Bin Suroor Mosque**. It is a tiny, restored mosque that was originally built in 1930 and is mainly used by the people working nearby. Next to this is the **Shaikh Saeed al-Maktoum House**; once the residence of the ruling family of Dubai, it has now been turned into a museum featuring mainly a photographic history of the city.

Next door to Al-Maktoum House are the new **Diving and Heritage Villages**. At the time of writing they were not finished, although visitors were still permitted to enter. Inside you will find displays on pearl diving and village life, a museum featuring archaeological relics found in Dubai and a small souq. This is where your walking tour of Bur Dubai ends. Now you'll probably feel like stopping for a drink at the Heritage Village, where you can sit and watch the Creek life float by.

If you have the stamina, you can make your way back to the abra dock, cross the Creek and begin a walking tour of Deira.

Walk 2: Deira

Begin this walking tour at the abra dock on the corner of Beniyas and Al-Sabkha Rds. Walk north along Al-Sabkha Rd and turn left onto Al-Suq al-Kabeer St, just past Al-Khaleej Hotel (which will be on your right). Turn right into 67 St then left onto 20D St. This will bring you into the hustle and bustle of Deira. As you head west along here you will pass shops selling various goods such as textiles, clothes, rugs and luggage. This area is known as the **Murshid Souq**. There is probably not a lot of merchandise here that you will want to buy or admire, but it is interesting to take in the sights and sounds of this ethnic melting pot.

When you get to Suq Deira St turn left and then immediately right back on to Al-Suq al-Kabeer St. This will bring you to the covered, wooden entrance of the **Deira Old Souq** or, as it is also called, the **Spice Souq**. This is where things get more interesting. You will know you are here when your nose is bombarded with the pungent aromas of cardamom, cloves and cinnamon. The alleyways here are narrow and intricate and there is no set route that you should take. Just wander around at will and enjoy the many exotic sights.

If you continue in a south-westerly direction you will eventually come out on to Al-Abra St. Turn right then turn left onto Al-Ras St, the next main street. Walk along here until you get to Al-Hadd St where you turn right. Al-Hadd St is lined with shops selling sacks of spices, nuts and pulses. When you get to the end of this street turn right into Al-Ahmadiya St. About 50m along you will come to a restored house called the **Heritage House**. Behind this is the restored **Al-Ahmadiya School**. Built in 1912, it was once a school for the sons of Dubai's wealthy merchants. The building is spacious and airy and is decorated with arches along a verandah on the ground floor.

Continuing along Al-Ahmadiya St, turn right into Old Baladiya St; ahead you will see the wooden latticed archway of the entrance to Dubai's famous **Gold Souq** where you will be bamboozled by the sheer mass of glittering gold. When you come out at the other end of the souq, continue in the same direction along Sikkat al-Khail St and you will pass the **Perfume Souq**, a string of shops selling Arabic and European perfumes. Try them out, though be aware that Arabic perfumes are extremely strong and you only need a little dab. After passing through the Perfume Souq, you will come to a roundabout. Turn right into 67 St where you will find lots of trinket shops selling kitsch souvenirs.

Tucked behind the shops lining the east side (left side) of 67 St is the **Deira Covered Souq** which sells everything from sheeshas to henna. Turn left and head through the souq. You will come out onto Al-Sabkha Rd near the bus station. Turn left here then turn right into Naif Rd. At this corner you'll see a crumbling old **windtower** in desperate need of restoration.

Follow Naif Rd and turn right into 9A St. As you round the corner you will see an **old fort** on your left, which is now used as a police station. A little farther along you will come to **Naif Souq**. This small, covered souq is frequented almost exclusively by women, as it sells abayas, headscarves, materials, perfumes and children's clothes. A walk through here will bring you to Deira St on the souq's south side. Turn left into Deira St and walk to Al-Musalla Rd. Turn left into Al-Musalla Rd and on the next corner is **Naif Park**, which is a nice place to rest and end your walking tour of Deira.

THE CREEK (MAP 2)

Dubai's waterfront epitomises the city's personality. If you do only one touristy thing in Dubai, make sure you visit the Creek – the best way to see a great trading port is from the water. Instead of booking an expensive cruise you can just hire an abra for an hour or so. For around Dh30 (for the whole boat, not per person) the captain should take you to Al-Maktoum Bridge and back. For Dh40 he ought to extend that route to include a trip to the mouth of the Creek and back. These prices take a bit of bargaining to achieve. The shorter trip takes just over half an hour, the longer one takes 45 to 60 minutes.

Also take some time to walk along the **dhow wharfage** on the Deira side of the

THINGS TO SEE & DO

ALEM GOSHIME

On the waterfront: modern offices overlook the abras awaiting their passengers.

Creek to the west of the abra dock. Dhows bound for every port from Kuwait to Bombay dock here to load and unload all sorts of cargo. You'll see tyres, jeans, kitchen sinks, cars and probably just about anything you can imagine.

MUSEUMS (MAP 2)
Dubai Museum

The Dubai Museum (☎ 353 1862) is one tourist site that should definitely not be missed, as echoed by one particular reader:

The Dubai Museum underneath Al-Fahidi Fort is a must see. It's a multi-million dollar investment, making use of new technology to portray the old Dubai of the 1960s and 1970s. Sometimes it's hard to distinguish the attendants in their local, everyday dishdasha costumes, from the models.

Norman Sheppard

The museum occupies Al-Fahidi Fort on the Bur Dubai side of the Creek, next to the Diwan. The fort was built in the early 19th century and is thought to be the oldest building in Dubai. For many years it was both the residence of Dubai's rulers and the seat of government, before it became a museum in 1971.

At the entrance is a display of **aerial photographs** showing the growth of Dubai over the years. Entering the fort's courtyard, you'll see a big tank which was used to carry fresh water on pearling boats. Several small **boats** are also in the courtyard, including a

shasha – a small fishing boat made of palm fronds, still used by fishermen on the east coast of the UAE, around Khor Kalba. There is also a **barasti house** with a windtower (see the special section 'Architecture' in the Facts about Dubai chapter for more information on barasti houses).

The hall along the right-hand side of the courtyard has a display on the fort itself and another display featuring *khanjars* (curved daggers) and other **traditional weapons**. The hall to the left of the courtyard has a video of traditional Emirati dances, a display of musical instruments and more weapons.

The tower at the far corner of the courtyard leads down to a large underground area where the rest of the museum's exhibits are. The first is a very slick multimedia presentation of the city's development. Then you come to very detailed **re-creations of a typical souq**, a home and school as they would have looked in the 1950s. These come complete with disturbingly lifelike dummies of people – you always have the feeling that someone real is standing right next to you. This is followed by a display on water and how it was conserved in the desert.

There is also an **interactive display** on the flora and fauna of the UAE, a display of seafaring life and the area's archaeology, including a complete grave from the Al-Qusais archaeological site. Another room features finds from the digs at both Al-Qusais and Jumeira (5th and 8th centuries AD respectively).

To get to the museum if you've come across the Creek by abra, walk inland from the dock for about 100m then turn left onto Al-Fahidi Rd. You'll see the museum on your left. Alternatively, go through the Bur Dubai Souq and out the other end through the narrow street and lanes heading inland and you'll eventually come to the museum. If you are catching a taxi, the word for museum is *mathaf*.

The museum is open Saturday to Thursday from 8.30 am to 8.30 pm and Friday from 3 to 9 pm. Admission is Dh7 for adults and Dh3 for children aged eight and under. All displays in the museum have explanations in Arabic and English. Photography is permitted. Bus No 19 goes past the museum.

Shaikh Saeed al-Maktoum House

The house of Shaikh Saeed (☎ 393 7139), the grandfather of Dubai's present ruler, has been restored as a museum of pre-oil times. It sits along the Creek waterfront on the Bur Dubai side in the Shindagha area. The 30-room house was built in 1896 during the reign of Shaikh Maktoum bin Hasher al-Maktoum. For many years it served as a communal residence for the Al-Maktoum family, in keeping with the Arabian tradition of having several generations living in separate apartments within the same house or compound. Shaikh Saeed lived here from 1888 until his death in 1958. The house was re-opened as a museum in 1986 and houses an **exhibition of photographs**, mainly from the 1940s, 50s and 60s, documenting the history and development of Dubai. It is amazing to see how different the place looked only a few decades ago and makes you realise just how quickly Dubai has developed from a sleepy Gulf fishing village into a leading metropolis in the region.

Some of the photos go back to late last century and there are some fascinating shots of traditional life in Dubai taken in souqs and at celebrations such as *Tawminah*, the festival carried out on completion of the recitation of the Quran by school children. Traditional Bedouin life is also represented, and there are models of the different sorts of dhows used in Dubai. There is also a model of Bur Dubai from the 1950s.

There is a display of **coins** that were once used in the region, including Indian rupees (the currency used in Dubai during British control of India). From 1948 until federation in 1971, a currency known as the 'Gulf Rupee' was the legal tender in the region.

The two storey house, built around a courtyard, has a windtower at each corner and is divided into four wings. Near the entrance is the main *majlis* (reception area or meeting room) and a room that was once set aside for the sheikh's clerk. The house is built of coral quarried from the Gulf and then covered with lime and plaster. Until recently this was a common building method along both the Gulf and Red Sea coasts of Arabia and you can see more examples of it around the Heritage Area of Sharjah (see the Excursions chapter). In Shaikh Saeed's era, the entrance on Al-Shindagha Rd (the one used by visitors today), was the back door to the house. The main entrance, opening onto the large, central courtyard, faced the sea.

The house lies next to the Heritage and Diving Villages on Al-Shindagha Rd in Dubai. It is open Saturday to Thursday from 8.30 am to 9 pm and on Friday from 3 to 10 pm. Admission is Dh2. The gift shop sells some souvenirs as well as a guide to the house (Dh5). You can catch bus Nos 8, 16, 19 or 20 to get to Al-Maktoum House.

Heritage & Diving Villages

These villages, next to Shaikh Saeed al-Maktoum House on Al-Shindagha Rd, were under construction at the time of writing, but visitors were still permitted to enter for free.

When finished, the Diving Village (☎ 393 9390) will have displays on pearl diving, once the livelihood of the city, and scale models of various types of dhows and pearling boats. There are a few shops selling and hiring (modern) diving equipment. A large outdoor **restaurant** and sheesha bar gives you a nice view of the Creek with Dubai in the background.

You will notice some signs along the waterfront here offering **boat cruises** for Dh100 per hour. If you want to take a boat ride it's better to make a deal with one of the many skippers who cruise up and down this area; you should only pay Dh30 to Dh35 for half an hour or Dh40 to Dh45 for one hour.

The Heritage Village (☎ 393 7151) recreates traditional Bedouin and coastal village life, complete with barasti homes, a traditional coffeehouse and a small souq where you can buy freshly made *dosa* (a flat, grilled bread made of flour and water) from Emirati women for Dh1. The other shops in the souq sell rather nice traditional handicrafts, Bedouin jewellery and pottery, as well as some tacky and rather overpriced souvenirs from India, Africa and Asia.

There is also a small **museum** here displaying artefacts and diagrams from archaeological sites at Al-Qusais, on the north-eastern outskirts of town; Jumeira, in Dubai; and Al-Sufouf, near Hatta (see also the Jumeira Archaeological Site later in this chapter). Finds from the Al-Qusais site (2500-550 BC) include human skeletons, bronze arrowheads, stone vessels, daggers, hooks, needles and pottery collected from around 120 graves. At Al-Sufouf a circular, collective tomb was discovered much like the one at the Hili Archaeological Gardens in Al-Ain. It suggests that this society belonged to the Umm al-Nar culture, which arose near modern Abu Dhabi. Little is known about them except that they were probably part of the Bahrain-based Dilmun Empire, which was then the ascendant power in the central and northern Gulf. More than 50 individual tombs were discovered, most of which were looted over the centuries. Finds from those found intact include jars, jewels, beads and weapons.

The Heritage and Diving villages are open daily from 7.30 am to 9 pm, but close between 2 and 3 pm. To get there you can catch bus No 8, 16, 19 or 20.

ART GALLERIES
The Dubai International Arts Centre (Map 5)

The Arts Centre (☎ 444 398) off Al-Jumeira Rd, opposite McDonald's, is open from 8.30 am to 4 pm. It is a nonprofit, membership organisation, which means it exhibits only the works of its members, all of whom are UAE locals. Having said that, its members represent over 60 nationalities. Some of the more interesting works are by Abdul Wahed al-Mawlawi, Susan Walpole, Fay Lawson, Alem Goshime (who drew all the illustrations in this book) and Margaret Henderson. It also runs courses for members in everything from pottery to framing to photography. Bus Nos 8 and 20 will take you there.

The Majlis Gallery (Map 2)

The Majlis Gallery (☎ 536 233) at Al-Fahidi roundabout in Bur Dubai exhibits the paintings of local artists. There are also some handicrafts such as cushion covers and bags, ceramics, glassware and sculpture. The gallery is open Saturday to Thursday from 9.30 am to 1.30 pm and 4 to 7.30 pm. Catch bus No 19 to get here.

The Orient Gallery (Map 4)

This gallery (☎ 558 832), in the Bur Juman Centre on the corner of Trade Centre and Khalid bin al-Waleed Rds, has paintings, sculptures and photographic works by local and overseas artists. An original photograph by Wilfred Thesiger, a well known explorer of the region during the 1940s, will cost you between Dh600 and Dh1600. Ramesh Shukla, the royal photographer from the 1940s until the 1980s, runs the gallery with his son. Ramesh's photographs will cost you between Dh500 and Dh1500. His paintings, depicting life in Dubai earlier this century, will cost you anywhere between Dh5000 and Dh40,000. Artists' supplies are sold here as well as some coffee-table books. The gallery is open everyday from 10 am to 10 pm. Bus Nos 3, 5, 16, 44, 61 and 90 go past here.

Profile (Map 5)

Profile (☎ 491 147) in Markaz al-Jumeira on Al-Jumeira Rd is primarily a framing shop, but it also has a number of works by well-known local artists such as Spencer Tart, Margaret Henderson, Patricia al-Fakhri and Abdul Qader al-Rais. Most of the works are watercolours and acrylics and depict traditional life in Arabia. Catch bus No 8 or 20 to get here.

HERITAGE & ARCHAEOLOGICAL SITES
Majlis Ghorfat Um-al-Sheef (Map 1)

It is unusual to find a traditional building still standing so far from the Creek, but this one, located just south-east of Jumeira Beach Park, has been well restored and is worth a visit. The two storey Majlis Ghorfat Um-al-Sheef was built in 1955 and was attended in the evenings by Shaikh Rashid bin Saeed al-Maktoum. Here he would listen to his people's complaints, grievances and ideas. It was a place of open discussion and exchange. A former British political resident of Dubai, Donald Hawley, saw the Majlis as 'an Arabian Camelot' and Shaikh Rashid as 'King Arthur'.

The majlis also provided a cool retreat from the heat of the day. It is made of gypsum and coral rock – traditional building materials of the Gulf – and the roof is made of palm fronds *(areesh)*. The ground floor is an open area surrounded by columns and the second floor consists of a verandah on one side and the enclosed majlis itself on the other. The columns, windows and doors are all made of teak from India. The majlis is decorated with cushions, rugs, a coffeepot, pottery and food platters, and is pretty close to the way it would have looked in Shaikh Rashid's day. Windows surround the room and, in the summer heat, the breeze circulates freely around the house, keeping it relatively cool.

A garden of date palms and fig trees has been constructed around the majlis, and a traditional barasti cafe sits in one corner of

---

The Majlis

Majlis translates as 'meeting place' or 'reception area'. The Majlis was a forum or council where citizens could come and speak to their leaders and make requests, complaints or raise any issue that was troubling them. In Dubai the majlis system was preserved until the 1960s.

A majlis, in its more domestic sense, is a reception area found in all of the older buildings in Dubai (such as Al-Fahidi Fort, now the Dubai Museum, and the Heritage House in Al-Ahmadiya). Its western cousin is probably the lounge room. The majlis is still an important room in an Arab household and is usually the domain of the male members of the family. It's a place where they can get together and talk without disturbing the women of the house. Some traditional houses had a separate majlis for women.

---

the enclosure. The garden, with its *falaj* (traditional irrigation system), needs to mature a little, but the sound of running water is very soothing and, though it's in the middle of a residential area, it's very peaceful. The majlis is located on 17 St which runs off Al-Jumeira Rd, on the inland side, just past the Jumeira Beach Park. It is open Saturday to Thursday from 8.30 am to 1.30 pm and 3.30 to 8.30 pm. On Friday it's open from 3.30 to 8.30 pm. Admission is free. You can catch bus No 8 and get off just south of Jumeira Beach Park.

The Bastakia Quarter (Map 2)

This district, on the waterfront east of the Dubai Souq and the Diwan, features a number of old, traditional windtower houses. Built at the turn of the century, these windtowers were once the homes of wealthy Persian merchants lured to Dubai by its relaxed trade tariffs. Most came from the Bastak district in what is now southern Iran, hence the name Bastakia. Windtowers were a traditional form of air-conditioning, whereby cool air was funnelled down into the house (see the 'Architecture' special section in the Facts about Dubai chapter).

The quarter has been declared a conservation area and restoration work is being carried out on a few of the houses. As you wander through the narrow, peaceful lanes you can easily imagine the life of the merchant residents at the turn of the century. Notice the original carved wooden doors that remain on some of the houses.

Two of the windtower houses have been fully restored and are homes to two western expat families. Some of the others are lived in by a few Indian families, but most of them are under restoration. If you pass one of the houses under restoration ask the workmen if you can have a look around, but don't go climbing any stairs unless you're sure they're safe. Another restored house is home to the Majlis Gallery and is well worth visiting to see some local artwork.

Al-Ahmadiya School (Map 2)

Al-Ahmadiya School, behind the Heritage House on Al-Ahmadiya St in the souq area of Deira will eventually be turned into a museum detailing early education in Dubai. The classrooms of the school lead off a central courtyard and inscriptions from the Quran sit above each doorway. The school was built by a philanthropic pearl merchant in 1912 and was attended by Shaikh Rashid bin Saeed al-Maktoum, the prime mover behind the development of modern Dubai. By the middle of the century the building fell into disrepair and it wasn't until the early 1990s that restoration work began.

The small area around the school is home to a number of traditional houses that have been restored of late, including some courtyard houses (see the 'Architecture' special section in Facts about Dubai). They are made of gypsum, sea rock, coral, wood (from East Africa) and the trunks of date palms. At the time of writing the houses were not officially open to the public, but if the doors are open you can wander inside and have a look. You can catch any of the buses that go along Beniyas Rd and around the Al-Ras district to get here. You'll need to get off at the Public Library and walk from here.

Heritage House (Map 2)

This restored traditional house, next to Al-Ahmadiya School in the souq area of Deira, was once home to a wealthy Iranian merchant and was built in 1890. It differs to the old houses in the Bastakia Quarter on the other side of the Creek as it has no windtowers. The house is characterised by many wooden shutters at street level and a balcony railing along the roof. Once inside, you find yourself in a large courtyard surrounded by rooms and a verandah at one end.

As you move around the courtyard you pass a majlis, a cattle pen, kitchen, bedrooms, the ladies' majlis and a bride's room. This last room was where a young bride to be would prepare for her wedding day with the help of other women of the harem. It is decorated with mattresses, pillows and Persian rugs.

Jumeira Archaeological Site (Map 1)

This site is considered one of the biggest and most significant archaeological sites in the UAE. Remains found here date to the 6th century AD and can be seen in the small museum at the Heritage Village in Shindagha. The settlement is particularly interesting in that it spans the pre-Islamic and Islamic eras. Surrounded by modern villas and shopping centres, this settlement was once a caravan station on a route linking Ctesiphon (in what is now Iraq) to northern Oman. It was first excavated by archaeologists from the American University of Beirut in 1969, then by a team from Iraq in 1975. Now the work is being carried out by a team from Dubai.

Remains at the site link it with the Persian Sassanid Empire, the dominant culture in the region from the 3rd to the 6th century AD. Other Sassanid settlements have been found at Kush and Julfar in what is now the northern emirate of Ras al-Khaimah (see the Excursions chapter). The Sassanids were wiped out by Arab tribes, notably the Umayyad dynasty, with the coming of Islam in the 7th century. The Umayyads extended and restored many of the original buildings and the site continued to exist until at least the 10th century.

Excavations have revealed a series of stone walls that surrounded a souq made up of seven shops and a storage room. There are also the remains of a few houses, including a large courtyard house with decorative plaster work that was most likely the governor's palace (this kind of decoration can still be seen on restored houses in Dubai, such as in the Al-Ahmadiya district and along the waterfront in Bur Dubai). There is also a large building made up of a series of small rooms with arched openings around the walls close to the ground. It is believed that these were fox traps. Once a fox was lured inside the room the openings would be closed off. This building is characterised by towers at each corner and smaller, round towers set at intervals along each wall.

Other findings include glazed pottery utensils, copper and iron items, small pieces of glassware, coins and pieces of decorated gypsum. Two coins dating to the 10th century were also found here.

There is no access to the site for the public since archaeologists are still working on excavating it. If someone is there you may be able to have a look inside, otherwise you'll just have to make out parts of the site through the fence.

To reach the site, head south down Al-Jumeira Rd and do a U-turn when you get to the Jumeira Beach Park, just past the Hilton Beach Club. Take the first street on the right, which is 27 St, and continue straight to the end, then turn right; you will see a large fenced-in area about 50m along on your left. You can also catch bus No 8 as far as the Jumeira Beach Park and then walk for five minutes.

SOUQS (MAP 2)
Compared to how it would have been only 20 or 30 years ago, not much of the old covered souqs remain, but they still operate in the early morning and in the evening from around 5 to 8 pm. The **Deira Covered Souq**, off Al-Sabkha Rd, sells just about everything, though it has more of an Indian feel than an Arabic one. Textiles, spices, kitchen wares, walking sticks, sheeshas, clothes and a lifetime supply of henna are all available here.

The **Deira Old Souq**, or **Spice Souq** as it is also known, is a wonderful place to wander around and take in the smells of spices, nuts and dried fruits. The spices are mainly found at the souq's eastern end, closest to the Creek. There are sacks brimming with frankincense, dried lemons, ginger root, chilli and cardamom to name but a few. Other shops in this souq sell tacky trinkets, kitchen wares, shoes, rugs, glassware and textiles.

Deira's **Gold Souq** is on and around Sikkat al-Khail St, between Suq Deira and Old Baladiya Sts. If you don't spot the glittering gold in the windows you'll recognise this souq by the wooden lattice archways at the entrances. The Gold Souq is probably the largest such market in Arabia and attracts customers from all over the Middle East and the Subcontinent.

At the eastern end of the Gold Souq, along Sikkat al-Khail St, is the **Perfume Souq**. A number of shops here sell a staggering range of Arabic and European perfumes. The European perfumes are a mixture of designer originals and copies.

The Arabic perfumes are much stronger and spicier than western perfumes. Near the intersection of Al-Sabkha and Al-Maktoum Hospital Rds is Dubai's famous **Electronics Souq**. Dozens of shops, all selling virtually the same stock, are packed together and do a roaring trade with visitors from the CIS who buy up big and take the goods back home to sell for a profit.

The **Dubai Souq** in Bur Dubai has been beautifully reconstructed to be more appealing to tourists, but it still seems to be frequented almost exclusively by the local Indian population. It sells mostly materials and shoes. There is very little in the way of Arabic antiques or souvenirs that might be of interest to you. If you want to have a sari made, however, this is the place to come.

For more on what to buy at these souqs and how much it costs, see the Shopping chapter.

MOSQUES (MAPS 2 & 5)
The multidomed **Grand Mosque (Map 2)** in Bur Dubai, immediately north of the Dubai Museum, is home to Dubai's tallest minaret. This mosque might appear to be a beautiful example of restoration work, but was in fact built in the 1990s. Maintaining the style of the original Grand Mosque, dating from 1900 and knocked down to make way for another mosque in 1960, its sand-coloured walls and wooden shutters blend in perfectly with the surrounding old quarter of Bur Dubai. As well as being the centre of Dubai's religious and cultural life, the original Grand Mosque was also home to the town's schools *(kuttab)* where children learnt to recite the Quran from memory.

The **Jumeira Mosque (Map 5)** on Al-Jumeira Rd is the most well known mosque in Dubai due to its size and elaborate design. The best time to see it is at night when it is spectacularly lit up. You can catch bus Nos 8 and 20 along Al-Jumeira Rd to get there.

It's worth a quick drive along Al-Wasl Rd in Satwa to see the stunning **Iranian Mosque (Map 5)** and, opposite it, the Iranian Hospital. The incredibly detailed design of the brilliant blue mosaic work is typical of Iranian building design. Bus Nos 7 and 12 go along Al-Wasl Rd.

Non-Muslims are not allowed to enter mosques in the UAE. However, during special tourist events, such as the Dubai Summer Surprises, the Shaikh Mohammed Centre for Cultural Understanding (see Cultural Centres in the Facts for the Visitor chapter) organises tours inside the Jumeira Mosque.

OTHER ATTRACTIONS
Dubai Zoo (Map 5)

What a sorry sight this is. Lions, tigers and bears, among many other animals, living on featureless, concrete slabs, panting and groaning in the excessive heat. A bowl of water and a fan are the only amusements for most of these animals. You can't help wondering why a city that has enough money to build giant water parks and luxury hotel after luxury hotel cannot spend a little more to ensure that these poor animals have a humane existence. There has been talk for quite some time about rebuilding the zoo, but it is yet to happen. The zoo, on Al-Jumeira Rd in Jumeira, is open from 10 am to 6 pm daily except Tuesday; admission is Dh2. Bus No 8 or 20 will get you there.

World Trade Centre (Map 1)

The World Trade Centre tower was once Dubai's tallest building. Even though it has been overshadowed by taller skyscrapers it is still a very important and recognisable landmark in the city. There is a viewing gallery on the 37th floor for those who want a bird's-eye view of the city but can't afford to hire a helicopter. You can only visit the gallery as part of a tour. These leave daily from the information desk in the tower lobby at 9.30 am and 4.30 pm. Admission is Dh5. For more information call ☎ 331 4200. You can catch bus No 6, 61, 90 or 98 to get here.

Dhow Building Yard (Map 1)

On the Creek waterfront, about 1km south of Al-Garhoud Bridge in the Jaddaf district, there's a dhow building yard where monstrous dhows are built in the traditional style. This means that the planks are curved and fitted, one on top of the other, and then

Dhows

Dhows are just as much a characteristic of Dubai now as they were centuries ago. The dhow wharfage along the Creek, piled with assorted goods from Iran, India, Pakistan and East Africa, lends the city an exotic, ancient flavour. Even though glistening steel and glass buildings now dominate the Creek waterfront, the dhows give the place an unmistakably oriental feel.

Dubai was once one of the most important dhow-building centres on the Gulf coast. The dhow builders (al-galalif in Arabic) used basic materials and methods to construct the enormous vessels. The advancement of Dubai's maritime culture is reflected in the large number of different boats they constructed for different purposes.

The larger dhows used for long distance journeys were called al-boom, al-bateel and al-baglah and were up to 60m in length. Some of them have now been turned into cruise vessels and floating restaurants. The sambuk was a smaller boat, never more than 30m long, which was used mainly for fishing. It was characterised by its single mast and square stern, which had decorative wings protruding from it. Pearling boats (baggara) were larger and had no mast. The abra is still used to ferry people across the Creek.

the frame is fitted on the inside. In the west, the frame is generally built first, and the planks are fitted to it. The enormous vessels are all built by hand, using just the most basic of tools – a hammer, saw, chisel, drill and plane. Teak, because it's so sturdy, and Shesham are the most commonly used woods. Both are imported from the Subcontinent. These days, of course, dhows are powered by modern engines, usually from Europe or Japan, rather than sails.

To get to the dhow yard from the Bur Dubai side of the Creek, head along

Al-Qataiyat Rd towards Al-Garhoud Bridge. Take the first exit to the right after the Dubai Police Headquarters. Go past the nursery and turn left onto a gravel track just before the Dubai Docking Yard. Follow this track for about 700m as it bends around to the left and you will come to a string of dhow building yards. You can't miss the enormous hulls of these dhows. If you are coming from the Deira side you will have to cross over Al-Garhoud Bridge then do a U-turn at the next roundabout to be on the other side of the road. Bus No 14 goes as far as the Dubai Docking Yard from where it's a five minute walk to the dhows.

Al-Boom Tourist Village (Map 1)

This is really just a nice place to go for a coffee and sheesha in traditional barasti surroundings or to have a meal on the Fishmarket Floating Restaurant (see the Places to Eat chapter). This enormous restaurant dhow is permanently moored here. The rest of the 'village' is just made up of function rooms, a couple of Lebanese restaurants and a gallery, which seems to be closed most of the time. The sheesha cafe, does get going in the evenings though. The village lies next to Al-Garhoud Bridge on the Dubai side of the Creek. Bus No 44 goes past here.

PARKS (MAP 1)
Jumeira Beach Park

This lovely park fronts on to Jumeira Beach and a walk on the grass is a real treat. There is a children's play area, barbeques, picnic tables, walkways and kiosks. The long stretch of beach is clean and lined with date palms for shade. Lifeguards are on duty here.

The park, on Al-Jumeira Rd, is open Saturday to Wednesday from 8 am to 10.30 pm and to 11.30 pm on Thursday and Friday. Saturday and Monday are for women and children only. I can highly recommend this beach for women who don't want to pay a small fortune to use one of the five-star hotels' beach clubs, but also don't want to risk the unwanted male attention they may receive at other public beaches. Admission is Dh5 or Dh20 per car. You can catch bus No

8 or 20, which run along Al-Jumeira Rd to the park.

Safa Park

On Al-Hadiqa St in Jumeira, this park stretches for 1km from Al-Wasl Rd to Shaikh Zayed Rd. It is one of the most colourful parks in Dubai and is very popular with the local residents. One attraction is its small scale models of famous landmarks from around the world, such as the Taj Mahal, the Colosseum and the Leaning Tower of Pisa. There is a lake where you can hire paddle boats, tennis courts, a soccer pitch, BBQs and an artificial waterfall.

The park is open Saturday to Wednesday from 6.30 am to 9.30 pm and on Thursday, Friday and public holidays from 7.30 am to 10.30 pm. Admission is Dh3. To get there catch bus No 12 along Al-Wasl Rd.

Creekside Park

This is the largest of Dubai's parks and it runs 2.6km from Al-Garhoud Bridge on the Dubai side towards Al-Maktoum Bridge. It has children's play areas, dhow cruises, kiosks, restaurants, an amphitheatre and beaches (though it's not advisable to swim in the Creek). It is open Saturday to Wednesday from 8 am to 11 pm. On Thursday, Friday and public holidays it is open until 11.30 pm. Wednesday is for ladies and children only. Bus No 3, 5, 6, 14 or 44 will get you close to the park, but you will have to cross a couple of major roads to get to the entrance.

Al-Mamzar Beach Park

This park covers a small headland on the northern outskirts of Dubai at the mouth of Khor al-Mamzar. There are beaches, jet skis for hire, a swimming pool, children's play areas, BBQs, free transport around the park and kiosks. Lifeguards are on duty.

The park is open Saturday to Wednesday from 8 am to 9.30 pm and on Thursday, Friday and public holidays from 8 am to 10.30 pm. Wednesday is for ladies and children only, unless there is a special event, in which case it's open to everyone. Admission is Dh5 per person or Dh30 per car. Bus No 22 goes as far as the park's entrance.

Mushrif Park

This is the largest of Dubai's parks and is on the eastern outskirts of Dubai, about 15km from the centre. To get here, continue along Airport Rd, past the airport, until it becomes Al-Khawaneej Rd. You will see signs for the park. The biggest attraction here is the 'World Village', which is a miniature reconstruction of buildings from around the world, including a Dutch windmill, Tudor cottages and Thai stilt houses. Kids are welcome to crawl around the models. There are camel and pony rides, swimming pools, BBQs and lakes.

The park is open Saturday to Wednesday from 8 am to 9.30 pm and until 10.30 pm on Thursday, Friday and public holidays. Admission is Dh2 per person or Dh10 per car. You can catch bus No 11 or 15 along Al-Khawaneej Rd, from where it's a few minutes walk to the park.

BEACHES (MAPS 1 & 5)

Most beaches along the Dubai coast are the private domains of the five star beach hotels and, unless you are a guest, you will pay dearly for the use of their facilities. The average cost for a day visit is Dh200 with Dh100 redeemable on food and drinks. Some are only open to hotel guests and members. Don't despair. There are a few nice stretches of public beach. Though for single women, the male attention can sometimes be more of a hassle than the private beach club fees.

Next to the Marine Beach Resort just off Al-Jumeira Rd, more or less opposite the Jumeira Mosque, there is a stretch of public beach with facilities – showers, shelters, toilets and plenty of newly planted date palms (although it will be some years until these are big enough to provide shade). A little farther away from town, on either side of Jumeira Beach Hotel, there are public beaches. The beach farther south has shelters and showers and the beach to the north has jet skis for hire.

On the Deira side of the Creek there is a public stretch of beach running along the bank of the Khor al-Mamzar, which looks out over Sharjah. Follow the signs for Al-Mamzar Park and you'll see the beach

about 50m past the entrance to the park. There are no sun shelters or lifeguards here, only rubbish bins.

ACTIVITIES

There are far too many activities and sports clubs in Dubai to list here. The best source for this sort of information is the *Dubai Explorer*. It has an alphabetical listing of all the activities available in Dubai, where to do them and how much it will cost you. *What's On* also has information on clubs and leisure activities in Dubai.

Golf

It costs a fortune to maintain grass courses in this part of the world. And yes, this cost *is* reflected in exorbitant green fees. Dubai has most of the Arabian Peninsula's real grass golf courses. There are three courses in Dubai.

The Emirates Golf Club (☎ 473 222), on Shaikh Zayed Rd at Interchange No 5, is the site of the Dubai Desert Classic, part of the European PGA Tour. Green fees are Dh330 for 18 holes plus Dh45 for cart rental. Bus No 90 goes along Shaikh Zayed Rd as far as the golf club, but you'll have to cross Shaikh Zayed Rd which is not recommended. Catch a taxi, for about Dh40, instead.

The Dubai Creek Golf & Yacht Club (Map 1; ☎ 295 6000), near the Deira side of Al-Garhoud Bridge, has the same green fees. It also has a nine hole, par-three course, which you can play for Dh180 plus cart rental. At night it is floodlit and costs only Dh30 per round. No bus route passes the club entrance, but bus Nos 4, 11 and 15, which travel along Al-Maktoum Rd, go close.

The newest golf course in Dubai is the Dubai Golf & Racing Club (☎ 336 3666) on the outskirts of town. Green fees are Dh220 and you need to book five days in advance. Head down Oud Metha Rd, as if you were driving to Al-Ain or Hatta, then follow the signs for Nad al-Sheba. You can catch bus No 16 directly to the course.

There is a 10% discount on all these courses if you have United Arab Emirates Golfers' Association (UGA) membership. To play you must be wearing a shirt with

ALEM GOSHIME

The Dubai Creek Golf Course with its ultra-modern clubhouse in the background.

sleeves and a collar and trousers. Jeans and 'beach wear' are not allowed. You will probably be asked for a handicap certificate if you book a round, but it's not compulsory to have one. To find out more about the design of the courses, go to the Web site at www.dubaigolf.com.

Water Sports

Water sports are popular in Dubai, and the tourist industry is increasingly promoting the city as a winter 'sea & sun' destination. Most water-sports facilities are tied either to a big hotel with huge fees or a private club, and thus are not generally accessible to budget travellers.

Jet-Skiing If your life depends on a spot of jet-skiing you can pay for the use of a five star hotel beach club for the day and then pay Dh100 per half-hour on top of that, or you can go to the Creek bank just south of Al-Garhoud Bridge on the Deira side. There are a number of jet skis for hire here everyday from about 10 am until it begins to get dark. They cost Dh50 for half an hour from Saturday to Thursday, Dh100 on Friday morning, and Dh75 on Friday afternoon. To get here from the Deira side of the Creek, take Al-Garhoud Rd past the bridge and follow the signs for Al-Rashidiya. Turn right at the first set of lights after the bridge and follow the road towards the Creek. If you are coming from the Bur Dubai side, you'll need to take the right-hand exit as soon as

you're over the bridge, then turn right at the next lights. You'd be better off getting a taxi here as the buses don't go close enough.

There is another jet-ski area to the north of the Jumeira Beach Hotel. Here they charge Dh100 per half hour.

Remember that jet-skiing can be a dangerous, environmentally unfriendly activity, so take care and drive sensibly.

Water-Skiing If you are staying at a five star hotel with a beach club you will pay Dh100 for a half-hour of water-skiing. If you are not a guest at one of these places you will also have to pay the exorbitant daily admission fee to the beach club – usually about Dh200.

The only place to water-ski other than five-star-hotel beach clubs is at the Dubai Water Sports Association (Map 1; ☎ 334 2031) on the Bur Dubai side of the Creek. There is an entry fee of Dh15 on weekdays and Dh25 on weekends to get into the club and use the pool, deck chairs, jacuzzi or hang out at the bar and restaurant. If you want to water-ski it will cost you Dh45 for a 13 minute tow. The club is open from 9 am until dusk every day, although there is no water-skiing on Sunday.

To get here from the Deira side of the Creek, head along Al-Qataiyat Rd towards Al-Garhoud Bridge. Take the first exit to the right after the Dubai Police Headquarters. Continue past the nursery and turn right just before the Dubai Docking Yard. The tarmac road ends here, but continue along a sand track for 1.4km as it skirts around a large fenced-in compound. At this point you'll see the lonely looking club ahead and to your right. You can get bus No 14 as far as the fenced-in compound, but you will have about a 10 minute walk from here.

Diving Although the waters around Dubai are home to some coral reefs, marine life and a few modern shipwrecks, visibility in the water is not very good. Most dive companies take you up to the east coast to dive in the waters off Khor Fakkan, Dibba and Lima on the Musandam Peninsula (which is part of Oman). Dives are offered

Safety Guidelines for Diving

Before embarking on a scuba diving, skin diving or snorkelling trip, careful consideration should be given to a safe, as well as an enjoyable, experience. You should:

- Possess a current diving certification card from a recognised scuba diving instructional agency (if scuba diving).
- Be sure you are healthy and feel comfortable diving.
- Obtain reliable information about physical and environmental conditions at the dive site (eg from a reputable local dive operation).
- Be aware of local laws, regulations and etiquette about marine life and the environment.
- Dive only at sites within your realm of experience; if available, engage the services of a competent, professionally trained dive instructor or dive master.
- Be aware that underwater conditions vary significantly from one region, or even site, to another. Seasonal changes can significantly alter any site and dive conditions. These differences influence the way divers dress for a dive and what diving techniques they use.

to people at all levels of expertise. If you are uncertified you might want to take a diving course (see Courses later in this chapter).

The best deal is with Al-Boom Marine Diving Unlimited (☎ 394 1267) behind the Eppco petrol station on Al-Jumeira Rd, 1.4km south of Jumeira Beach Park. It only offers dives off the east coast and charges Dh130 for one dive or Dh200 for two dives with full equipment hire.

Inner Space Diving Centre (Map 2; ☎ 331 0203) at the Diving Village in Shindagha will arrange a dive off the Dubai coast if you really want, although it will warn you that it's not the best diving in the country. The cost ranges from Dh125 to Dh215 (with equipment). Inner Space can also take you up to the east coast and into the waters of off the Musandam Peninsula; dives range from Dh200 to Dh500 (with equipment), depending on how far up the coast you go.

Scuba International (Map 5; ☎ 420 553) on Al-Wasl Rd, just south of the Iranian Mosque, and Scubatec (Map 4; ☎ 348 9888) in the Sana building, on the corner of Trade Centre and Al-Adhid Rds in Karama, both arrange dives off the east coast for around Dh220 to Dh250, including equipment hire.

Fishing Fishing is not allowed in the Creek and, considering the amount of pollution released by the endless number of boats plying

the waterway, you wouldn't want to fish here anyway. As for deep sea fishing, there are a few options, all of which are very expensive. If luck is on your side and the weather conditions are right, you're likely to catch flying fish, tuna, barracuda, kingfish and sailfish. The best time to fish off the coast of Dubai is from September to April when the water is not so warm. You will probably have to leave a deposit, usually about Dh50 per person, when you book one of the following trips.

The Dubai Creek Golf & Yacht Club (Map 1; ☎ 295 6032) rents out a 36 foot boat with skipper for up to six passengers. The cost of Dh1500 for four hours or Dh2200 for six to eight hours includes fishing tackle, bait, lunch and beverages. Prices are similar at the exclusive Dubai International Marine Club (☎ 399 4111), 21.5km south of the centre. It costs Dh1300 for four hours and Dh1800 for six to eight hours. A somewhat pricier fishing trip can be arranged on the *Discovery*, which is operated by Creek Cruises (☎ 721 937) from the docks just west of the Sheraton Dubai (Map 3). This 42 foot yacht can accommodate up to seven passengers. It's more expensive than the others, however, at Dh2500 for a four hour trip.

Wild Wadi Waterpark

Attached to the Jumeira Beach Hotel, this 12 acre water park opened to much fanfare in 1999. Two million gallons of water are pumped through the park's various tunnels, tubes, slides, caves and pools every day. The 24 rides are all interconnected so that you can get off one and jump straight onto another. Some of the hairier rides reach speeds of 80km/h, while the 'Jumeira Sceirah' is the highest and fastest free-fall water slide outside North America. There are wave pools for swimmers and surfers as well as more sedate rides for younger kids and slightly nervous adults.

The design of the park, with its sand and stone-coloured structures, is based around a legend in which the Arabic adventurer Juha and his friend, Sinbad the sailor, are ship-wrecked on a lush lagoon, beyond which lies a magical oasis. The design blends in with the natural surroundings fairly well and it is attractive, as far as water parks go. There are two restaurants and a few kiosks. The park is an expensive day out at Dh120/95 for adults/children. Bus No 8 along Al-Jumeira Rd will get you there.

Creek Cruises
Coastline Leisure (☎ 398 4867, fax 398 5497) offers one hour guided tours of the Creek by dhow daily at 11.30 am, 3.30 and 5.30 pm for Dh35 per person. The boats depart from the docks in Deira. It also offers dinner cruises on Tuesday and Sunday for Dh240, and the charter of larger boats.

Danat Dubai (☎ 223 5755) has a 34m catamaran that cruises the Creek every day of the week for lunches and dinners for Dh180 (half-price for children under 12). A one hour cruise without a meal costs Dh50. You can also book a cruise along the coast between Sharjah and Jebel Ali. Private functions for up to 300 people are also available.

Arabian Sail Charters (☎ 332 9567) can take you for a two hour catamaran ride for Dh150 per person including refreshments. Discounts are offered for children.

For Dh260 with Arabian Adventures (☎ 343 9999, next to the Metropolitan Hotel, Interchange No 2, Shaikh Zayed Rd), or Dh250 with Relax Tourism (☎ 451 881), you can take a dhow dinner cruise along the Creek.

For something different, take a ride on Seascope to see some of the marine life around Dubai. This semisubmersible lives at the Diving Village in Shindagha (Map 2) and can take up to 24 people for a 45 minute cruise along the Dubai coast. The cost is Dh55 per person; call Sam Tours on ☎ 592 930 for bookings.

Ice Skating
Believe it or not, Dubai has two ice rinks – indoors of course. The one at the Hyatt Galleria (Map 1) is open Saturday to Thursday and sessions are from 10 am to 1.30 pm, 2 to 5.30 pm and 6 to 9.30 pm. It closes at 8 pm on Friday, and costs Dh25 per session with skate hire and Dh15 with your own skates. Socks are mandatory and unless you bring your own you will have to pay an additional Dh5 to buy some. You can catch bus No 8, 16, 19 or 20 to the Hyatt.

There is another rink at Al-Nasr Leisure-Land, off Umm Hureir Rd in Karama. Entrance to this complex is Dh10, then you pay another Dh10 to skate. Sessions are from 1 to 3 pm, 4 to 6 pm and 7.30 to 10 pm. Bus No 14 goes past here.

Health Clubs
All five star hotels and most mid-range hotels have health clubs, which are free for guests. The facilities of the larger places include a gym, sauna, squash courts, tennis courts and swimming pool. Generally, if you are not a guest you must be a member or a member's guest to use the facilities. Two, however, accept day visitors for a very reasonable fee. Athena at the Sheraton Deira (Map 1) and Inter-Fitness at the Dubai Inter-Continental (Map 2) charge Dh50 for the day during the week and Dh75 on weekends. If you decide to use one of the hotel beach clubs for the day you will have access to their gym facilities as well. This is not cheap though and the average day fee is Dh200.

If you are going to be in Dubai for a week or more you can join the exclusive Wafi Pyramids Pharaohs Club (☎ 324 0000), opposite the Wafi Pyramids Shopping Centre. This place is truly awesome, from the sphinxes and hieroglyphic columns at the entrance to the artificial beach and 'lazy river' on the rooftop. One week's membership is available for Dh250, which is a lot cheaper than paying Dh50 per day at the hotels or Dh200 per day to use the facilities at the beach clubs. Massages, spas and beauty treatments are all available for both men and women in luxurious surroundings – for a price of course. If you are in the area, it's worth dropping in just to have a look at the facilities or to have lunch at one of the complex's restaurants.

Desert Safaris

Desert safaris are popular activities for tourists and expats alike and a great way to experience the rugged terrain of the UAE. Driving over the dunes is exhilarating and sometimes quite frightening, though it is easy to roll down the side of a dune if the driver is not experienced. There are dozens of off-road 4WD jaunts from Dubai that take in amazing desert and mountain scenery, wadis (seasonal river beds), ruins, archaeological sites and remote villages. Having said this you should keep in mind that 'bashing' around the place in a 4WD is potentially damaging to the environment and there are a number of things you should keep in mind (see the Responsible Tourism section in the Facts for the Visitor chapter).

The best way to enjoy a desert or wadi drive is to book a trip with one of the many tour operators (see the Organised Tours section in the Getting Around chapter). In general, a half-day desert safari or wadi drive with lunch/dinner costs around Dh250 per person. They usually leave Dubai in the afternoon so that you can see the sunset over the desert. Overnight desert trips cost Dh350 to Dh450. This will get you some dune driving, a camel ride, a BBQ dinner (maybe with a belly dancer for entertainment) and a night at a Bedouin-style camp site. Desert Rangers (Map 5; ☎ 453 091) in the Dune Centre, Al-Dhiyafa Rd, Satwa, offers a dune-buggy trip that puts you behind the wheel. However, it's pretty pricey at Dh350 for the day, not including lunch.

You could also rent a 4WD, but at around Dh950 a day, this option is out of reach of

Dune Driving

It's not a good idea to drive on the dunes unless you know what you are doing, or you are accompanied by an experienced desert driver. Even if you are experienced, you should always travel with another vehicle in case you get seriously stuck in the sand and need help getting out. If you do go dune driving yourself, remember these basic tips:

- Always let someone know where you are going and how long you expect to be.
- Deflate your tyres by one-third to a half.
- Always engage low 4WD.
- Descend the slope of a dune diagonally, unless it is particularly steep, in which case you should descend straight down.
- Always carry a spade, at least two flat pieces of wood (to stick under the tyres if you get stuck), a tow rope, a tyre pump, a jack and spare petrol and water (for you and the car).

most travellers' budgets. Also, unless you are an experienced desert driver, it's not a good idea to go into the sands on your own. Desert driving courses are available, however. If you do know what you're doing and want to do some off-road driving you should get a copy of *Off-Road in the Emirates* and *Off-Road in the Emirates II*.

There are a number of desert driving rallies throughout the year, the most popular of which is the *Gulf News* Fun Drive. In 1999 there were 2000 participating vehicles in a two day drive over the dunes from Dubai to Al-Ain. If you are interested in the Fun Drive, get your tickets well in advance; call ☎ 447 100.

Sand-Skiing

This sport involves a monoski and an arduous climb up the highest dune you can find. Arabian Adventures (☎ 343 9999, 331 4696) next to the Metropolitan Hotel, Interchange No 2, Shaikh Zayed Rd, charges

Dh195 for a half day of sand-skiing and camel riding. Orient Tours (☎ 06-535 7323, PO Box 24947, Sharjah) will also take you sand-skiing and camel riding for Dh180/125 for adults/children.

Go-Karting
The best facilities in Dubai, and in the Middle East for that matter, are at Go-Karting, just beyond the main entrance to the Jebel Ali Hotel, where it costs Dh75 for 15 minutes. It's open everyday from 2 pm until dusk, although floodlit functions can be arranged. The Dubai Kart Club (☎ mobile 050-651 5945) is also based here. Membership is Dh850 per annum, and competition days are held 14 times a year, culminating in the UAE championship. If you are catching public transport, minibuses only go as far as Jebel Ali Port so you will have to catch a taxi the rest of the way. Alternatively, it will cost you around Dh60 one way in a metered taxi from the centre of Dubai.

Formula One Dubai (☎ 338 8828) on Shaikh Zayed Rd, near the Oasis Centre at Interchange No 2, is open from 10 am to 10 pm and charges Dh40 for 10 minutes. To get there turn left at the Interchange, then immediately right at the sign that says 'Oasis Centre'. Turn right at the first street then left and continue along this road for 2.1km.

WonderLand (Map 1; ☎ 334 1222), next to Al-Boom Tourist Village, near Al-Garhoud Bridge on the Dubai side of the Creek, has a go-kart track. It costs Dh30 for 10 minutes plus the entrance fee to Wonderland, which is Dh10 (Dh20 on Friday).

COURSES
Language Courses
Most language courses on offer are in English. There are only a handful of places where English speakers can study Arabic. This is because of the great demand by National students and expats from the Subcontinent who want to improve their employment opportunities in the world of business, which is dominated by the English language.

Polyglot Language Institute (☎ 222 3429/2596) on Al-Maktoum Rd, Deira offers beginner courses and conversation classes in Arabic, French, German and English. It also offers computer courses.

The Dubai World Trade Centre (DWTC; Map 1; ☎ 308 6036) offers courses in Arabic from beginner to advanced levels. The British Council (Map 1; ☎ 337 1540) on the Dubai side of the Creek, just to the right of the entrance to Al-Maktoum Bridge, has intensive courses in Arabic for beginners. Berlitz Language School (Map 5; ☎ 440 034) on Al-Jumeira Rd offers courses in a number of languages including Arabic and Urdu. The latter is useful to know to some extent as this is the language of so many of the Pakistani expats in the UAE.

Diving
There are half a dozen companies or so in Dubai offering diving courses. The companies listed below all offer Professional Association of Divers International (PADI) certified courses, ranging from beginner to instructor level.

At Al-Boom Marine Diving (☎ 849 858) an open-water course costs Dh1200 and advanced courses cost Dh800. Courses and diving trips are not available on Friday mornings. The Inner Space Diving Centre (Map 2; ☎ 310 203) at the Diving Village in Shindagha has beginner courses for Dh1400 and advanced courses for Dh900. Scuba International (☎ 420 553) has a beginner's course for Dh1600 that takes about 4 days to complete. If you don't have your own mask, fins and snorkel you can hire them for Dh100.

Dubai Explorer has a full listing of dive courses on offer in Dubai.

4WD Desert Driving
Everyone wants to experience the thrill of driving over the dunes, but this is one activity that takes a certain amount of practice and skill since it is potentially very dangerous. Generally, half-day courses cost Dh250 to Dh300, including lunch. You will need to have your own 4WD or hire one for the day. Planet Tours (☎ 822 199, PO Box 55645, Dubai) offers courses for beginners and for more advanced drivers. Five hours of instruction costs Dh255 per person.

Places to Stay

With around 250 hotels and more on the way, Dubai is definitely not short of accommodation options. The only really busy time is during the Dubai Airshow (a trade show for the aircraft industry) in November, when you'll need to book well ahead.

Dubai has a range of accommodation to suit all budgets. The area around the Deira Souq (Map 2) contains the real budget hotels. It's handy because of its central location, though it's likely to be quite noisy. Bur Dubai (Map 2) and Rigga (Map 3) are also quite central, though there are not as many cheaper hotels. The luxury beach hotels down past Umm Suqeim are great if you are just after a beach holiday, but they are a long way from the centre and you'll find yourself notching up a Dh50 taxi fare each time you want to go into town.

The hotel prices quoted in this book are inclusive of municipal tax (10%) and service charge (10%). Keep in mind that these are the hotels' rack rates. This means they are the standard, published, high-season rates. With the exception of many budget hotels around Deira, discounts are almost always offered on the rack rates so make sure you ask. During summer the tourist traffic really drops off so from mid-May to mid-September hotels drop their rates, often by between 50% and 70%. Throughout Ramadan (see the Table of Holidays in the Facts for the Visitor chapter) and on weekends during the Dubai Shopping Festival (March/April) most hotels drop their rates by about 50%.

All mid-range and top-end hotels require you to leave your passport in their safe for the duration of your stay. They also require you to leave a credit card authorisation of about Dh500 per night. If you don't have a credit card you will have to leave a cash deposit. This can make things very difficult if you don't have a lot of cash, or if your credit card is nearly at its limit. Remember that while the authorisation is being held on your credit card, you will not have that amount available to spend.

Few of Dubai's cheap hotels still arrange visas, which is probably just as well considering the chequered record some of these places had in terms of getting the paperwork done properly and on time. In any event, our experience has been that if you're coming to Dubai on a hotel-sponsored visa you're far better off coming in via a more upmarket place and sleeping cheap later on. Most mid-range and top-end hotels will sponsor visas, though some will be reluctant to sponsor Russians and other visitors from the CIS. There is a fee for this service but it should not be more than Dh180. See Visas in the Facts for the Visitor chapter for more information.

PLACES TO STAY – BUDGET
Camping
There are no official camp sites in or around Dubai. Camping in the desert or on beaches is quite common outside Dubai, but this is usually done in the more mountainous areas around the east coast. The best time to camp is November to March, when it's not too hot.

Hostels
Dubai's *Youth Hostel* (Map 1; ☎ 625 578, Qusais Rd) is on the eastern outskirts of the city, near the Jamiat al-Islah relief agency. To get there from central Deira take Salah al-Din Rd to Al-Giyada roundabout, turn left into Al-Ittihad Rd, and then right onto Qusais Rd. The place on the left with a stadium is the Al-Ahli Club, the hostel is another 100m along on the same side of the road. Beds in clean, comfortable two and three-bed dorm rooms are Dh35 per night. Breakfast is available for Dh10 and lunch and dinner for Dh15. Women, as well as men, can be accommodated and there are separate rooms for families, though the manager reserves the right to turn away unaccompanied women if the hostel is full of rowdy young males (which, he says, is rare). The doors do not have locks but each bed has a wardrobe/locker with a key that

Gulf women wear a *shayla* to cover their faces in public.

A traditional gun belt

Preparing a home-made fishing net.

A *khanjar* (dagger) is seldom used today.

Traditional Dubai (clockwise from top left): a National plays a *mimzar,* a traditional oboe-like instrument; the *Ayyalah* is a typical Bedouin dance, celebrating courage and strength; an old man, his face etched with the sands of time, in traditional Arabic dress; a young girl bears a traditional gold offering.

you can take with you when you go out for the day.

You'll need an Hostelling International (HI) card to stay here, and a working knowledge of Arabic would be useful. If you don't have an HI card you can always pay for a year's membership (Dh75), but with the cost of the bed on top of this you might be better off staying closer to the action at one of the cheap hotels in Deira. Membership cards are available from the hostel and from Danata outlets around town and at the Airline Centre (Map 3) on Al-Maktoum Rd. There is no age limit.

Bus No 13 runs from the Deira bus station to the hostel every 10 minutes from 6.00 am until 11.45 pm. The fare is Dh1. A taxi from central Deira will cost about Dh14.

Hotels

Dubai's hotels are scattered over a wide area. The cheapies are concentrated in the Deira Souq (Map 2), particularly along Al-Sabkha Rd and in the side streets off Suq Deira St. All of the hotels listed have fridges and TVs.

The budget hotels bottom out around Dh70 to Dh80 for a single and Dh100 to Dh120 for a double. There are a handful of places with quasi-permanent male guests that are Dh10 to Dh15 cheaper, but we don't recommend them to single women travellers.

If you don't want to be turned away from a particular hotel it is worth stating at the outset that you are not Russian. Deira is simply riddled with Russians and other visitors from the CIS on shopping trips. Some hotels will not accept Russian guests because, I was told by one hotel manager, 'they bring in criminal elements'. These elements are, no doubt, prostitutes from the CIS, who have their 'offices' in Deira hotels. Single women travellers staying in the really cheap hotels run the risk of being mistaken for a prostitute, but that's as far as the problem goes. It is unlikely you will suffer any harassment beyond a whispered, misguided solicitation. Women should aim to stay at those places that advertise themselves as 'family hotels'. This means that they will not accept single men but will usually accept single women and couples, and have strict

The Russians are Coming

With the demise of Stalinism and the break up of the USSR, large numbers of Russian traders descended on Dubai in the 1980s and 90s in search of cheap goods to resell at home, and many young Russian women also came to work as prostitutes. Today the Deira Souq area has become a second home for many Russians, as testified by the preponderance of Cyrillic shop signs here.

Unfortunately, Russia's reputation for crime and Mafia activities has accompanied this influx and the police attribute much of Deira's criminal activity to Russians. As a result, most hotel managers in the Deira Souq area now refuse to take Russians and the Immigration Department refuses visitor visas to CIS and Russian women within a certain age group, unless they are accompanied by their husbands or fathers. Of course, many Russians come to Dubai simply for a holiday and the restrictions have meant a drop in the number of Russian visitors. Some travel agencies have complained that much of their business has dropped off since the crackdown.

policies about visitors in guests' rooms. If you are a non-Russian man, you may be accepted at the family hotels, as long as you do not bring home company or alcohol.

Deira Souq (Map 2) With the exception of the first two listings, most of the following hotels are all very much the same so if your budget is a concern, don't hesitate to simply go with the cheapest.

Al-Karnak Hotel (☎ 226 8799, fax 225 2793, Naif Rd) is probably the best value hotel in Deira, with large, clean rooms at Dh120 for singles and doubles.

Al-Noor Hotel (☎ 225 5455, fax 229 1682) just off Sikkat al-Khail St is also highly recommended. Singles/doubles in this recently refurbished place are large and cost Dh120/165.

Al-Khail Hotel (☎ 226 9171, fax 226 9226, Naif Rd) next to Al-Karnak Hotel is one of the cheaper hotels in Deira at Dh100 for singles and doubles, but rooms are only just OK.

Swiss Hotel (☎ 221 2181, fax 221 1779, Al-Musalla Rd) is a very friendly place and is better value than most of the hotels closer to the Deira Souq area. Singles/doubles cost Dh120/150. The hotel caters mainly to Indian clientele – its two bars even cater specifically for south and north Indians.

Deira Palace Hotel (☎ 229 0120, fax 225 5889, 67 St) advertises itself as a family hotel and has decent rooms for Dh150 for singles and doubles. The hotel reception is always bustling with guests and there is a good restaurant on the first floor.

Al-Sheraa Hotel (☎ 226 5213, fax 225 4866, Al-Buteen St) credibly claims to be able to arrange visas, but at Dh80/120 for singles/doubles without baths it is definitely a step down from many of the other Deira hotels.

Shams al-Sahraa Hotel (☎ 225 3666, fax 225 3647) on the corner of Al-Buteen and Old Baladiya Sts, has cheap singles/doubles for Dh80/120. The pink walls and retro-red carpets give the place a strange but fun aspect. Rooms are a bit smelly.

Gold Plaza Hotel (☎ 225 0240, fax 225 0259, Suq Deira St) on is a family hotel right at the entrance to the Gold Souq and has singles/doubles for Dh120/150 with balconies. Be warned, the rooms are very cramped.

Metro Hotel (☎ 226 0040, fax 226 2098) is in an alley between Sikkat al-Khail and Al-Soor Sts. It charges Dh80/100 and has OK rooms, but accepts only families.

Shiraz Hotel (☎ 225 4800, fax 225 4867, Al-Khor St) opposite the bus station has relatively decent singles/doubles for Dh120/150, but it's very noisy here. Also, there seems to be a lot of single men staying here so women might want to stay elsewhere.

New Avon Hotel (☎ 225 8877, fax 225 2061, Al-Sabkha Rd) near Al-Soor St charges Dh140/180, but is a little overpriced for what you get.

Sina Hotel (☎ 225 2323, fax 225 2606) is behind Al-Sabkha Rd bus stop in an alley inside the Deira Covered Souq. The rooms are small and not very clean and cost Dh120/150 a single/double, but this rate seems to be negotiable. The hotel seems to cater mainly to single men who appear to be long-term residents and we can't recommend it to single women travellers.

Royal Prince Hotel (☎ 223 9991, fax 221 9757, Al-Sabkha Rd) has singles/doubles for Dh130/160. The single rooms are a bit pokey but the doubles are very good value.

Vienna Hotel (☎ 221 8855, fax 221 2928, Al-Sabkha Rd) can arrange visas and has good, clean singles/doubles for Dh130. The staff are refreshingly pleasant here.

Mariana Hotel (☎ 225 9333, fax 225 9185) across the street has singles/doubles for Dh150/160. Both this hotel and the Vienna Hotel cater mostly to Russians.

Green Line Hotel (☎ 226 8661) opposite the Metro Hotel, between Al-Soor and Sikkat al-Khail Sts, is very cheap at Dh80/100. The rooms are absolutely crammed with furniture and the toilets have no seats.

Arbella Hotel (☎ 222 6688, fax 227 2645) is on the edge of the bustling souq area of Deira on the corner of Naif and Al-Musalla Rds. It's pretty basic but rooms and bathrooms are clean. Still, it's a bit overpriced at Dh135/180/220 for singles/doubles/triples.

Beniyas Square (Map 2) This area, just east of the Deira Souq, is very vibrant. As it sits between old and modern Dubai, you get the best of both worlds when you stroll around. There are a number of shopping centres, plenty of travel agents and cheap restaurants here.

The only budget hotel, however, is *Piccadilly Hotel (☎ 222 2113, fax 222 2145, Beniyas Square)*. It's a fairly ordinary hotel with rooms for Dh170/200. Although the rooms are good value, I got the feeling that I wasn't really welcome here, which may have had something to do with the fact that it is almost exclusively frequented by Russians.

Bur Dubai (Map 2) This area, strictly speaking, runs north-south from Khalid bin al-Waleed Rd to the Creek and east-west from Al-Khaleej Rd to Trade Centre Rd, although the entire area on this side of the Creek is often also referred to as Bur Dubai.

Swiss Plaza Hotel (☎ 393 9373, fax 393 9370, 38 St) is one of the very few real budget hotels on this side of the Creek. It is basic but clean and comfortable and well located near Al-Ghubaiba bus station. Rooms cost Dh150/180.

Time Palace Hotel (☎ 532 111, fax 539 948) is the only other cheap hotel in Bur Dubai and has a good location on the edge of Dubai Souq. Singles/doubles cost Dh150/240 and they are pretty shabby, although the management has done a good job of jazzing up the hallways.

PLACES TO STAY – MID-RANGE
Some hotels in this price range are reluctant to sponsor visas. It's often just up to how the management feels when you book the hotel. Generally speaking, most are reluctant to sponsor visas for Russians or visitors from other CIS states.

Unless otherwise stated, all hotels in this price range have business centres with Internet access and secretarial services. Most offer courtesy buses to and from the airport.

Deira Souq (Map 2)
St George Hotel (☎ 225 1122, fax 226 8383) is near the mouth of the Creek in the Al-Ras district, behind the public library. It is very near the Spice Souq and has nice views over the Creek towards Bur Dubai. Singles/doubles cost Dh588/708. Their rather large suite is reasonably good value at Dh1000. This place is ideal if you want to be right in the heart of the souq area of Deira and your budget allows you a little luxury. There are no business facilities here.

Victoria Hotel (☎ 226 9626, fax 226 9575) in an alley near the intersection of Al-Sabkha and Al-Maktoum Hospital Rds is a decent, if dull, place. Singles/doubles cost Dh200/250 and the hotel doesn't have business facilities.

Hotel Delhi Darbar (☎ 733 555, fax 733 737, Naif Rd) is, as its name implies, an Indian-oriented establishment. Singles/doubles are a little overpriced at Dh201/287.50,

but rooms are large and spotless. There are no business facilities here.

Beniyas Square (Map 2)
Landmark Hotel (☎ 228 6666, fax 228 2466) on the north side of Beniyas Square is one of the newest hotels in the area. The staff are very friendly and keen to please and the hotel has parking for guests. The hotel is aimed at business travellers and singles/doubles cost Dh575/690.

Ramee International Hotel (☎ 224 0222, fax 224 0221) just off Beniyas Square is very good value given the standard of rooms. Singles/doubles in this constantly busy hotel cost Dh262.50/367.50.

Phoenicia Hotel (☎ 222 7191, fax 222 1629) has a prime location on Beniyas Square. At Dh345/460 a single/double, the rates for the rather ostentatious rooms are OK by local standards.

The Creek (Map 2)
Carlton Tower Hotel (☎ 222 7111, fax 222 8249, Beniyas Rd) has a great location on the Creek and plush singles/doubles starting at Dh460/575. If you want a Creek view you may have to pay a little more, but you should be able to work out a good discount if the hotel isn't full.

Riviera Hotel (☎ 222 2131, fax 221 1820) next door to the Carlton Tower is less plush and does not serve alcohol, but is better value at Dh300/375 for a souq view and Dh350/425 for a Creek view.

Rigga (Map 3)
This area runs from Abu Baker al-Siddiq Rd to Omar ibn al-Khattab Rd and from Al-Maktoum Rd to Al-Muraqqabat Rd. There are lots of restaurants and shops around here. You're just a short stroll from the Creek front as well as being close to Al-Maktoum Bridge, so getting to places on the other side of the Creek is quick and easy.

Lords Hotel (☎ 228 9977, fax 227 3772, Al-Jazeira St) has huge rooms and bathrooms and is very good value at Dh540/660 or Dh1200 for an executive suite. It's much better value than the Howard Johnson Hotel farther up the street.

Orchid Hotel (☎ 228 9289, fax 228 448) off 37 St, between Al-Rigga and Al-Maktoum Rds near the Clock Tower roundabout, is popular with Russians and Arab travellers. It has good-value rooms at Dh350/400/550 for singles/doubles/triples, but has a slightly sleazy atmosphere.

Nihal Hotel (☎ 227 8800, fax 228 6655) is across the road from the Orchid Hotel and is a better option for women travellers. It offers single and double suites, each with a small sitting room, enormous bathroom, bedroom and a kitchen with all the trimmings for Dh325/450 or Dh525 for an executive suite. This is very good value if you like a little more space and you intend to do your own cooking.

Sheraton Deira (Map 1; ☎ 688 888, fax 688 876) on Al-Mateena St is situated on the outskirts of the interesting part of Deira and is very much geared towards business guests. It has a business and conference centre and some rooms have fax machines. It is fairly close to the airport and singles/doubles cost Dh562.50.

Bur Dubai (Map 2)

Admiral Plaza (☎ 521 111, fax 523 333, Al-Nahda St) costs Dh250/350 for singles/doubles, but the rooms are rather cramped.

New Penninsula Hotel (☎ 393 9111, fax 393 7070), next to Al-Ghubaiba bus station and handy to the abra dock, charges Dh437.50/562.50.

Ambassador Hotel (☎ 531 000, fax 534 751, Al-Falah Rd) is one of the oldest hotel in Dubai (established 1968), and has singles/doubles for Dh312.50/475.

Astoria Hotel (☎ 534 300, fax 535 665, Al-Nahda St) has been around for ever and a day. It's a large, ugly place, and charges Dh345/517.50. It's popular with groups from Russia and Western Europe.

Regent Palace Hotel (Map 4; ☎ 396 3888, fax 353 080, Trade Centre Rd) is opposite the Bur Juman Centre. It's a quiet hotel with a relaxing and leafy lobby area. Rooms are very reasonable at Dh360/420.

Dubai Marine Hotel (☎ 520 900, fax 521 035, Khalid bin al-Waleed Rd) is one of the best value hotels in Dubai. It has a good lo-

The Call to Prayer

If you haven't visited a Muslim country before, be prepared to be awoken at about 4.30 am each morning by an inimitable wailing. This is the call to prayer. At the first sign of dawn, you'll hear a cacophony of droning sounds as muezzins chant the call to prayer through speaker phones which are positioned high up on the minaret of each mosque. Before speaker phones were used to tear people from their beds, the muezzins used to climb the minarets and call out from the top.

There are five prayers each day: at dawn; when the sun is directly overhead; when the sun is in the position that makes the shadow of an object the same length as that object; at the beginning of sunset; and at twilight when the last light of the day disappears over the horizon. Of course, things are worked out a little more technically than this and exact times are printed in the daily newspapers.

Once the call has been made, Muslims have half an hour in which to pray. If they are not near a mosque, they can pray anywhere, so long as they face Mecca. You'll find a *qibla* (a niche that indicates the direction of Mecca) in each hotel room in Dubai.

If someone cannot get to a mosque, they will stop wherever they are to pray – by the side of the road, in hotel lobbies, in shops – so you may have to step around people occasionally. This is OK, just be as unobtrusive as you can. All public buildings, such as government departments, libraries, shopping centres, airports etc, have prayer rooms or designated areas where people can pray.

The phrase that you will be able to make out most often during the call to prayer is *Allah-u-akbar* which means 'Allah the Great'.

cation on the edge of the Bur Dubai Souq. The rooms, although not large, are very comfortable and tastefully decorated. The staff here are helpful and friendly and this is one place we highly recommend. Rates are Dh627/748 for singles/doubles.

President Hotel (Map 4; ☎ *334 6565, fax 396 8915, Trade Centre Rd)* in Karama has large, clean rooms for Dh250/350, which is excellent value. It's in a good location if you intend to spend at bit of time in Jumeira and the Karama shopping district and there are plenty of good, cheap restaurants within walking distance.

Capitol Hotel (Map 1; ☎ *460 111, fax 460 333, Al-Mina Rd, Satwa)* is a subtly tasteful hotel popular with business travellers from the US. Huge and beautifully furnished rooms go for Dh385/506. This place is very good value, even if it is a little out of the way. The neo-art deco lobby is stunning.

PLACES TO STAY – TOP END

Unless otherwise noted, all of the hotels in this category will arrange visas. They all have business centres and conference facilities unless otherwise stated.

Deira Souq (Map 2)

Al-Khaleej Hotel (☎ *221 1144, fax 223 7140),* between Beniyas Square and Al-Sabkha Rd is the only hotel that falls into the top-end category in this area. It has singles/doubles for Dh625/750 but I was able to negotiate a 30% discount on these rates during the tourist season. Don't confuse this place with its namesake in Rigga.

The Creek (Maps 2 & 3)

The following two established five star hotels, although in an enviable position on the Creek, are a bit past their prime. With the proliferation of so many other top-end hotels in the city with better rates and newer furnishings, you're not really getting your money's worth here.

Dubai Inter-Continental Hotel (Map 2; ☎ *222 7171, fax 228 4777, Beniyas Rd)* overlooks the Creek and has rooms for an overblown Dh1360/1486. It's a well established hotel and is still a mainstay for business travellers.

Sheraton Dubai (Map 3; ☎ *228 1111, fax 221 3468,* Beniyas Rd*)* has the best position

in the city, right on the edge of the Creek. Singles/doubles cost Dh930/1030.

The Airport (Map 1)

Distances are all fairly small around Dubai, but if you really want to be sure you don't miss your plane the following hotels are only three minutes from the airport by taxi.

Le Meridien Dubai (☎ *824 040, fax 825 540, Airport Rd)* is opposite the airport. Singles/doubles cost from Dh1200/1320; suites begin at Dh1600. Unfortunately, the hotel is in desperate need of a face-lift.

Al-Bustan Rotana (☎ *820 000, fax 828 100, 16 St)* backs on to Le Meridien; rooms cost Dh1125/1375. It's one of the nicer hotels in Dubai and is better value than Le Meridien.

Rigga (Map 3)

This district is the most densely populated as far as four-star hotels go.

Quality Inn Horizon (☎ *227 1919, fax 228 8175, Al-Rigga Rd)* has decent-sized singles/doubles for Dh630/750. The staff here are very friendly and keen to please. The hotel appears to be popular with business travellers from other Arab countries.

Avari Dubai Hotel (☎ *295 6666, fax 295 9459)* is set back off the west side of Abu Baker al-Siddiq Rd, near the Clock Tower roundabout. It has nice singles/doubles for Dh770/870 with coffee/tea facilities. The staff are very helpful and the two-roomed suite at Dh1200 is very good value compared with suites at other hotels in this price range.

Mayfair Hotel (☎ *228 4444, fax 227 228, 42A St)* just behind Al-Maktoum Rd is well set up for the business traveller and has nice singles/doubles for Dh780/894 or a suite for Dh1194. Every room has tea and coffee-making facilities.

The Royalton Plaza (☎ *295 9171, fax 295 9091)* has a convenient location just off Abu Baker al-Siddiq Rd near the Clock Tower roundabout. It's a lovely hotel and is better value than most in this price range. Singles/doubles cost Dh600/720; a suite costs Dh840. There is a phone and fax in every room and the hotel has that very sought after commodity – an underground car park.

PLACES TO STAY

The Mariedas Hotel (☎ 228 9393, fax 228 8600, Salah al-Din Rd) has clean rooms with comfortable furnishings for a very reasonable Dh600/720, or Dh960 plus 20% for an executive suite.

Al-Khaleej Palace Hotel (☎ 223 1000, fax 221 1293, Al-Maktoum Rd) has large but bland singles/doubles for Dh790/880. It also offers two and three-bedroom apartments for Dh1500/2300. The staff are friendly, however, and the hotel has a good central location in Rigga. Don't confuse it with its namesake in Deira.

Holiday Inn Downtown (☎ 228 8889, fax 228 0033), north of Al-Rigga Rd, has large and luxurious singles/doubles for Dh550/650. You could do a lot worse in this price range. It also has one suite for Dh1000.

Hyatt Regency Dubai (Map 1; ☎ 209 1234, fax 209 1235) is the monstrous construction you'll have trouble ignoring between Al-Khaleej Rd and the Corniche. Rooms here have great views over the Arabian Gulf, Dubai and Sharjah. The hotel seems to be most popular with East Asian business travellers and standard singles/doubles cost Dh1176/1296. Various suites range from Dh2100 per night to Dh7500 per night. It has business and conference facilities for up to 2000 people, as well as a cinema auditorium.

JW Marriott Hotel (☎ 624 444, fax 626 264, Abu Baker al-Siddiq Rd) is one of the most impressive five star hotels in Dubai. It's beautifully decorated and standard rooms are very luxurious and spacious. Singles/doubles begin at Dh1260, executive suites cost Dh3000 and the 'Royal' suite will set you back a mere Dh18,000. If you are prepared to spend over Dh1000 for a room then this is your best bet in Dubai.

Renaissance Dubai Hotel (☎ 625 555, fax 697 358, Salah al-Din Rd) is a luxury hotel run by the Marriott chain and a well known Dubai establishment. The staff are very friendly, but at the time of writing were unable to give me their winter rates. You can count on them being similar to prices at the JW Marriott, however.

The Metropolitan Palace Hotel (Map 1; ☎ 227 0000, fax 227 9993, Al-Maktoum Rd) is a stunning hotel with a phone/fax, and coffee/tea facilities in every room. Standard singles/doubles cost Dh1260/1440 and executive rooms, which all have Internet access, cost Dh1440/1620. Suites begin at Dh2040 and go up to Dh15,000 for the 'Presidential' suite.

Bur Dubai (Maps 1 & 5)

Ramada Hotel (Map 1; ☎ 521 010, fax 527 589, Al-Mankhool Rd) hasn't kept up with the competition in this price range and the single/double rooms are average at Dh875/1000. Make sure you walk around the other side of the lobby elevators to look at the magnificent stained-glass window that stretches the entire height of the hotel.

Heritage International Hotel (Map 2; ☎ 590 111, fax 590 181) on the corner of Al-Mankhool and Khalid bin al-Waleed Rds is one of the newer hotels in Bur Dubai and has singles/doubles for Dh660/780.

Dubai Hilton (Map 1; ☎ 331 4000, fax 331 3383) is in the World Trade Centre complex at the Za'abeel roundabout and is like a second home to some regular business travellers. Singles/doubles cost Dh787.50/937.50.

Crowne Plaza (Map 1; ☎ 331 1111, fax 331 5555, Shaikh Zayed Rd) is very popular with business travellers as it is well set up for conferences and meetings. Standard singles/doubles cost from Dh1250/1375 and there are a variety of suites ranging from Dh3000 up to Dh14,400 for the 'Royal' suite.

Rydges Plaza (Map 5; ☎ 398 2222, fax 339 8700) on the corner of Al-Dhiyafa and Al-Mankhool Rds in Satwa is part of an Australian chain of hotels and has rather sumptuous singles/doubles for Dh850 or executive suites for Dh1000.

The Beach Hotels

If you come to Dubai on a package tour you will probably stay at one of the five star hotels along the beach on the way to Jebel Ali. As luxurious as they are, these hotels are about 30km from the centre of Dubai and getting into town will cost you about Dh50 in a taxi. All of the hotels provide shuttle buses to major shopping centres and to expensive, hotel in Dubai. The furnishings here are so exquisite that one would be scared to even sit on the bed, let alone sleep in it. Standard rooms cost Dh1700 and standard suites cost from Dh4404 to Dh7340.

Ecotourism

For something very different and very exclusive there is an ecotourism resort about 20km south-east of Dubai off the Dubai-Al Ain highway. *Al-Maha Resort (☎ 303 4224, fax 343 9696)* was receiving its final touches at the time of writing and exact prices were not yet available, but it will cost around US$900 per night including meals and activities such as dune driving, camel trekking and falconry. It is set in 16 sq km of sculptured oasis among the dunes. Each guest room is a luxurious, tent-style suite complete with Bedouin antiques and a private plunge pool.

The idea is that the area will also be home to endangered species such as the Arabian oryx and gazelle, Arabian foxes and caracals. The resort uses recycled paper and packaging, biodegradable products and solar energy. There are also permanent exhibitions of paintings, sculptures and handicrafts by UAE artists. Children under 12 are not allowed at the resort.

LONG-TERM RENTALS

The Bur Dubai and Mankhool areas are riddled with 'suites' and 'residences' renting rooms by the day, week, month or year. These places offer larger rooms than normal with kitchens complete with cooking utensils. They also have pool and gym facilities. Most places will offer discounts on the rates quoted below for stays of more than a week. The largest concentration of these 'residences' is found between Al-Mankhool and Trade Centre Rds, just south of Khalid bin al-Waleed Rd.

Rolla Residence (Map 2; ☎ 592 000, fax 592 111, Al-Rolla Rd) is one of Dubai's more upmarket residences, and rooms cost Dh500 per day or Dh800 for an executive suite.

Savoy (Map 4; ☎ 553 000, fax 551 330, 12A St) is rather luxurious and has the

The Arabian Tower at the Jumeira Beach Hotel is built on an artificially constructed island.

Beniyas Square but these operate only two or three times a day.

The *Jumeira Beach Hotel (☎ 480 000, fax 482 273, Al-Jumeira Rd, Jumeira)* is easily recognised by the spectacular Arabian Tower (*Burj al-Arab*) that rises up out of the water and has become a landmark of the city. Singles/doubles are very expensive at Dh1375/1500. It's well worth visiting the hotel for a view of Dubai from one of the top floors. The luxurious rooms in the Tower are due to open for guests in December 1999. If you want to stay in this part of the hotel you will need to be made of money. The decor is incredibly opulent – marble from Brazil, linen from Ireland, gold from Italy etc. Al-Mahara Restaurant on the bottom floor of the hotel is actually under the water so you can view marine life swimming by as you eat.

Oasis Beach Hotel (☎ 399 4222, fax 399 4200, Al-Sufouh Rd, Mina al-Siyahi) is another 10km farther south along the coast. It has singles/doubles for Dh687.50/812.50, and seems to be *the* place for German package tourists.

The more upmarket *Le Meridien Beach Hotel (☎ 399 3333, fax 399 3111, Al-Sufouh Rd, Mina al-Siyahi)* costs Dh1062.50/1187.50, and the *Radisson SAS (☎ 399 5533, fax 399 5577)*, also on the same road, has singles/doubles for Dh750/875. All these hotels have beach clubs, pools and water sports.

The Ritz-Carlton (☎ 399 4000, fax 399 4001, Al-Sufouh Rd, Mina al-Siyahi) is probably the most luxurious, and the most added bonus of a washing machine in each room. Rooms cost Dh495 per night.

Royal Imperial Apartments *(Map 2; ☎ 553 668, fax 591 743, Al-Rolla Rd)* is good value at Dh300.

Baisan Residence *(Map 4; ☎ 554 545, fax 551 707, 10B St)* is a little shabby in comparison to other places in the area, but is much cheaper at Dh275. The only drawback is that bathrooms tend to be a bit grotty and very cramped.

Pearl Residence *(Map 4; ☎ 558 111, fax 550 530, 18B St)* is one of the newer places in the area. Rooms are large, but very bland, and cost Dh450 a day or Dh2000 per week. There is a washing machine in each room.

Al-Hina Residence *(Map 4; ☎ 555 510, fax 592 838, 7 St)* is good value at Dh300 per day or Dh1800 per month. Rooms are spacious and have washing machines.

Bourivage Residence *(Map 2; ☎ 393 4718, fax 393 6441, Al-Rolla Rd)* is one of the cheaper places along this stretch, with rooms at Dh250/300. Rooms have washing machines but the attitude of most of the residents here is probably a little relaxed for most people's liking (eg leaving their doors wide open while they get dressed).

Places to Eat

FOOD

There is very little in the way of a national cuisine in Dubai. Middle Eastern dishes are largely borrowed from other countries in the region, in particular Lebanon and Iran. The diet of the Bedouin who inhabited the area that is now Dubai consisted only of fresh fish, dried fish, dates, camel meat and camel milk. Traditional Emirati cuisine doesn't lend itself to mouthwatering interpretations of these ingredients. Fortunately, the cultural mix of people in Dubai is well reflected in the city's restaurants and cafes.

As you'd expect, cheap Indian and Pakistani restaurants are ubiquitous. Filipino food is also very common, especially around the Karama shopping district. Chinese food is widely available, although its authenticity is rather questionable (often Chinese food tastes suspiciously like the nationality of the cook, who is usually Indian or Filipino). Lebanese and Persian food is easy to find in all price ranges. At the top end of the market, you can satisfy just about any craving, from Mexican to Thai to French. As you would expect, American fast-food chains have successfully infiltrated the streets of Dubai – you'll find them all over the city.

Pork is not eaten by Muslims. It is *haram*, or forbidden by Islam. Dishes containing pork generally only appear on the menus of top-end restaurants. Meat consumed by Muslims must be *halal*, meaning religiously suitable or permitted. The animal must be killed by having its throat cut and the blood drained out before it is butchered. This is why much of the red meat in Gulf supermarkets (ie the meat butchered in the Gulf) is very pale in colour. If you are a red-meat eater you might find the taste of your steak a little bland here.

Indo-Pakistani Food

Indo-Pakistani fare in Dubai is tasty and cheap and Indo-Pak restaurants can be found all over the city. Dishes such as biryani (rice with chicken or meat,

flavoured with cardamom and other spices) are ubiquitous, but you'll also find *kima* (minced meat with peas and tomato served with salad and *paratha*, an Indian bread), *dahl* (lentils), *dosa* and roti (Indian breads). *Puri baji*, another common dish, is a delicious Indian breakfast meal of curried vegetables and flaky bread, usually served with a coconut dipping sauce, but you can only get it before 10.30 am. Indo-Pak restaurants have also adopted a number of Arabic staples into their menus such as *moutabel* (eggplant and sesame seed dip) and *fuul* (mashed and stewed fava beans).

In general, the small Indian places that call themselves 'cafes' serve only sandwiches, fresh fruit juices and snacks such as samosas and *pakora* (bite-size pieces of vegetable dipped in chickpea-flour batter and deep fried). The term 'sandwich' covers a variety of snacks. If you ask for a chicken or mutton sandwich, you're usually asking for a *shwarma*. Sometimes, you'll get the meat in a European-style roll or you may even get a chicken or mutton burger with chips. If you want to be sure of what you're getting, just look around at what other people are eating, or ask to be shown the bread. Omelette sandwiches make a great snack or breakfast. One or two-egg omelettes are wrapped in Indian paratha bread with tomato, cucumber, onion and chilli. If you want the less greasy Arabic bread instead, be sure to ask for it. The staff in these places are not afraid to make a sandwich out of anything – you can also have a kima sandwich, fuul sandwich, moutabel sandwich or even a samosa sandwich if you ask for it.

Lebanese Food

Lebanese cuisine in Dubai is slightly different to Lebanese cuisine anywhere else as it has adopted some of the traditional aspects of cooking from this part of the Arabian Peninsula. Found all over Dubai, Lebanese restaurants occur in all price ranges. For some reason a large number of them are called 'Automatic Restaurant'. The ones that serve alcohol are only found in hotels.

Shwarma and felafels are the favoured snack and are available from most street cafes for about Dh2.50 each – just look for the huge grills outside restaurants. They always come with a small serve of pickled cucumbers and radishes. Lebanese appetisers are known as *mezze*. They include *homous* (chickpea and garlic dip), which is also available with pine nuts mixed through and/or small pieces of lamb, *arayes* (mince meat with spices spread inside Arabic bread then fried), *fatayer* (baked pockets of pastry filled with mince meat, cheese or spinach) and *kibbeh* (delicious deep-fried balls of mince meat, with pine nuts, onion and cracked wheat), which is also served raw, like steak tartar. A thick and creamy, cheesy yoghurt called *labneh* is very popular among Arabs as a dip at the beginning of a meal, but it can also be bought in a slightly less viscous form as a drink. *Fattoush* is a salad of lettuce, tomato, cucumber, croutons made from Arabic bread, and a lemon, garlic and olive-oil dressing. Another well known Lebanese salad is *tabouleh*, which is made from finely chopped parsley, tomato, cracked wheat and mint.

Main dishes include *kofta* (a grilled skewer of spicy minced lamb), various incarnations of *shish kebab* (pieces of grilled meat on a skewer) and *shish tawouk* (delicious spiced pieces of char-grilled chicken), which is a little like the Indian chicken tikka. If you want a little taste of everything, you should order a mixed grill, which is invariably on every menu. All Lebanese dishes are served with pickles, piles of Arabic bread and a big plate of fresh salad. You do get value for money at Lebanese restaurants.

Iranian Food

Even though there are similarities with Lebanese cooking, Iranian food has it's own style and flavours. The Iranians are big on *berenj* (spicy rice dishes which are usually topped with nuts and raisins) and *koresh* (tasty meat stews with vegetables). Kebabs are also a staple of Iranian cuisine, but the Iranian kebab is bigger, flatter and slightly denser than a Lebanese kebab, and it is

served in many different ways. You'll find *chelow kebab* on every menu. It is a grilled kebab served on top of rice (*chelow* means a dish in which the rice has been cooked separately from the other ingredients). There are many different types of kebab, for instance *chelow kebab barg* is a thinner than usual kebab, *chelow kebab makhsous* is a thicker than usual kebab, *bakhtari kebab* is served with grilled capsicum and a *lari kebab* is marinated and cooked in yoghurt.

An Iranian-style biryani is called *Istanboli polow* and consists of rice with haricot beans and chicken or mutton on top. Other Iranian dishes include *baghleh polow* (rice with dill, broad beans and chicken or mutton) and *zereshk polow* (rice mixed with barberry and chicken).

A favourite in Iranian cooking is the buttery crust left at the bottom of the pan after rice is cooked. Anyone who doesn't serve this part of the rice dish to guests is considered either a bad cook or a bad host.

Iranian food is usually served with a plate of lettuce, cabbage, tomato and onion and a minty yoghurt dipping sauce. *Naan* (Iranian bread) is baked in different ways, but the most common variation in Dubai is *lavash*, which is thin, square and somewhat elastic.

Fast Food

Fast food is unfortunately becoming more and more popular with young Emiratis, who prefer to munch on burgers than healthier, home-cooked meals. Unlike in the west, there is very little public awareness about the dangers of eating too much fast food. The fast-food invasion is blamed for many social problems (youth are spending more time away from their families) and health problems in Dubai, including obesity and diabetes. Of course, there are other contributing factors to these problems, such as a lack of exercise in a very sedentary society, but fast food is at the top of the list.

If you have an itch you just have to scratch, there are various fast-food chains along major roads and shopping centres around the city. Along Al-Rigga Rd in Rigga (Map 3) you'll find **Wendy's**, **KFC**, **Pizza Hut** and the English fish-and-chip chain, *Harry Ramsden's*. On Al-Dhiyafa Rd in Satwa (Map 5) there's plenty of fast-food eateries, including *Burger King*, *Hardees* and *Round Table Pizza*.

McDonald's can be found on Al-Jumeira Rd in Jumeira, next to the Crowne Plaza Hotel (Map 5) on Shaikh Zayed Rd; at Khaleej Shopping Centre (Map 4) on Al-Mankhool Rd in Bur Dubai; and at the Al-Ghurair Centre (Map 3) on the corner of Al-Rigga and Omar ibn al-Khattab Rds in Deira. There's a *Subway* at Wafi Shopping Centre (Map 1), Deira City Centre (Map 1) and Al-Rigga Rd (Map 3) in Rigga.

Bakeries & Sweet Shops

If you are a bit of a foodie, you'll find that one of the great pleasures of eating in Dubai are the delicious Lebanese, Iranian and Indian delicacies on offer at the many bakeries and sweet shops around town. The best time to go to a bakery is early in the morning (they usually get going at about 4 am) when everything is warm and fresh and the smell is marvellous. Most bakeries make western-style loaves of bread, but they are usually laden with sugar. French-style bread sticks and croissants are your best bet as they are usually pretty authentic.

The best place to go for Indian sweets is Trade Centre Rd between Khalid bin al-Waleed Rd and 25a St. One of these is *Puranmal* (Map 4), which has such delicacies as milk cake, cream chum chum and the delicious-sounding chocolate barfi! *Feras Sweets* (Map 5) on Al-Dhiyafa Rd in Satwa specialises in very sticky Jordanian sweets and pastries. *King Pastries* (Map 3) on Al-Rigga Rd in Rigga is a bakery and coffee shop serving western and Lebanese pastries and sweets. Coffee here costs you Dh6 to Dh8 and a serve of sweets is Dh5. One of the best places for coffee and sweets is *Iranian Sweets* (Map 3) on Omar ibn al-Khattab St, next to the taxi and minibus stand. Coffee and a selection of sweets for two people costs Dh9.

Self-Catering

Those interested in self-catering will find plenty of small grocery stores around Deira,

Bur Dubai and Rigga. They sell a good range of basic groceries as well as a small selection of fruit and vegetables, but these are not always of the best quality. Fresh fruit can be purchased at stalls around the bus stop on Al-Sabkha Rd (Map 2) and from Shindagha Market (Map 2) in Bur Dubai. However, we don't recommend you buy meat from the market in Shindagha as it hangs in the open air within the reach of hungry flies for far too long; instead buy the wrapped and refrigerated meat from one of the supermarkets.

For Arabic breads and sweets, there are a number of bakeries around town (see Bakeries & Sweet Shops earlier). For European breads, head straight to *La Brioche* in the Al-Khaleej Shopping Centre (Map 4) on Al-Mankhool Rd. Bread is baked daily and there is a large selection of white and brown loafs. Western-style bread from supermarkets is usually sweetened as well as stale.

The biggest and best supermarket is *Continent* at Deira City Centre (Map 1) but it gets so crowded in the late afternoon and evenings, it's just not worth it. If you can get there early you'll be treated to a great selection of fresh seafood. *Spinney's* (Map 2) is the most popular supermarket with western expats, though it is a little more expensive than the rest. There is one on Abu Baker al-Siddiq Rd in Deira (Map 4), just north of Salah al-Din Rd, and another opposite Al-Rolla Rd on Al-Mankhool Rd in Mankhool (Map 2). *Choitram's*, another chain supermarket, is the only one that sells pork products. You'll find one at the Hyatt Galleria (Map 1) on Al-Khaleej Rd and a 24-hour store on the corner of Al-Rolla and Al-Mankhool Rds in Bur Dubai (Map 1). *Safestway* (Map 1) on Shaikh Zayed Rd, near Interchange No 1, has a better bakery and deli section than Choitram's, but it is a little out of the way for most people. The *Union Co-op Society* (Map 5) opposite Ravi Restaurant in Satwa, has a good selection of cheap groceries.

DRINKS

Nonalcoholic drinks are widely available in Dubai. Throughout much of the year, the

PLACES TO EAT

heat in Dubai can dehydrate you very quickly, which is why there are drink vending machines on just about every street corner. Mineral water and soft drinks cost Dh1 while most fruit juices cost Dh1 to Dh2. Freshly squeezed (and usually sweetened) juice is available from Indian cafes, which are plentiful in the souq areas of Bur Dubai and Deira. A glass costs Dh5.

Alcohol can only be sold in restaurants and bars attached to hotels (in practice, three-star hotels or better). The selection is what you would expect to find in any well stocked bar. The prices are pretty outrageous – expect to pay around Dh16 for a pint of beer or a glass of wine. Even the most ordinary table wine will cost you at least Dh85 a bottle.

Non-Muslim expatriates must obtain an alcohol licence (with the permission of their sponsor) to purchase booze for consumption at home. These licences allow the holder to spend a limited amount each month depending upon their salary. There are also a number of 'holes in the wall' around the city where alcohol is sold to those without licences. The police tend to turn a blind eye to these places, which do a roaring trade.

For a really refreshing pick-me-up, try a cup of *chai* (tea) from any Indian cafe or restaurant. For 50 fils you get a cup of Lipton's with a good dash of Rainbow milk (sweetened milk in a tin) and loads of sugar. It'll really get you going.

Coffee

In Arabic, coffee is called *qahwa*. Arabic coffee is flavoured with cardamom, which makes it green, or sometimes greenish-brown, in colour. The version served in Dubai is fairly tame, but should you ever find yourself out in the desert with Bedouin be prepared for an extremely bitter taste. Arabic coffee is served in tiny handleless cups that hold only two or three sips worth. In many offices and in the lobbies of some hotels you'll see a thermos of coffee and a few cups. This is not for display so help yourself if you feel like it, but try to grab a clean cup.

In an Arab Home

If you are invited into someone's home, the following tips may be useful guidelines:

- It is appropriate to take a small gift such as sweets or pastries.
- Do not sit in such a way that the soles of your feet are pointing at someone else.
- Do not eat or offer things with your left hand.
- It is considered polite to let your host set the pace in any conversation.
- Be careful of openly admiring any of your host's ornaments or other such things. It is an Arab custom to make a gift of anything that a guest admires.
- It is polite to take a second or third helping, but don't leave your plate completely empty. This implies that you are still hungry and that your host has not been attentive to your needs.
- It is considered very impolite to refuse an offer of coffee or tea in any social or business setting. After finishing your coffee hold out the cup in your right hand for more. If you have had enough, rock the cup gently back and forth to indicate that you're through. It is generally considered impolite to drink more than three cups, unless the conversation drags on for an extended period of time.
- Don't overstay your welcome. If you are dining at someone's house it's best to leave soon after coffee is served.

In restaurants and hotels in Dubai it is most likely that you will be offered Turkish coffee. This will usually be served *mazboot* (with medium sugar), unless you specify otherwise. If you only want a little sugar ask to have the coffee *areeha; khafeef* means with a lot of sugar and *saada* with no sugar at all. Those unfamiliar with Turkish coffee should be aware that it is very thick and strong. Even if you drink regular coffee black and strong you will probably want to have at least some sugar in your Turkish coffee. Turkish coffee is served in small cups similar to those used for espresso. You will find a layer of grounds, possibly quite thick, in the bottom of the cup.

A good cup of American-style coffee is hard to find in Dubai. Everyone seems reluctant to put a decent amount of coffee in the plunger, or the dripolator, and the result is consistently weak and watery coffee. *Costa*, an Italian coffeehouse next to the Irish Village (Map 1), is one exception. A regular costs Dh7, while a 'French Bowl' costs Dh10. Our highest recommendation though goes to *Cafe Mozart (Map 2; ☎ 221 6565)*, which recreates the atmosphere, food, coffee and service of a Viennese coffeehouse, right down to the change purse carried by the waitress. The pastries and croissants cost about Dh3 each and are very good. The coffee and cappuccino are excellent.

At *Cafe de Paris* (Map 5) the coffee is acceptable and costs about Dh6. The coffee at *Dome* at the Bur Juman Centre (Map 4) on Khalid bin al-Waleed Rd and *La Marquise* at Twin Towers Shopping Centre (Map 2) on Beniyas Rd is only so-so.

PLACES TO EAT – BUDGET
Deira (Map 2)

Cafeteria al-Abra next to the Abra Dock in Deira, at the intersection of Al-Sabkha and Beniyas Rds, is ideal for a snack while watching the activity on the Creek. It has good shwarma and samosas, along with fruit juice and soda. The coconut juice is even served fresh in the shell.

Popeye, a little further east along Beniyas Rd, has shwarma, burgers and other snacks. It has a pretty good offer of two shwarma and one drink for Dh5.

Al-Burj Cafeteria, near the main entrance to the Gold Souq, is a stand-up affair offering excellent shwarma, fresh fruit juices, soda and popcorn.

Golden Fork (☎ 224 3834, Beniyas Square) has an odd combination of oriental (mainly Filipino) and western fast food. The western food is cheaper and better; you can get three pieces of fried chicken with fries and bread, or a burger, salad and fries, for Dh10.

Entezary Restaurant a few doors down also offers good-value food. A dinner of

Vegetarian Meals

With the proliferation of Indian restaurants, vegetarians will have no trouble finding places to eat, and they are all terrific value. Nevertheless, vegetarians can still enjoy plenty of dishes from any Lebanese and Iranian restaurant, for example homous, labneh, tabouleh, spinach and cheese mezze and salads.

The greatest number of all-vegetarian Indian restaurants can be found in Bur Dubai just north of Khalid bin al-Waleed Rd.

Emirates Restaurant (Map 2; Al-Esbij St, Bur Dubai) specialises in south Indian vegetarian dishes. It's clean and comfortable and dishes range from Dh2.50 to Dh5.

Bhavna Deluxe Restaurant (Map 2; ☎ 530 707, 25C St, Bur Dubai) is a well known establishment where vegans are also catered for. No egg or dairy products are used in the cooking.

India House (Map 2; ☎ 526 006, Al-Hisn St, Bur Dubai) has a great selection of north and south Indian vegetarian dishes and a more upmarket interior than most restaurants around here. Mains cost Dh5 or Dh6.

Chhappan Bhog (Map 4; ☎ 599 652, Trade Centre Rd, Karama) serves mainly north Indian dishes. It is very popular with the local Indian population and has a fast-food counter downstairs if you're in a hurry. Main dishes cost around Dh8.

Sarovar Restaurant (Map 2; ☎ 225 5549, 39 St, Deira), just off Sikkat al-Khail St in the Gold Souq, is one of the best places in Deira for a quick, cheap meal. It is a very small and basic, all-vegetarian restaurant with north and south Indian dishes. It's excellent value at Dh2.50 to Dh5 for meals and is one place we can highly recommend.

Swagath Restaurant (Map 2; ☎ 222 4695) just down the street from the Ramee International Hotel, off Beniyas Square, is a little more expensive. It is a north Indian vegetarian restaurant with mains for Dh6 to Dh8.

kebab, rice, soup, salad, homous, bread and tea costs only Dh15. Judging by the signs and menus in Russian, this place is very popular with tourists from the CIS.

Hatam Restaurant on Beniyas Rd is one place we can highly recommend. Several readers have also been very happy with the place. It serves excellent Persian food at very reasonable prices. A traditional chelow kebab (which appears on the menu as sultan kebab) costs Dh17, including soup and salad. Other full dinners cost Dh14 to Dh25 with most under Dh20.

Pizza Corner (☎ 222 2671, Beniyas Rd), not far from the abra dock, is a reasonably priced place with pizzas for Dh16 to Dh18. Their burgers and sandwiches go for Dh9 to Dh16.

Bab al-Sabkha on Naif South St has good, cheap Pakistani food.

Gulf Restaurant & Cafeteria at the intersection of Al-Sabkha Rd and Deira St, is another good Indo-Pak restaurant. Lots of chicken, lamb or fried fish on a pile of rice with salad costs Dh12. You can also get freshly squeezed juice for Dh5 a glass.

La Marquise on the third floor of the Twin Towers Shopping Centre on Beniyas Rd is the place to go in this area if you feel like something western. It's a French-style cafe with an outdoor terrace and a nice view over the Creek. Huge baguette sandwiches cost Dh12 to Dh15 and pastries and cakes range from Dh5 to Dh10.

Bur Dubai (Maps 4 & 5)

Pars Iranian Kitchen (Map 5), behind the Rydges Plaza Hotel on Al-Dhiyafa Rd in Satwa, is an Iranian restaurant; it's also a sweet shop and bakery. Most main dishes cost Dh17 to Dh20. See Iranian Food earlier in this chapter for the kinds of meals you'll find on the menu.

Istanbouli Restaurant (Map 5; ☎ 450 123, Al-Dhiyafa Rd), just west of the Satwa roundabout, is an excellent Lebanese restaurant. Mezze cost Dh7 to Dh12 apiece and main dishes begin at Dh15.

Ravi Restaurant (Map 5; ☎ 331 5353) is a Pakistani restaurant just off Al-Dhiyafa Rd in Satwa that comes highly recom

mended by readers and this author. The restaurant is very clean and a meal consisting of a curry, biryani, or chicken tikka with bread, salad, raita and a drink comes to about Dh15. Chinese dishes are also served.

La Brioche (Map 4; ☎ 553 726, Al-Khaleej Shopping Centre) near the corner of Al-Rolla and Al-Mankhool Rds is a french-style bakery and cafe, with enormous baguette and focaccia sandwiches for Dh8 to Dh15, cakes and pastries for Dh3.50 to Dh6.50, and hot meals such as pastas or chicken cutlets for Dh20 to Dh25. Their Dh15 breakfast is also very good value.

Gerard (Map 5; ☎ 443 327, Magrudy Shopping Centre, Al-Jumeira Rd) is *the* place to see and be seen. Yes, even in Dubai, there is a poser culture. This French-style patisserie and coffeehouse is the haunt for those who are referred to locally as the 'Jumeira Janes' (the nonworking wives of well-to-do expats).

All Spice Fast Food (Map 4; ☎ 337 2555, Trade Centre Rd, Karama) is the place to go for Indian snacks such as *chole* (curried chickpeas), puri samosas, roti and sandwiches. Most snacks cost from Dh2 to Dh4.

Karama shopping district is the place to find good, cheap Filipino food. *Fiesta Filipino* (Map 4; ☎ 334 4121, 45B St) has main meals for Dh12, or seafood for Dh15. The service is friendly here and the food is good value. Try *kare-kare* (oxtail curry), a very popular dish, or *lapa-lapa*, a baked fish dish, usually served with *sinigang*, a kind of tamarind soup.

Shezan (Map 4; ☎ 337 8701, 16 St, Karama) is an Indian restaurant with a small and clean upstairs area and a very extensive menu that also features Chinese dishes. Starters, such as *paneer pakoda* (deep-fried fritters of chickpea and cheese) and *alu chana chaat* (spicy potato and chickpea snack), cost around Dh7, and mains, such as fish tikka and *gosht sagwalla* (lamb with spinach and spices), are Dh10 to Dh15.

PLACES TO EAT – MID-RANGE
Deira (Maps 1, 2 & 3)

The Irish Village (Map 1; ☎ 824 750, Al-Gharoud Rd), behind the Aviation Club and opposite the Dubai Creek Golf & Yacht Club, is a real slice of Britain and is a very popular lunch place with western expats. The pub and large outdoor area is as traditional as the food (stew, bangers and mash, baked potatoes, and fish and chips). Mains cost Dh20 to Dh30. Attached to the pub is a shop selling Irish arts and crafts.

Hana (Map 2; ☎ 222 2131, Riviera Hotel) is an enormous place offering three different menus: Japanese, Thai and Chinese. The food is authentic and reasonably priced at about Dh30 for mains, but alcohol is not served.

Sadaf (Map 3; ☎ 223 7049, Al-Maktoum Rd), a Persian restaurant, is not attached to a hotel and, therefore, serves no alcohol, but the food is excellent. Large chelow kebab meals cost Dh25 to Dh30 and appetisers cost Dh7 to Dh12. It also offers an enormous buffet, at both lunch and dinner, for Dh54. There is a separate room for families and women.

The Pub (Map 2; ☎ 222 7171, Dubai Inter-Continental Hotel) is about as good an imitation of the real thing as you'll find in the Gulf. It serves a varied menu of sandwiches and 'traditional pub food' (shepherd's pie, roast beef etc). The sandwiches cost Dh20 to Dh30 and other main dishes run from Dh30 to Dh50.

Automatic Restaurant (Map 3; ☎ 227 7824, Al-Rigga Rd) is clean and comfortable and is not too brightly lit as are so many restaurants in Dubai. Mezze cost Dh12 to Dh15 and mains, such as a mixed grill, cost Dh25. Fish dishes are a little pricier at Dh35 or Dh45. There are two 'Automatic' restaurants along here. This one is closer to Omar ibn al-Khattab St. In fact, there are dozens of 'Automatic' restaurants in Dubai.

Harry Ramsden's (Map 3; ☎ 221 9980, Al-Rigga Rd) is an upmarket fish-and-chip chain from the UK. It's the only place in Dubai where you can get English-style battered fish, mushy peas and pickled onions. A piece of fish, chips, bread and a drink will cost you about Dh25.

Little Italy (Map 3; ☎ 223 1000, Al-Khaleej Palace Hotel) has excellent and simple Italian meals for Dh25 to Dh30. This place is easy to come back to again and again.

San Lorenzo (Map 1; ☎ 227 0000, Metropolitan Palace Hotel) is very similar and has excellent Italian food at Dh25 to Dh30 for pastas, and Dh20 to Dh25 for pizzas. Other mains cost Dh30 to Dh40.

Curry House (Map 3) just off Al-Rigga Rd is an Indian restaurant with warm and welcoming surrounds, which tend to be spoilt a bit by the TV blaring out Hindi movies. The food is good at Dh15 for mains and Dh6 to Dh9 for starters. I can recommend the *murgh dakshini* (chicken in a spicy coconut gravy with curry leaves).

Barrio Fiesta (Map 3; ☎ 221 1872, Omar ibn al-Khattab Rd), near the taxi station, has reasonably priced Filipino food, with an emphasis on seafood. Soups and rice dishes cost Dh12 and most mains cost Dh18. The menu also offers some Chinese and Indonesian dishes, as well as the good old Arabic grill for Dh20.

Bur Dubai (Maps 1, 2, 4 & 5)

Pancho Villa's (Map 2; ☎ 532 146, Astoria Hotel) is a Tex-Mex restaurant. It's a bit of a legend and one of the Gulf's best known restaurants (its bumper stickers can be seen far and wide). Appetisers and main dishes cost Dh20 to Dh50. The restaurant is a bit cheaper at lunch, when it offers a variety of specials.

Kowloon (Map 2; ☎ 598 777) on Al-Rolla Rd next to the Rolla Residence is highly recommended. It serves excellent Chinese food at a very reasonable price. Mains cost around Dh18. The buffet lunch on Friday and buffet dinner on Sunday are very good value at Dh30 per person, but the a la carte meals are of a higher standard. The place has a nice atmosphere and the staff are very friendly. Alcohol is not served.

TGI Friday's (Map 1; ☎ 331 8010, Shaikh Zayed Rd), next to the Crowne Plaza, is usually popular with large groups. It has western food such as burgers (Dh20 to Dh23) or steaks (Dh60), fish, salads and some Cajun dishes, always served with fries. The menu changes slightly every six

PLACES TO EAT

weeks. Keep in mind that alcohol is not served here.

Henry J Beans *(Map 1;* ☎ *458 350, Capitol Hotel Al-Mina Rd, Satwa)* has American fare, too. Tex-Mex meals and huge burgers cost around Dh25. Steaks cost Dh50. Lunch specials are offered, which usually consist of soup or salad, a main course and desert for Dh30. The atmosphere is dark, dingy and in the vein of an American sports bar.

Kitchen Restaurant *(Map 5;* ☎ *398 5043)* is tucked away behind Al-Dhiyafa Rd in Satwa. This atmospheric little Indian restaurant also serves Chinese dishes and Arabic-style grills. Starters cost around Dh6 and main dishes, such as murgh green masala and fish tikka, are around Dh18. They also have lots of offerings for vegetarians for Dh12 to Dh14.

Thai Terrace *(Map 4;* ☎ *336 7356, Trade Centre Rd, Karama)* is a favourite for connoisseurs of authentic and interesting Thai food. The food is a little expensive at Dh28 to Dh34 for mains, but the servings are generous and the food is excellent. Especially good is the crispy fish salad – try it. As it is not part of a hotel, alcohol is not served.

PLACES TO EAT – TOP END

At the top end of the market almost any kind of cuisine can be found in Dubai, but in most cases 'top-end' food means eating at the five-star hotels and this can end up being very expensive, especially if you want alcohol with your meal. If you are looking for mid-priced food, especially Thai, Chinese and Lebanese, try the restaurants along Trade Centre Rd between Khalid bin al-Waleed and Al-Adhid Rds. As these places are not attached to hotels they don't serve alcohol.

Deira (Maps 1, 2 & 3)

Casa Mia *(Map 1;* ☎ *824 040)*, behind Le Meridien Hotel, once won an award from the Italian consulate for the best Italian Restaurant in Dubai. The menu is interesting and the carefully concocted wine list is unlike any other in Dubai. It is run by an Italian couple – he commands the kitchen and she, with lots of charm, commands the dining room. This is one place that keeps the regulars coming back for more. Mains cost Dh50 to Dh75. You'll need to book ahead if you plan to eat after 8.30 pm.

The Blue Elephant *(Map 1;* ☎ *820 000, Al-Bustan Rotana)* serves just about the best Thai food you can find anywhere outside Thailand. The restaurant is decked out like a Thai village, complete with a pond and bridge, and the service and food are impeccable. Mains will set you back about Dh40 to Dh50.

Minato *(Map 2;* ☎ *205 7333, Dubai Inter-Continental Hotel)* is reputedly Dubai's best Japanese restaurant. A meal here is likely to run to well over Dh100 per person.

Aeroplane Restaurant *(Map 1;* ☎ *722 999)* on the first floor of the deserted-looking pink building at Burj roundabout is something rather different. The restaurant is divided into three rooms, each done up like the cabin of an aeroplane. You can choose between a 747, a Cessna and a Falcon (just for men). The waiters are dressed as cabin crew and the chairs are aeroplane seats and there is even a TV screen at the front of the cabin. It's a pity that the effort that has gone into the decor is not reflected in the food, which is very old-fashioned and what you would expect from a highway cafeteria.

Cafe Mozart *(Map 2;* ☎ *221 6565)* just off Beniyas Rd, near the Riviera Hotel, is most famous for its great coffee and cakes, but it has a full menu of Austrian specialities to choose from. Most mains are around Dh40. It's open for both lunch and dinner.

Fairways *(Map 1;* ☎ *295 6000, Dubai Creek Golf Club)* is an international restaurant with an interesting menu and spectacular views over the golf course and the Creek. Appetisers are around Dh30 to Dh45 while mains are from Dh60 to Dh80. It's best to dine early here so you can enjoy the sunset views.

Tahiti *(Map 3;* ☎ *205 1364, Metropolitan Palace Hotel, Al-Maktoum Rd)* is a blend of Polynesian, South Pacific and Japanese cuisine. It has a range of set menus beginning at Dh85. A la carte meals include potato-wrapped prawns with wasabi dip, teriyaki beef and crispy Maui potato-and-curd cheese fritters with nutmeg.

Al-Dawaar (Map 1; ☎ 209 1100, 25th Floor, Hyatt Regency) is a rotating restaurant. As it spins you get fantastic views of the Arabian Gulf, Sharjah, Port Rashid and Deira. It is buffet only and costs Dh144 per head, or Dh115 if you're out before 9pm. The food on offer is international – salads, seafood, carvery and soups.

Bur Dubai (Map 1, 2 & 4)

The Steakhouse (Map 1; ☎ 331 1111, Crowne Plaza Hotel, Shaikh Zayed Rd) is an upmarket restaurant with a steakhouse-style menu. Most mains here are Dh70 to Dh90, but the steaks are cooked to perfection.

At *Fishmarket Floating Restaurant (Map 1; ☎ 324 3438, Al-Boom Tourist Village)* you choose the fish you want from a display and the chef will cook it any way you like. Be prepared to spend about Dh150 per person for three courses. There is also a dinner cruise along the creek every night from 8.30 to 10.30 pm, costing Dh110. Phone ☎ 341 000 to make a booking.

Sphinx (Map 1; ☎ 324 9603, Wafi Pyramids), off Al-Qataiyat Rd, features decor that is as opulent as its menu. The theme is international, which means such dishes as chilled lobster consomme, fruit tempura, braised lamb shank with lentils and breaded Dover sole adorn the menu. Starters range from Dh45 to Dh60, while mains are around Dh56 for seafood and up to Dh85 for something like fillet steak.

Dynasty (Map 4; ☎ 521 010, Ramada Hotel, Al-Mankhool Rd) is a very classy Shanghai-style Chinese restaurant with an excellent wine list. Mains cost around Dh55, but the servings are very large. Give the honey and sesame spare ribs a try.

Marco Polo (Map 2; ☎ 520 900, Top Floor, Dubai Marine Hotel) has a small but well chosen menu of Thai, Chinese, Indian and Japanese dishes. The decor is 'South Pacific' and the lighting is nicely dim. The food here is excellent and the prices very reasonable – about Dh25 to Dh30 for entrees and Dh35 to 50 for mains. There is also a leafy terrace for non-summer nights.

Sakura (Map 1; ☎ 331 1111, Crowne Plaza Hotel) vies with Minato for the best Japanese restaurant in Dubai. You can eat at the sushi bar, the teppanyaki grill or choose from the a la carte menu. A meal here for two, with alcohol, will cost around Dh400.

PLACES TO EAT

Entertainment

There is no shortage of after-hours social life at the bars and discos in Dubai's big hotels. A night out on the town, however, is not going to be cheap. If you're drinking, plan on spending well over Dh150 and even nondrinkers could easily go through half that in cover charges and overpriced glasses of Pepsi.

The entertainment scene in the big hotels is constantly changing. The best way to keep up is to get a copy of *What's On* magazine, which is available from bookshops and most four and five star hotels. Almost everything – country & western, rock, karaoke, deafening disco or a quiet piano bar – is available somewhere. The problem is that, with the exception of a few perennials, the hotels keep changing the theme in their clubs in an attempt to keep everything contemporary. For example, you might have karaoke night, curry night, football night, quiz night, ladies' night, happy night (whatever that means) and nurses' night, all in one week. If you have the time and money to explore, it could be rather interesting.

PUBS & BARS

Considering that the possession or the consumption of alcohol can land you in jail in most other Gulf countries, it's hard to believe that Dubai has so many pubs and bars. Don't be surprised when you see Gulf Arabs enjoying a pint just as much as non-Muslims. Yes, it's illegal for them to purchase alcohol, but who cares? This is Dubai.

Pubs and bars in Dubai are open until 1 or 2 am. They are well stocked with spirits and all the major beers are available. The wines are invariably the same as the wines at licensed restaurants – mostly table wines from France, Italy, Australia and California. Expect to pay about Dh16 to Dh18 for a pint of beer or a glass of wine. The posher pubs at the five star hotels charge around Dh22 plus tax and a 20% service charge for each drink. Most bars and pubs have a happy hour where all drinks are around

Dh10 to Dh12. Happy hour times vary from place to place. All the pubs and bars mentioned here serve meals as well.

At most places, Tuesday and Sunday are 'Ladies' Night', which means those of the right sex get not one, but two free drinks. Not surprisingly, ladies' night tends to attract more men than women. The biggest problem with many of Dubai's bars is that the managers all seem to feel that a bad, loud lounge singer or two is an absolutely essential part of any drinking establishment. This usually means that your quiet conversation over a pint of beer will be completely drowned out by a loud rendition of a Whitney Houston song.

One of the exceptions to this is *Duke's Bar* (Map 2; Top Floor, Al-Khaleej Palace Hotel), between Beniyas Square and Al-Sabkha Rd. It has pool tables, prices are not as grotesque as at some of the five star hotels and the view over the Creek at sunset and is really worth a beer or two.

The Irish Village (Map 1) behind the Aviation Club off Al-Garhoud Rd, Deira is the best of the Irish pubs. It's very popular with the Brits in Dubai and is a good, casual watering hole. It is expensive though – Dh18 for a pint and Dh9 for a soft drink. The pub has a large outdoor area with wooden tables and chairs and serves good, honest pub grub.

Harry's Place (Map 4; Renaissance Hotel) is a bit of a legend in Dubai and one place you should visit. It's a shrine to Hollywood in a most unusual way – the walls are covered in framed mug shots and arrest reports of many Hollywood celebrities. From Jane Fonda to Robert Downey Jr, no-one is spared exposure. This is a sophisticated place with experienced and friendly bar staff and a great menu. Tucked away in a little room off to the side is the Cigar Room, adorned with leather couches and Arab men enjoying the good life.

The Old Vic (Map 1; Ramada Hotel) is another good place for a drink. The bar has nicely subdued lighting and the walls are decorated with theatre posters from London's West End. The atmosphere is very relaxed, but prices are pretty inflated.

Bordertown *(Map 2; Al-Rolla Rd, Bur Dubai)*, opposite Rolla Residence, is a Mexican pub known for its margaritas and any kind of tequila cocktail you can think up. There is a band most nights from about 9.30 pm until 1 am.

Legends Bar *(Map 5; Rydges Plaza, Satwa)* is Dubai's first Australian pub. It's pride and joy is the enormous TV screen that pumps out Aussie Rules Football and cricket at all times of the day and night. The bar is decorated with footy souvenirs and its bistro offers moderately priced, modern pub grub.

Red Lion Pub *(Map 1; Metropolitan Palace, Shaikh Zayed Rd)* is another popular Brit pub. It's a little more casual than, say, the Old Vic, and is perfect for lunch or an afternoon drink. It has an outdoor terrace overlooking the grassy courtyard of the hotel.

Jules Bar *(Map 1)* behind Le Meridien Hotel, near the airport, is a southern USA-themed bar very popular with Filipino expats. It's lively and loud and there is an original rock band most nights from about 10.30 pm. The menu here features Cajun, Tex-Mex, Filipino and Mediterranean meals.

Planet Hollywood *(Map 1)* next to the Wafi Pyramids, off Al-Qataiyat Rd, is the ultimate in American kitsch. There is a band most nights, drinks are hideously expensive and you are encouraged to spend as much money as possible on gimmicky Planet Hollywood souvenirs.

Boston Bar *(Map 5; Jumeira Rotana Hotel, Satwa)* is, obviously, an American bar. It seems to be most popular with families and older expats. It doesn't get too loud and boisterous here – a good place for a quiet, casual drink, though the atmosphere is lacking a little.

Uptown *(Map 5; 24th Floor, Jumeira Beach Tower Hotel)* is also down this way. You can sit outside on the terrace and enjoy spectacular views across to the Arabian tower and along the coast towards the centre of Dubai. As with everything else in this hotel, the prices are rather high.

Chelsea Arms *(Map 1; Sheraton Deira)* is an elegant English pub with wooden panelling and subtle lighting. It's very popular with Nationals and other Gulf Arab men and we cannot recommend it to women who want to be left alone.

Up on the Tenth *(Map 2; Dubai Inter-Continental Hotel)* is a very cool piano bar with superb views over the Creek. Some of the best jazz duos from Chicago, New York and New Orleans entertain here most nights of the week. It's open until 3 am. As with all bars at five star hotels the prices are outrageous, but it's worth dropping in for one after-dinner drink.

NIGHTCLUBS

Dubai's nightclubs tend to be segregated into Arabic, western, Filipino and Indian clubs. This is just the way people socialise in Dubai – apart. Wednesday, Thursday and Friday nights are the biggies, with music rocking until 3 or 4 am.

Pancho Villa's *(Map 2; Astoria Hotel, Bur Dubai)* has long been one of Dubai's most popular nightspots. There's a dance floor as well as a bar and restaurant and live music is featured several nights a week, often with bands from the UK playing 80s covers.

Atlantis *(Map 1)* off Shaikh Zayed Rd, past Interchange No 4, is attached to the Hard Rock Cafe. It's a long way from the centre, but if you're staying at the beach hotels it's only a two minute taxi ride. Atlantis was the newest and slickest nightclub at the time of writing, but this probably won't be the case for long. It holds about 1000 people and, even though it's so far from everything else, there are still long queues to get in on Thursday and Friday night.

Cave des Rois *(Map 3; ☎ 222 2333, Vendome Plaza Hotel)*, behind Al-Maktoum Rd, Rigga, has a belly-dancing dinner show each evening. It's not cheap though at Dh125 per person.

Even pricier is **Escoba** *(Map 2; ☎ 223 1000, Al-Khaleej Palace Hotel)*. Here the belly-dancing show costs Dh175 with dinner or Dh100 without.

The Cage *(Map 3; Avari Dubai Hotel, Rigga)* is a medium-sized club and, refreshingly, it attracts an ethnically mixed crowd. There's a band each night and a small dance floor to strut your stuff on. It's slightly more conservative than the other nightclubs mentioned here in that it only allows couples and women on the dance floor. It closes at 2.30 am.

Scream *(Map 1; Ramada Hotel, Abu Hail Rd, Hor al-Anz)* is a serious techno nightclub that thumps to house and drum 'n' base. The interior design has a warehouse theme. At present it's the only club of its kind in Dubai. There is a cover charge of Dh50 on Thursday night only.

COFFEEHOUSES

When in Dubai you really should try one of the city's traditional pastimes. A *sheesha* (also known as a hubbly bubbly) is a long-stemmed, glass-bottomed smoking implement that's about two feet high. They are common in much of the Middle East, but the ones used in Dubai are most similar to those found in Lebanon and Egypt.

Sheeshas, packed with apple-flavoured tobacco, are part of Dubai's coffee culture.

Sheesha smoking at public cafes is banned in some of the Emirates. The governments here believe it to be detrimental to health and destructive of family life as it lures men away from the home.

Sheeshas are packed with apple-flavoured tobacco, unless you ask for something different such as strawberry, coffee, liquorice or tropical. Although coffeehouses are still popular with Emirati men it seems that they are being abandoned more and more for pints at the many pubs and clubs instead.

The going rate for a sheesha is Dh10. The nicest place to enjoy one in Dubai is at the oddly named **Fatafeet Cafe**, *(Map 2; Al-Seef Rd, Bur Dubai)* where you get great views across the water to Deira. The best time to go is at sunset when the glass and steel buildings on the opposite side of the Creek reflect the water and the whole city takes on a golden glow.

Al-Areesh Restaurant *(Map 1; Al-Boom Tourist Village)* offers a peaceful setting on the lawn among palm trees overlooking the eastern end of the Creek.

There is an **outdoor sheesha bar** *(Map 2; Al-Sabkha Rd, Deira)* on the ground level of Al-Khaleej Palace Hotel but it's closed during summer, and is very noisy the rest of the time.

Al-Khan Café *(Map 1; Ramada Hotel, Abu Hail Rd)* has a sheesha cafe on the roof, set inside a traditional Bedouin-style tent. The atmosphere is nice, but you will have to spend a minimum of Dh25 per person.

Granada Coffeshop *(Map 1)*, on the corner of Abu Hail and Al-Rasheed Rds, Al-Hamriya, is a bit out of the way, but it has a casual garden setting and only charges Dh7 for a sheesha.

CINEMAS

You can catch relatively recent western flicks at a number of cinemas around town. The films shown are all mainstream Hollywood movies, with an emphasis on action.

Films are subject to censorship and, as sex and romance is an ingredient of most Hollywood recipes, they are usually cut to shreds. The films are subtitled in Arabic and French. Cinemas are comfortable and clean; the biggest complex, Almassa, has eight cinemas. Programs are published in the 'Tabloid' section of the *Gulf News* and in the entertainment section of the *Khaleej Times*. Tickets cost Dh25. The following is a list of English-language cinemas:

Al-Nasr
(Map 1; ☎ 337 4353)
Off Oud Metha Rd, near Rashid Hospital
Almassa
(Map 1; ☎ 343 8383)
Next to the Metropolitan Hotel, Shaikh Zayed Rd at Interchange No 2
Galleria
(Map 1; ☎ 209 6469)
Galleria shopping centre, attached to the Hyatt Regency Hotel, Al-Khaleej Rd, Deira
Lamcy
(Map 1; ☎ 336 8808)
Lamcy Plaza, Al-Qataiyat Rd, Bur Dubai

CONCERTS & THEATRE

The people of Dubai just can't get enough 1970s and 1980s music. If it's not enough that the English-language radio stations are stuck in the past, every couple of months there is usually a visit from a band that has long since departed the scene in other parts of the world.

Around the time of writing, for instance, there were concerts by Boney M, James Brown, Ian Dury and the Blockheads, Human League and, who could forget, Kajagoogoo. Almost every month you can see some such international act. These concerts are usually held in the large hotels or at the Dubai Tennis Stadium, behind the Aviation Club. Check the papers for details.

There is very little in the way of live theatre in Dubai. The British Airways Playhouse does come to Dubai every so often, usually to perform a 'rollicking' comedy in one of the major hotels. There is always plenty of pre-publicity for these events so watch the papers.

SPECTATOR SPORTS
Camel Racing

Since camels, with their long, loping gait, are the most common animal in the UAE, it is unsurprising that camel racing is the main spectator sport. While it sounds like fun, however, it is not for the faint-hearted.

Since the races begin on a 4km straight, the moment the gun sounds, dozens of Emi-ratis go screaming down the side of the track in their 4WDs, paying far more attention to the camels than to where they are going. It would be *very* easy to get run over in these circumstances, so be careful. The jockeys themselves are also at risk from these unwieldy ships of the desert. Due to allegations of child abuse, a decree was issued in 1993 prohibiting children from racing camels. In keeping with the international standards set for horse jockeys, the decree stated that all jockeys must

The Ubiquitous Camel

The most common animal in the UAE has to be the camel. As a symbol of the Emirates, a symbol of the desert and a symbol of the Bedouin, camels are very important creatures in the UAE.

However, unless they are for eating or racing, camels don't seem to be of much use. They just wander around, and when they wander onto the road, they can get hit. As you can imagine, a road accident involving a camel is not a pretty sight. If you hit a camel you must pay the owner for its loss, as well as the damage to your car. If you hit a camel and just injure it, chances are it will become your responsibility. We heard a story about an expat doctor who got himself into just such a situation. He had to load the camel onto the back of a pick-up and keep it in his backyard until he could find someone to take it off his hands.

ALEM GOSHIME

Visitors can either go on a camel safari or watch Dubai's weekly camel races.
❀❀❀❀❀❀❀❀❀❀❀❀❀❀❀❀❀❀❀

weigh at least 45kg, though it is unclear whether this ruling has been fully embraced by the operators of the industry.

Races take place early on Friday morning during winter and spring and on public holidays at the track (Map 1; ☎ 422 208) south of the centre off 2nd Za'abeel Rd on the Dubai side. Admission is free. The races usually start around 7 am and continue until about 9 am. If you miss out on a race meeting you can usually catch training sessions each morning at about the same time or at around 5.30 pm.

Desert Rallies

Not quite the Paris-Dakar, the Desert Challenge is still a high-profile international driving event that attracts top rally drivers from all over the world. It is held in the first week of December and is a part of the World Cup in Cross Country Rallying. There are a number of smaller rallying events during October and November including the Drakkar Noir 1000 Dunes Rally, the Federation Rally and the Spring Desert Rally, which are all 4WD events. Contact the Emirates Motor Sports Federation (☎ 827 111) for details.

Golf

It's not surprising that the Dubai Desert Classic attracts some of the world's best players, it's the richest golf tournament in the world with prize money of over US$1 million. Held at the Emirates Golf Club (☎ 473 222, Shaikh Zayed Rd) each February, it runs for four days and costs Dh75 for the day. The Dubai Open, with its relatively paltry prize money of US$300,000, is held at the Dubai Creek Golf & Yacht Club (Map 1; ☎ 822 789, Al-Garhoud Rd) in October. Throughout the year there are small amateur tournaments at the golf clubs in Dubai. See the daily newspapers for details.

Tennis & Cricket

The Dubai Duty Free Tennis Open, held in February, is a part of the ATP world series tour and total prize money is just over US$1 million. It is held at the Dubai Tennis Stadium (☎ 206 2425, The Aviation Club, Al-Garhoud). Tickets get more expensive as the tournament progresses. It's about Dh100 for the first few matches and goes up to Dh250 for the finals. Tickets for the whole tournament, with food and beverage included, cost Dh2000 per person.

To see international cricket you will have to go to nearby Sharjah (see the Excursions chapter), which hosts the Sharjah Cup in April. Participating teams change every year, but there are three competing nations each time. It is held at the Sharjah Cricket Stadium (☎ 06-329 219/5, PO Box 88, Sharjah) and admission prices range from Dh20 to Dh100.

Horse Racing

A number of sheikhs have taken a liking to racing horses and many have stables replete with some of the finest horses in the world. Shaikh Mohammed, Dubai's crown prince, is somewhat of a racing celebrity and he is quite well known in the international racing community. The Dubai World Cup, held in March, is well known as the world's richest horse race with prize money of US$12 million. It is held at the Nad al-Sheba Racecourse (☎ 329 888) 5km south-east of Dubai. To get there head south down Oud Metha Rd until you get to a large roundabout with signs for Al-Ain and Hatta and you will see the sign for Nad al-Sheba. It is also signposted from Shaikh Zayed Rd.

The racing season lasts from November to March. Racing is also held at night from about 7 pm (9 pm during Ramadan). General admission is free, though if you want to enjoy the members' stand you will have to pay Dh70. Call the club for the exact dates of race meetings throughout the year.

There are also dozens of desert endurance races during the winter. Stunning Arabian horses compete in these events as they are most suited to this kind of terrain. The most prestigious of these races is the Emirates Championship Cup, which is run over 130km. Many sheikhs enter these races and, funnily enough, they usually seem to win.

Marine Events

If fast boats give you a bit of a thrill you should come to Dubai during autumn and spring when the city plays host to the Class

One World Championship Power Boat races. These are held at the Dubai International Marine Club, now known as Club Mina (☎ 399 4111) in Mina al-Seyahi, 35km along the coast south of the centre. Entry is free and entertainment is provided for kids. Heats are held in October, November, March, April and May.

It's hard to imagine it but they do race those big dhows. Up to fifty of them take part in a race. When they're all lined up with their sails hoisted, ready to begin, it's quite a spectacular sight. Races take place every weekend from late September to May at Club Mina. Entry is free but you won't really see much from the club as the races take place five miles off the coast. Many people watch from boats just beyond the breakwater.

Every year in March is the President's Cup Dubai-Muscat Sailing Regatta. It begins in Dubai at Club Mina and finishes in Muscat at the Marina Bandar al-Rowdha.

You can call the Race Department of Club Mina for more information and exact dates of any of the above events.

COMPUTER ARCADES

If you can't resist trying out all the new shoot 'em up computer games that are churned out each week, and you don't want to pay a small fortune to buy them, go to Express Network Games (Map 5; the Dune Centre, Al-Dhiyafa Rd, Satwa). Here you can play any number of brand-new games on large screens for Dh10 an hour. It's open every day from 4 pm to 1 am.

Shopping

Dubai is a shopper's paradise. The lack of duty and taxes, in addition to the relatively cheap shipping costs, mean that travelling here for a shopping expedition is well worthwhile. The Dubai Shopping Festival, held every March/April, is promoted aggressively and brings in thousands of tourists, especially from other Arab countries and the CIS.

The major shopping districts in Dubai are Beniyas Square in Deira (Map 2), Al-Rigga Rd in Rigga (Map 3), Al-Dhiyafa Rd in Satwa (Map 5) and the areas around Dubai Souq in Bur Dubai and the various souqs in Deira (Map 2). The best of Dubai's shopping, though, is contained within the many shopping centres (see Shopping Centres later in this chapter).

Dubai is probably the cheapest place (outside of Iran) to buy Iranian caviar. Most supermarket delicatessens and five star hotels sell caviar. Specialty caviar shops are located at the airport, in Markaz al-Jumeira on Al-Jumeira Rd (Map 5) and at the Jumeira Beach Hotel.

Honey is another special product you can buy in Dubai. It comes from Oman and you can find lots of it in Al-Ain, in south-west UAE. In Dubai you'll find it in the odd grocery store or spice shop around the souq areas of Bur Dubai and Deira (Map 2). It ranges in colour from light golden to almost black, and is usually packaged in old Vimto bottles. Believe it or not it sells for anywhere between Dh100 and Dh700 a bottle. Though it seems to taste just like ordinary honey, the reason it is so expensive is that it is collected by hand from remote areas in the mountains and deserts of Oman.

WHAT TO BUY
Gold
Dubai has earned itself the well-deserved reputation as the City of Gold. Even seasoned veterans of Middle East gold markets are likely to be blown away by the sheer scale of Dubai's Gold Souq (see Gold Souq under Souqs later in this chapter).

Just about every conceivable kind of gold jewellery is on offer here. There are earrings, rings, necklaces, bracelets and pendants. Designs can be traditional or modern, bold or conservative, chunky or delicate. Different shades of gold are also available. The craftsmen can alter the composition of alloys in the gold to create pink, white, yellow or green hues in the one piece of jewellery. Items can have a dull or a shiny polish applied to them. And it is not solely gold jewellery that is on offer. You can also buy ingots or coins.

In most Gulf countries, a bride must be laden with gold jewellery on her wedding day. Antique or second-hand gold passed down from previous generations is not considered good enough as a gift. Gold presented to a bride must be new, so this keeps a constant flow of customers coming to Dubai's Gold Souq. It also means that a lot of gold is recycled.

There are very strict laws involving authenticity: gold traders are quickly put out of business if they try to dupe a customer. If a shop attendant tells you that a particular piece of jewellery is 22 carat (meaning that 22 of the 24 parts of the alloy are gold; the remaining parts are zinc, copper and silver) you can be confident that it is.

Gold is sold by weight and prices fluctuate almost daily. There is room to bargain so don't accept the first price, and be sure to shop around. Prices also vary depending on whether the piece was made by a machine or a craftsman.

A 22 carat machine-made bracelet costs around Dh300, while an intricately handcrafted one costs around Dh500, after bargaining. A necklace can cost as much as Dh1500. Small items, such as simple earrings or a pendant, can be purchased for under Dh150 in lower grades of gold and can go up to Dh500 for 21 or 22 carat gold.

Carpets
Dubai and Sharjah are among the best places outside Iran to buy Persian carpets.

Turkish kilims and Turkoman, Kashmiri and Afghan rugs are also widely available.

Whenever you buy a rug you will be given a Certificate of Authentication, which is guaranteed by the Dubai Chamber of Commerce & Industry, so you can be sure that the Turkoman rug you're about to spend Dh4000 on is actually a Turkoman rug.

For more useful information on the history of Persian carpets, how they are made and what to look for when buying one, see the boxed text 'The Art of Carpet Buying', or read *Oriental Carpets: A Buyer's Guide* by Essie Sakhai.

There is no doubt that the best range of carpets is at the Sharjah Central Souq, which is only a 10 minute drive from Dubai (see the Excursions chapter for more information). The only problem is that each year the prices seem to creep up as more and more tourists come here to shop. There is room to bargain though, and if you're having trouble getting the price you want, just go to the next shop – there are dozens of them. Be aware that the carpet sellers here are not exclusively retailers, there are a few wholesalers as well. If you can seek out these shops you'll get much better prices.

If you can't make it to Sharjah, one of the best carpet shops is Red Sea Exhibitions (Map 5) in the Beach Centre on Al-Jumeira Rd. It has an excellent selection of oriental carpets, including many antiques, at very reasonable prices.

All the shopping centres listed later in this chapter have carpet shops. Deira City Centre has the greatest number of rug shops. One of the best here is Pride of Kashmir (Map 1) in Deira City Centre on Al-Garhoud Road. It has the largest range and very good prices.

In Deira try the Deira Tower (Map 2) and Dubai Tower (Map 2) on Beniyas Square, both of which have lots of small carpet boutiques. Khyber Carpet in the Hyatt Galleria (Map 1) has an enormous selection of high quality carpets from Iran. They are expensive, however, and the vendors do not seem very interested in bargaining.

If you are interested in Afghan carpets in particular, you'll find the greatest selection

The Art of Carpet Buying

Buying carpets without getting ripped off takes great skill and patience. And it involves an understanding of the intricacies of the trade. These tips are designed to help you navigate your way through the rigours of the purchasing process:

• Do not feel embarrassed or obliged to buy just because the shop attendant has unrolled 40 carpets for you; this is part of the ritual.

• Ask a lot of questions and bargain hard over a long period of time (preferably two or three visits). You will be very disappointed if you make a hasty purchase then see the rug you really wanted for a better price at the shop down the road.

• Remember that rugs from Iran are generally more valuable than those from Kashmir or Turkey. Silk rugs are more valuable than wool ones.

• The more knots there are per square inch, the more valuable the rug (flip the corner of a rug over and have a look at the back).

• Look closely at the detail in the design of the carpet and compare it with others. Often the value of a carpet is raised by the name of the family who made it.

• Natural dyes are more desirable, and more expensive, than artificial dyes. Antique rugs are always naturally dyed. A naturally-dyed rug will appear to be slightly faded, but this is not considered a flaw. The settling down of natural dyes creates a carpet that is well balanced in colour and tone.

• If you are buying an artificially coloured carpet check that the colours have not bled. Artificial dyes are used widely now and can be just as attractive as the natural dyes. Unless you are a real purist it really doesn't matter.

at Afghan Carpet Palace in the Hamarain Centre (Map 3) on Abu Baker al-Siddiq Rd. If you've only got eyes for Persian carpets, go to Sadaf Carpet, next to the restaurant of the same name (Map 3), on Al-Maktoum Rd in Rigga. It only has rugs from Iran, both silk and wool, as well as a number of antiques. The prices are very reasonable here and they won't try to sweet talk you.

Arabian Souvenirs

Typical souvenirs include copper coffeepots (*dalla* in Arabic), which cost from Dh50 for small ones (about 8cm high) to Dh500 for large ones (about 50cm high). Antique dallas cost from Dh300 to Dh1000, depending upon their condition. Decorated metal food platters, used for special occasions, such as wedding banquets, can cost Dh150.

Carved wooden or leather stuffed camels are also a common souvenir; they cost anywhere from Dh30 to Dh350. Don't pay any more than Dh20 for a brass candle holder. Wooden Quran holders come in various sizes and fold up flat so they're not too bulky in your luggage. Most of them come from India and cost from Dh30 to Dh50.

Woollen camel bags, which are slung over a camel's back and have a large pocket on either side, mainly come from Afghanistan and cost anywhere from Dh250 to Dh500, depending on their quality and size.

Sheeshas (water pipes) are nice Middle Eastern souvenirs, but they are not very practical to transport. Large sheeshas with a hose cost from Dh120 to Dh150. Some cost as little as Dh75, but they might not work very well. Always check that air flows well through a sheesha before you buy it. If you intend to smoke through your sheesha there are a number of accessories you'll need, but they cost only a few dirhams each.

Bedouin Jewellery

Most of the Bedouin jewellery you will find comes from Oman. If you are travelling on to either Oman or Saudi Arabia, this sort of jewellery is much cheaper in those countries and the selection tends to be better. If you decide to make an excursion to Al-Ain you can cross to Buraimi on the Omani side

of the border (without a visa) and shop for Omani jewellery, though the selection there tends to be pretty limited.

Some of the beautiful things you can buy are *khanjars* (Omani curved daggers), gunpowder horns and silver bracelets and necklaces. But be sure to look closely at the workmanship. Is the work detailed and intricate? Do the movable parts come on and off or slide around easily? Is the item dented or split?

As a rule any khanjar under Dh500 tends to be pretty nasty, but you should not invest more than Dh1200. Many shops sell khanjars and jewellery in a display box so if you don't want to pay the extra price for this make it known.

Silver bracelets and necklaces from Oman are sold by weight, but often the shopkeeper has a fixed price for these items. The going rate is Dh1.8 per gram. For a simple studded bracelet you will pay around Dh200 after bargaining. For larger and more ornate items, such as a bride's chest and head piece, you will probably be quoted around Dh1500. Make sure you ask for a discount, or for their best price before you agree to purchase. Larger silver prayer holders (about 20 to 25cm in length) and gunpowder horns will cost around Dh350, but you could pay as much as Dh500 for really well-crafted items in good condition. Quality prayer holders made of white metal are not as valuable as the silver ones, but they still make a nice, and much more affordable, souvenir. You can get a small one for around Dh25.

ALEM GOSHME

Bedouin jewellery, *khanjars* and silverware are popular gifts available in the souqs.

Khanjars

Khanjars (also spelt 'khanja') are curved daggers worn mainly by Omani men, but also by Emirati men in the rural east and north of the country. Traditionally the handles of these daggers were made from rhino horn, though today they are almost always made from either plastic or wood. Khanjars come in two basic designs: regular khanjars are identified by two rings where a belt is attached; *Sayidi* khanjars have five rings.

Regular khanjars are decorated entirely, or nearly entirely, with thin silver thread. The intricacy of the thread pattern, and the skill with which it is executed, are among the main determinants of value. Sayidi khanjars are often covered entirely in silver sheet with little or no thread used.

The most important things to look for in assessing a khanjar's quality are weight and the workmanship on the scabbard. A khanjar is a substantial item and ought to feel like one when you pick it up.

Some khanjars have a second knife inserted in a small scabbard attached to the back of the main scabbard. Don't pay too much of a premium for one of these – the knives in question are often cheap steak knives that have had a bit of silver wrapped around the handle.

Do not believe anything anyone tells you regarding the age of individual pieces. Few khanjars will be more than 20 to 40 years old, and quality of workmanship, not age, should be your main criterion for assessing value.

If you have the time, the best place to shop for old Arabian souvenirs is actually in Sharjah at Al-Arsah Souq (see the Excursions chapter for more information). All of the shopping centres mentioned later in this chapter have shops selling souvenirs. Sometimes you will have to wade through the merchandise from India, Africa and Thailand to be able to find any genuine Arabian bits and pieces.

In Dubai you can buy Omani jewellery at Al-Kananah (Map 1) in the Hyatt Galleria off Al-Khaleej Rd in Deira. They also have some of the nicest khanjars available in Dubai, ranging from Dh500 to Dh1500, as well as various Arabic objects and souvenirs at a range of different prices depending on the quality.

Abu Amed Antiques (Map 5) on Al-Dhiyafa Rd in Satwa has khanjars and Bedouin jewellery from Oman as well as wooden chests and coffeepots. There is also some very nice silver from Italy. The prices are very high here so you should make sure you have shopped around a bit first.

You can also try the shops in the Heritage Village (Map 2) on Al-Shindagha Rd. As this is a touristy place prices tend to be a little high and bargaining doesn't bring them down by much. Although most five star hotels have shops selling good quality souvenirs, jewellery and carpets, remember that you are paying about 50% more than you should. Art & Culture, a crowded shop in the lobby of the Dubai Inter-Continental Hotel (Map 2), has high quality souvenirs and Bedouin jewellery. It also has very well made *kandouras* (a Gulf version of a caftan) and robes.

You should steer clear of Al-Jaber Novelty Store on Beniyas Rd, between the Carlton Tower Hotel and the Twin Towers shopping centre. The stuff in here is pretty tasteless and the only authentic Arabic antiques are in a very poor state and very overpriced.

Sheesha pipes are available from tobacconists, hotel souvenir shops, shopping centres and some of the small grocery stores. One of the cheapest places is the tobacconist shop on the south side of Beniyas Square.

Perfume & Incense

When you pass a black-cloaked Emirati women on the street you will no doubt be overwhelmed by the intense perfume that wafts all around her. Arabic perfumes *(attar)* are very strong and spicy, unlike western perfumes, which tend to be flowery and light. For centuries, Arab women have smothered themselves in perfumes. When there was no air-conditioning, and precious little water in the deserts of Arabia to wash clothes and bodies, people needed something to cover up the smell of perspiration.

You'll find perfume shops in all the shopping centres, but the best place to buy is the Perfume Souq (Map 2) on Sikkat al-Khail St in Deira, just east of the Gold Souq. Shopkeepers will want to daub you senseless with various perfumes, but a word of warning – the Arabic perfumes are oil based and once on your clothes they can leave a stain. You can buy perfumes in bottles ranging from 12mL to 36mL. It is sold by the *tolah* (12mL or 12g) and prices vary, depending on the perfume. The cheapest is about Dh10 per tolah while the most expensive is an incredible Dh1500 per tolah. This expensive stuff, made from agar wood from Malaysia, is extremely concentrated. In fact, it's so strong that you will probably find it rancid and quite disgusting when you smell it in the perfume shop. When it settles down though it's a lovely, spicy fragrance and one drop is enough to last the whole day.

The perfume shops also sell an enormous range of incense. It can be in the form of compressed powder, crystals, rock or wood. Frankincense (*luban* in Arabic) is probably the most common form of incense. The quality varies – frankincense from Japan is not as valuable as the stuff from Iran or Dhofar (in southern Oman). The cheaper frankincense is about Dh20 per kilogram and the more expensive stuff is about Dh50. The wooden incense (*somok* in Arabic) is the nicest and most valuable of all incenses and comes from agar wood in Malaysia. When burned it gives off a sweet, rich logfire smell. Agar wood ranges in price, depending on quality, from Dh10 per tolah to Dh30.

To burn incense you can either buy an electric incense burner, which has a metal plate that heats up, or you can buy a box of heat beads. The heat beads need to be set alight, then when they have settled down to a glow you put your piece of incense on top. You should consider, however, that travelling on a plane with these in your luggage is illegal as they are flammable. One option is to contact a church supplier when you get home – most Christian churches use special heat beads to burn frankincense.

Electronics

The UAE is the cheapest place in the Middle East to buy electrical goods. If it plugs into the wall you can buy it here, but the selection of these types of goods tend to be limited. Most shops stock the same three or four varieties of something (say, VCRs or DVDs) at pretty much the same prices. You'll also discover that the shop attendants are not very knowledgable about their stock so it helps to have a good idea of what you want before setting off on a shopping expedition. It is also a good idea, and it is accepted practice in the UAE, to plug your new gadget in at the shop to make sure that it works properly.

If you are looking for cheap electronics, try the area around the corner of Al-Sabkha and Al-Maktoum Hospital Rds, near Beniyas Square (Map 2). A medium-sized CD stereo with detachable speakers should cost about Dh550; a 20 inch TV will cost about Dh600. Basic, multisystem videos should cost about Dh250 to Dh350.

For computers and software go to Khalid bin al-Waleed Rd (Map 2) in Bur Dubai between Al-Mankhool Rd and the Falcon roundabout.

Textiles

The best place to buy fabrics is the Dubai Souq (Map 2) and along Al-Fahidi St in Bur Dubai. In fact, that's practically all you can buy here. All kinds and qualities of fabrics from India, Indonesia, Thailand, Japan and Korea are available at very cheap prices. Cotton fabrics, depending on the weave, cost anywhere from 30 fils to Dh5 per metre. Silk costs around Dh8 per metre and linen about Dh7 per metre.

There are also plenty of tailors around here, all of whom are very good at what they do. They also work very quickly so if you only have a few days in Dubai you'll still have time to have something made. A simple women's skirt may cost about Dh30, while a more complicated skirt, blouse or trousers will cost from Dh40 to Dh50 to make. A men's shirt costs about Dh25, while you can get a suit made for about Dh150.

Kitsch Souvenirs

If you're looking for the ultimate kitsch souvenir from the UAE, it has to be the tacky mosque clock, which belts out the *azzan* (call to prayer). It costs Dh20, and if it doesn't get you out of bed in the morning, then you must be dead! You can buy it from just about anywhere, but try the shops around the Deira and Dubai Souqs (Map 2) first. Another version of this clock comes in the form of a Quran.

Then there's the camel lighter – press its hump and it spits fire – which is available from some of the trinket shops on 67 St, Deira (Map 2), for Dh10.

Kitschy, though not cheap, are the little silver Emirati objects in frames, available from souvenir shops in shopping centres. These little objects include dhows, dallas, incense burners, camels and khanjars. They cost about Dh80 for the smallest ones (about 8 sq cm) and up to Dh500 for large ones.

WHERE TO SHOP
Bookshops

Dubai's best bookshop, Magrudy Books (Map 5), is in the shopping centre of the same name on Al-Jumeira Rd. It also sells books through its Web site at www .magrudy.com. Note that the bookshop is open all day on Wednesday and Thursday from 8.30 am to 8 pm.

In the centre, try Book Corner (Map 5) at the Dune Centre, Al-Dhiyafa Rd in Satwa and the Hyatt Galleria (Map 1). There is also the Books Gallery at Al-Ghurair Centre on the corner of Omar ibn al-Khattab and Al-Rigga Rds. Most of the larger hotels have small selections in their bookshops. The House of Prose (Map 5) is an excellent second-hand bookshop in the Jumeira Plaza on Al-Jumeira Rd.

Shopping Centres

A sea of shops, filled with the latest of everything, can be found in Dubai's many shopping malls. These open at the rate of about one per year with each one being bigger and flashier than the last. If you're really

serious about hitting the shops you could get the *Dubai Shopping Centres Directory*, available in bookshops and most upmarket hotel rooms. There are too many shopping centres to list here so we have just included the major ones:

Deira City Centre (Map 1) on Al-Garhoud Rd, near the Dubai Creek Golf & Yacht Club, is Dubai's most popular shopping centre, especially with teenagers and young families. It has the greatest range of shops in Dubai, including department stores and the biggest supermarket in the city. It is open everyday from 10 am to 11 pm; catch bus No 3, 4, 6, 11 or 15 to get there.

Bur Juman Centre (Map 4) on the corner of Trade Centre and Khalid bin al-Waleed Rds is one of the most popular shopping centres due to its central location. It stocks mainly men's and women's international clothes shops, sports shops and home wares. It is open Saturday to Thursday from 10 am to 10 pm and Friday from 2 to 10 pm; catch bus No 3, 5, 16, 44, 61 or 90 to get there.

Wafi Shopping Centre (Map 1) on Al-Qataiyat Rd, just before Al-Garhoud Bridge on the Dubai side of the Creek, is a rather ugly shopping centre with lots of exclusive, upmarket shops. It's main attraction seems to be Galactica and Lunarland, which provide entertainment for kids (see Dubai for Children in the Facts for the Visitor chapter). It is open Saturday to Thursday from 10 am until 10 pm and from 2 to 10 pm on Friday; catch bus No 14, 16 or 44 to get there.

Lamcy Plaza (Map 1) on Al-Qataiyat Rd, near the corner of Za'abeel Rd, Za'abeel, offers lower prices than most other big shopping centres. It has a couple of good department stores, a large CD shop and a cinema complex. It is open everyday from 10 am to 10 pm; catch bus No 44 to get there.

Al-Ghurair Centre (Map 3) on the corner of Al-Rigga and Omar ibn al-Khattab Rds, Deira, was Dubai's first shopping centre and was under renovation at the time of writing. When the upgrade is finished this will be the biggest shopping centre in Dubai and will house a multiplex cinema. It is open from 9 am to 1 pm and from 5 to 10 pm, closed Friday morning; catch bus No 5, 6, 13, 19 or 20 to get there.

Markaz al-Jumeira (Map 5) on Al-Jumeira Rd, Jumeira, is a small shopping centre with a number of specialty shops, including designer home ware, art, framing and jewellery stores, a caviar shop and cafes. It is open from 9 am to 1 pm and from 4 pm to 9 pm; catch bus No 8 or 20 to get there.

Karama Centre (Map 4) between Trade Centre Rd and Za'abeel Rd, Karama, caters mainly to Indian clientele. The rest of the shops in the area are very cheap, selling copies of label jeans, watches and jewellery. There are also a few shops selling musical instruments. The centre is open from 9 am to 1 pm and 4 pm to 9 pm; catch bus No 6 to get there.

Twin Towers (Map 2) on Beniyas Rd, Deira, is a quiet, upmarket shopping centre with lots of designer shops. It is open from around 10 am until 9 pm; catch bus No 4, 5, 8 or 11 to get there.

Souqs

The souqs of Dubai are also covered in the Things to See & Do chapter.

Gold Souq (Map 2) Even if you have no plans to buy anything, it is worth a visit to the Gold Souq simply to take in the atmosphere, and to ogle at the size of some of the jewellery on offer. Many westerners find the bright yellow colour of the gold here to be too gaudy for their tastes.

The main drag of the Gold Souq runs along Sikkat al-Khail St, between Suq Deira and Old Baladiya Sts, in Deira. The other part of the souq runs along 45 St, which comes off Sikkat al-Khail to form a T-shape. Wooden lattice archways and roofs cover the entire area (see the Gold section under What to Buy earlier in this chapter).

The souq is aggressively promoted during the Dubai Shopping Festival and Dubai Summer Surprises, which both send gold sales into orbit. During the 1999 Dubai Shopping Festival, a record was set when Dubai gold manufacturers created a 4.1km-long gold chain that weighed 206kg!

Spice Souq (Map 2) Also known as the Deira Old Souq (since it doesn't just sell spices), this is one place you must wander around for a real taste of traditional Dubai. The spices are mainly found at the souq's eastern end, in the area closest to the Creek. Sacks overflow with frankincense, dried lemons, ginger root, cardamom, dried fruit, nuts and pulses. For a few dirhams you can take home a bag of whatever exotic ingredi-

Henna

In the Middle East, as in the Subcontinent, women paint their hands, nails and feet with henna. The intricate painting is usually done for a special event, such as a wedding, and stays on for about six weeks. In the more conservative and traditional areas of the Dubai Emirate, such as Hatta, most Emirati women will have some form of henna decoration on their hands and feet.

Men also use henna to dye their hair and beards, and this seems especially popular with Pakistani expats in Dubai.

There are many beauty salons in Dubai that do henna decorations for clients; just look for signs with painted hands on them. You'll find a number of such shops around Deira's souqs and in Karama.

ent you want. Other shops in this souq sell tacky trinkets, kitchen wares, rugs, glassware and textiles, all at very low prices (though you will be expected to haggle a little). The alleyways here are narrow and intricate and there is no set route that you should take.

Deira Covered Souq (Map 2) This souq is enclosed in the square between Al-Sabkha Rd and 67 St, and Naif Rd and Al-Maktoum Hospital Rd. The most interesting area is right in the middle, just west of the bus station. The goods here are predominantly from India, as are the vendors. You will find textiles, spices, kitchen wares, walking sticks, sheesha pipes, clothes and a lifetime supply of henna. Attractively patterned muslin headscarves and shawls cost about Dh10. A small box of henna costs Dh5. The prices of textiles here are the same as in the Dubai Souq.

Dubai Souq (Map 2) This souq, on the Creek waterfront in Bur Dubai, offers little in the way of Arabic antiques or souvenirs. If you want to have a sari made, however, this is the place to come. There are dozens of shops selling all kinds of materials from India, Thailand, Indonesia and Korea. They

For a taste of traditional Dubai, spend some time wandering through the city's souqs.

are broken up only by the odd tailor shop (see the Textiles section earlier in this chapter for prices). You can also buy shoes and Indian snacks here. Note that the Dubai Souq is a little slow to get going in the morning and does not open up until around 9 or 9.30 am.

Satwa Souq (Map 5) This area, which lies to the south of Al-Dhiyafa Rd near the Satwa roundabout, is the place to buy shoes, textiles, tacky souvenirs, imitation brand watches and sunglasses. There are also a number of electronic spare-parts shops and lots of sweet shops. If you don't have time to visit this souq you won't be missing out on much but if you are in the area it is worth a wander around to feel the buzz of activity.

SHIPPING

There's probably more shipping and cargo agencies in Dubai than anywhere else in the world. You won't have any trouble finding them. All cargo is handled through the Dubai Cargo Village next to the airport. Most travel agencies can usually arrange cargo shipping to any part of the world. Alternatively, you can contact a cargo company directly. They are all quite reliable – we haven't heard any horror stories of damaged or lost goods – but prices do vary quite considerably so ring around for quotes.

To give you a rough idea of air freight charges, the average cost per kilo to Australia is Dh8.50 for under 45kg, Dh7.50 for more than 45kg. To the UK it costs around Dh4.75 per kilogram for 50 to 100kg or Dh6 for under 50kg. You could pay double these rates for door to door service. There is also a handling charge and a fee for packing up your items. This could be anywhere from Dh50 to Dh350, depending on the company. Sea freight is about half the cost of air freight.

There are dozens of cargo companies. Look under 'Shipping' in the UAE Business Directory, which should be available in your hotel. Some cargo companies we recommend are:

Danata
 (☎ 702 3666, fax 822 683)
Kanoo Group
 (☎ 472 860, fax 472 869)
Allied Pickfords
 (☎ 334 5567, fax 334 4515)
TNT Homepack
 (☎ 823 306, fax 823 439)
Rainbow Cargo & Tourism
 (☎ 634 728, fax 614 188)

Excursions

If you are going to be in Dubai for more than a couple of days it's well worth taking a day trip or overnight visit to a few of the surrounding villages and towns. Once you're out of Dubai city, the landscape changes dramatically as you cruise through deserts and mountain oases. The people and their way of life are much more traditional.

All the trips mentioned here can be arranged with any tour company in Dubai but we suggest you just hire a car or catch a minibus to your destination and do it on your own. You'll get much better value for money and you won't be as rushed.

Insurance Warning

Keep in mind that unless you make other arrangements, the insurance on your rental car will only be valid inside the UAE. This means that if you go into Buraimi while on an excursion to Al-Ain – which can be done without an Omani visa – you had better not have even a minor accident while you are on the Omani side of the border. It is possible to add Oman to a rented car's insurance (if, say, you want to rent a car in Dubai and drive to Muscat), but insurance will go up by Dh10 or Dh20 per day and the cost of renting the car itself may double.

ORGANISED TOURS

The following tour prices are per person and often there needs to be a minimum of four people to fill a 4WD. Bear in mind that you could hire a car for two or three days and take yourself to lots more places in your own time for the same price as a tour.

Orient Travel & Touring (☎ 06-535 7323, PO Box 24947, Sharjah) has a one day east coast tour that takes in Masafi Market, Dibba, Badiyah Mosque, Khor Fakkan Souq and Fujairah for Dh175 or Dh85 for children. Arabian Adventures (☎ 343 9999,

AROUND DUBAI

Interchange No. 2, Shaikh Zayed Rd, Dubai) has a Grand Canyons tour for Dh340 per person that takes in Masafi Market and Dibba, then goes off-road through wadis in the Hajar Mountains and on to Ras al-Khaimah via a camel farm. One of their overnight tours (Dh425 per person) takes you to a camel race, then over sand dunes by 4WD to a camp site in the desert where you'll have a BBQ. It goes back to Dubai the next day through the Hajar Mountains.

Desert Rangers (☎ 453 091, Dune Centre, Al-Dhiyafa Rd, Satwa) has a tour to the archaeological sites in Ras al-Khaimah then across to Dibba, Khor Fakkan and Fujairah for Dh190. It also has an Al-Ain city tour for Dh190 or a desert safari to the rock pools in the mountains around Hatta for Dh200.

Relax Tourism (☎ 451 881, Dune Centre, Al-Dhiyafa Rd, Satwa) charges Dh175 for either a city tour of Al-Ain or a trip to the east coast. Their Sharjah tour is Dh110. A full day tour of the wadis and mountains around Hatta costs Dh340, including lunch.

CHRIS MELLOR

CHRISTINE OSBORNE

RUSSELL MOUNTFORD

CHRISTINE OSBORNE

LOU CALLAN

Shop 'til you drop (clockwise from top left): Persian carpets, potent perfumes, gold bracelets, henna and pipes, and colourful cosmetics are all available in Dubai's souqs.

Top: The Bur Juman Shopping Centre is one of the most popular shopping malls in Dubai.
Middle: Sharjah's Central Souq has one of the best selections of oriental carpets in the country.
Bottom: The Fish Souq, where expats clean fish for a fixed fee set by the government.

JEBEL ALI
☎ 09

If you really want to get away from it all, the beach at Jebel Ali is like a desert island paradise, that is if you can ignore the industrial skyline of Jebel Ali Port in the distance. It takes 25 minutes to drive here from the centre and costs about Dh60 in a metered taxi. It's better to have your own car as getting back to Dubai means walking to the nearby Jebel Ali Hotel and calling a Dubai Transport taxi (☎ 331 3131) from there.

To get to this beach follow the signs for the Jebel Ali Hotel from the main Dubai-Jebel Ali highway. Instead of pulling into the hotel's main entrance, continue along a sandy path that follows the coast. You'll see dozens of tracks leading off to the beach on your right. Most saloon cars can make it, but if the track looks a little too sandy just leave your car on the path and walk across the dunes. The beach is long and wide and, generally, very clean. There are barasti shelters, though you will have to get there early to nab one for yourself. You might see a few campers along here as it's a popular overnight getaway for Dubai residents. The farther you get from the hotel, the fewer people there are.

If you opt for an overnight stay in Jebel Ali, and you don't have camping gear, the only place to stay is the pricey *Jebel Ali Hotel & Golf Resort (☎ 836 000, fax 835 543)*. The hotel extends over a large area and includes a nine hole golf course, stables, a marina, a shooting range, tennis courts, a long private beachfront, wooded gardens (complete with wandering peacocks) and two pools. Rooms cost Dh984/1104 for singles/doubles, but there are often special weekend package deals that include a round of golf for those inclined to travel with golf clubs!

The hotel provides a free shopping shuttle to Deira (though the shuttle does not go to the airport and will not let you take luggage). It costs about Dh60 to get there in a metered taxi or just Dh7 in a shared taxi, which you can catch from Al-Ghubaiba bus station in Bur Dubai.

SHARJAH
☎ 06

The most interesting sites to see in Sharjah can be covered in just half a day. It's a place that many tend to miss out on when they visit Dubai, but it's cheap and easy to get to and is worth a visit, if only for the fantastic shopping it offers. The third largest Emirate, Sharjah pushes itself as the cultural capital of the UAE, and with the proliferation of new museums and galleries in the last couple of years, it's easy to see why.

Sharjah has long been seen as Dubai's poor cousin, though Dubai's ascendance in terms of wealth and political power is actually relatively recent. During the first half of the 19th century, Sharjah was the most important port on the Arabian side of the lower Gulf, and during the latter half of the century its rulers vied with those of Abu Dhabi for the area's leading political role.

Orientation & Information

The centre of town is located between the Corniche and Al-Zahra Rd, from the Central Market to Shaikh Mohammed bin Saqr al-Qasimi Rd (or Mohammed Saqr St). This is not a huge area and it's pretty easy to get around on foot if the heat's not too debilitating. It is a dreadful place for driving, however, because the streets are so crowded.

Moneychangers and banks can be found on and around Burj Ave (also called Bank St). The main post office is on Government House Square. It's open Saturday to Wednesday from 8 am to 8 pm and Thursday from 8 am to 6 pm. The Etisalat office is on Al-Safat Square (formerly Kuwait Square). It's open 24 hours a day.

Al-Hisn Fort

This fort, originally built in 1822, has been fully restored and houses a fascinating collection of photographs and documents, mainly from the 1930s, showing members of the ruling family of Sharjah, the Al-Qasimis, and the British Trucial Oman Scouts who were stationed here at the time. As you enter the fort there is a room on your left showing

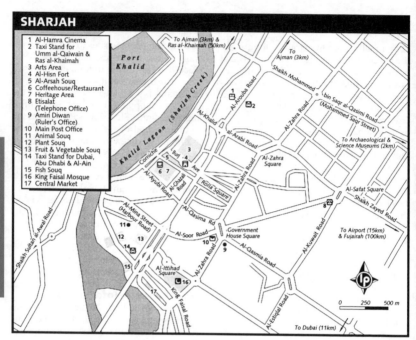

SHARJAH

1 Al-Hamra Cinema
2 Taxi Stand for
   Umm al-Qaiwain &
   Ras al-Khaimah
3 Arts Area
4 Al-Hisn Fort
5 Al-Arsah Souq
6 Coffeehouse/Restaurant
7 Heritage Area
8 Etisalat
   (Telephone Office)
9 Amiri Diwan
   (Ruler's Office)
10 Main Post Office
11 Animal Souq
12 Plant Souq
13 Fruit & Vegetable Souq
14 Taxi Stand for Dubai,
   Abu Dhabi & Al-Ain
15 Fish Souq
16 King Faisal Mosque
17 Central Market

footage of the first Imperial Airways flights from London, which landed here in 1932 on their way to India. The difference between Sharjah then and now is really incredible.

The fort sits in the middle of Burj Ave and is open from 8 am to 1 pm and 5 to 8 pm. On Friday it is open from 4.30 to 8.30 pm and it is closed on Monday. Admission is free.

Heritage Area

All the buildings in this block, just inland from the Corniche, between Burj Ave and Al-Ayubi Rd, have been faithfully constructed incorporating traditional designs and materials such as sea rock and gypsum. Coming from Burj Ave, the first place you will come across is **Literature Square**. It was under construction at the time of writing, but when completed it will house a library and be used as a meeting place for writers. Across from here is **Bait Shaikh Sultan bin Saqr al-Qasimi**, a house built around a courtyard and displaying traditional cos-

tumes, jewellery, ceramics, cooking utensils and furniture. The **Heritage Museum** displays much the same thing. Next door is the **Islamic Museum**, which should definitely not be missed. It includes a large collection of coins from all over the Islamic world and a number of handwritten Qurans and writing implements. There are ceramics from Turkey, Syria and Afghanistan, as well as a display on the covering of the Qaaba stone at Mecca, the most holy sacred shrine for Muslims, including a copy of the embroidered cloth.

All of the museums are open from 8 am to 1 pm and from 5 to 8 pm; they are closed on Monday. Wednesday is usually for women only. Admission is free, but it seems you are obliged to sign each and every visitor's book.

Arts Area

Tucked away on the north side of Burj Ave from the Heritage Area is the Arts Area, where there is a large **Art Museum** exhibiting modern art from local as well as foreign artists and some 19th century European paintings. It's open from 9 am to 1 pm and from 5 to 8 pm everyday except Friday.

The **Bait Obeid al-Shamsi** next to the Art Museum is a restored house that is now used as artists' studios. It is a lovely building featuring intricate pillars on the upper level. The **Arts Cafe** on the main square serves traditional snacks such as hot milk with ginger (delicious) for about Dh1.

Souqs
Just in from the Corniche on the south side of Burj Ave is **Al-Arsah Souq**. It was restored by the government after large sections of it fell to pieces during the 1970s and 80s. The *areesh* (palm frond) roof and wooden pillars give it a traditional feel and it's a lovely place to wander around and buy Arabic and Bedouin souvenirs. Despite the efforts to recreate a traditional atmosphere you can buy all kinds of non-Arabic souvenirs here too, including Princess Di phone cards and old Coke bottles. There is also a traditional **coffeehouse/restaurant**.

The **Central Market** (also called the New Souq, the Blue Souq or the Sharjah Souq), on the Corniche just south of the King Faisal Mosque, has the best selection of oriental carpets in the country, and also hundreds of shops selling souvenirs and antiques from Oman, India, Thailand and Iran. The **Animal Souq, Plant Souq** and **Fish Souq** may also be worth a visit.

Getting There & Away
The trip takes about 10 minutes from Dubai city, unless you encounter traffic, in which case it could take you 40 minutes. Avoid peak hours (1 to 2 and 5 to 7 pm). Minibuses go from the Deira taxi and minibus stand on Omar ibn al-Khattab St and cost Dh5. A taxi will cost you about Dh25. You won't be able to get a minibus back to Dubai though. You'll have to get a Sharjah taxi from the stand next to the fruit and vegetable souq. These cost Dh25 (engaged) or Dh5 (shared).

Getting Around
Since Sharjah has no bus system, getting around without your own car means either taking taxis or walking. The taxis have no meters and trips around the centre should cost Dh5 to Dh10 (agree on the fare before you get in). Sharjah's arts and heritage areas can be covered on foot quite easily.

HATTA
☎ 085

Hatta, an enclave of Dubai nestled in the Hajar Mountains, is a great weekend getaway spot. It is 105km from Dubai by road, about 20km of which runs through Omani territory. There is no customs check as you cross the border, but remember that if you are driving a rental car your insurance does not cover accidents in Oman. Hatta's main attractions are its relatively cool, dry climate (compared to the coast) and the mountain scenery. It is also a good spot for off-road trips through the mountains.

Rock Pools
Most people go to Hatta only to visit the magnificent rock pools, one of the UAE's highlights, about 20km south of the town. They are actually across the border in Oman, but access is from Hatta. The miniature canyon has water all year round, and it's an amazing experience to swim through these narrow rock corridors and play at the waterfalls.

You don't need a 4WD to get to the rock pools from Hatta, but if you want to continue past the pools and on to the town of Al-Ain you will need one. To get to the rock pools, turn right at the Fort roundabout on the edge of town and head into the centre. After 2.7km take the turn-off to the left for the 'Heritage Village'. Then turn left when you get to the T-junction at the mosque, fifty metres past the entrance to the Heritage Village. Follow this road, as it bends around to the left, for 1.4km. At this point take the turn-off onto the tarmac road to the right. There should be a blue-and-white sign in Arabic pointing in the direction you want to go. Continue along this road for 7.2km until the tarmac road ends. At this point there is a turn-off to the right onto a graded track. There is a stop sign here as well. The pools are in a large wadi, 7.5km from this turn-off.

Alternatively, the Hatta Fort Hotel offers 4WD safaris to the rock pools. A three hour trip for four people costs Dh600. An eight hour trip for four people costs Dh1400, including a picnic lunch (see Places to Stay and Eat later in this section).

Other Attractions

There is a huge **rug market** about 12km west of Hatta on the main highway. This is the only other large country market besides the one at Masafi (see East Coast later in this chapter). If you're looking for rugs, it's worth a stop as you can pick up great bargains.

At the time of writing, the government had almost finished building a **Heritage Village** in Hatta, a re-creation of a traditional mountain village from the pre-oil era. Even if the village is still not officially open when you visit, it is still possible to walk through the site. Climb up some stairs to the top of the watchtower here for some great views over the valley. There is a functioning *falaj* (a traditional irrigation system) that irrigates small but lush agricultural plots just below the Heritage Village. The turn-off for the village is signposted to the left off the main street, 2.7km from the Fort roundabout.

Places to Stay & Eat

The only place to stay in Hatta is the ***Hatta Fort Hotel*** (*☎ 085-23211, fax 23561*) where singles/doubles cost Dh400 on weekdays, Dh450 on weekends, plus a 10% tax and service charge. The hotel has a fine dining restaurant which, although pricey, outdoes just about anything else in Dubai. There are also extensive sports facilities.

There isn't much choice when it comes to eating in Hatta, but for a great omelette sandwich, try the ***Hatta Mountains Restaurant***, which is on the main street, near the bus stop.

Getting There & Away

From Dubai buses leave every hour for Hatta from 6.10 am to 9 pm (Dh10, 1 hour). In Dubai they leave from the Deira bus station. In Hatta, the buses depart from the red bus shelter near the Hatta Mountains Restaurant. Buy tickets from the driver. Buses leave Hatta for Dubai every hour from 6 am to 9 pm. Shared/engaged taxis leave from Al-Ghubaiba bus station in Bur Dubai and cost Dh20/100.

Bedouin Hospitality

Bedouin hospitality towards strangers is legendary. These traditions have not been lost on the new generation of Emiratis and invitations into people's homes for tea and coffee are common. Unlike many in the west who are reluctant to share themselves too much, or to make the effort to get to know strangers, the Bedouin are welcoming, friendly and helpful. You may find yourself invited to *fudell*, especially in rural areas outside Dubai. This is an invitation to share food with someone. Often it means that they want you to take the food right off their plate.

You'll also find that people will be very willing to help if you are in any kind of trouble. And they won't leave you until the problem is sorted out. If you are looking lost, people will stop and offer their assistance. Once a couple of young Emiratis drove 25 minutes out of their way to guide me back to a main road when I was a little lost on an off-road jaunt. They could have just pointed me in the right direction.

EAST COAST

The east coast is without doubt the most beautiful part of the UAE. The Hajar Mountains provide a stunning backdrop to the incredible blue waters of the Indian Ocean. There is a lot of greenery here too as the run-off from the mountains provides natural irrigation throughout most of the year. There are networks of wadis to explore through the mountains, and waterholes that are full all year round. Artificial coral reefs have been constructed along the east coast in an attempt to encourage natural reef formations. As a result, the area has become well known for diving and snorkelling.

Fujairah
☎ 09

This city is the capital of the emirate of the same name. There is not a great deal to see in Fujairah itself, but it makes a good base for exploring the rest of the east coast and it only takes 1¼ hours to get here from Dubai.

The main business strip is Hamad bin Abdullah Rd, between the Fujairah Trade Centre and the coast. Along this stretch of road you'll find the Etisalat office, several banks and, at the intersection with the coast road, the Central Market. The main post office is on Al-Sharqi Rd, just off Hamad bin Abdullah Rd.

The coastal road changes its name three times, which can be confusing. Passing through the city from south to north it is called Regalath Rd, Gurfah Rd and Al-Faseel Rd, in that order.

The **old town** is best described as spooky. It is home to a cemetery and a fort (at least 300 years old) overlooking the ruins of old Fujairah. Relics found in the old town date back to the 15th and 16th centuries. At the time of writing the **museum** had been closed for six months. It will eventually

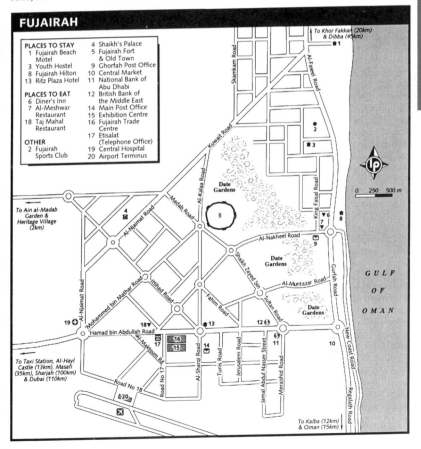

FUJAIRAH

PLACES TO STAY
1 Fujairah Beach Motel
3 Youth Hostel
8 Fujairah Hilton
13 Ritz Plaza Hotel

PLACES TO EAT
6 Diner's Inn
7 Al-Meshwar Restaurant
18 Taj Mahal Restaurant

OTHER
2 Fujairah Sports Club

4 Shaikh's Palace
5 Fujairah Fort & Old Town
9 Ghorfah Post Office
10 Central Market
11 National Bank of Abu Dhabi
12 British Bank of the Middle East
14 Main Post Office
15 Exhibition Centre
16 Fujairah Trade Centre
17 Etisalat (Telephone Office)
19 Central Hospital
20 Airport Terminus

To Khor Fakkan (20km) & Dibba (45km)

Skamkam Road
Al-Faseel Road
Kuwait Road
Al-Kalaa Road
Madab Road
Al-Njaimat Road
King Faisal Road
Date Gardens
Al-Njaimat Road
Mohammed bin Mathar Road
Ittihad Road
Shaikh Zayed bin Fahim Road
Date Gardens
Al-Nakheel Road
Al-Muntazar Road
Sultan Road
Date Gardens
Gurfah Road
Hamad bin Abdullah Road
Al-Maktoum Rd
Al-Sharqi Road
Tunis Road
Jerusalem Road
Jamal Abdul Nasser Street
Merashid Road
New Coast Road
Regalath Road

To Ain al-Madab Garden & Heritage Village (2km)

To Taxi Station, Al-Hayl Castle (13km), Masafi (35km), Sharjah (100km) & Dubai (110km)

Road No 17
Road No 18

GULF OF OMAN

To Kalba (12km) & Oman (15km)

0   250   500 m

reopen in the restored fort, which was under restoration at the time of writing.

Ain al-Madab Garden on the edge of town is a sorry sight, but the swimming pools here are clean, cool and segregated into men's and women's sections. The garden is open from 10 am to 10 pm and the pools are open from 10 am to 7 pm. Admission to the park is Dh2; Dh5 if you want to swim. There is a small **Heritage Village** across from the garden, which is open from 9 am to 6 pm every day. Here you'll find a reconstructed coastal desert village, complete with a real cow.

Places to Stay & Eat Fujairah's *youth hostel* (☎ 222 347) is just off Al-Faseel Rd, near the sports club. Beds are Dh15. The hostel will only accommodate women if it is empty enough to segregate them from men. Considering how small the hostel is, this means a single woman stands a fairly high chance of being turned away.

Fujairah Beach Motel (☎ 228 111, fax 228 054) is 3km north of the centre on the coast road and has rooms for Dh262.50. It is frequented mainly by Russians. The *Fujairah Hilton* (☎ 222 411, fax 226 541) is closer to the centre and is very popular with Americans and Europeans; rooms cost Dh598/666.

The *Ritz Plaza Hotel* (☎ 222 202, fax 222 203) on Hamad bin Abdullah Rd has comfortable but small singles/doubles for Dh460/575.

Taj Mahal on Shaikh Hamad bin Abdullah Rd, at the back of the building directly opposite the Etisalat office, serves excellent Indian and Chinese food and is cheap with main courses from Dh10. It is also clean, cool, comfortable and the service is good.

Diner's Inn on Al-Faseel Rd, across from the Hilton, has good cheap Indian and Chinese food served in reasonably large helpings. Meals can cost as little as Dh8.

Al-Meshwar, on King Faisal Rd, in the block behind Diner's Inn, is a more upmarket, medium-priced Lebanese restaurant. It has mezze from Dh7 to Dh12 and mains from Dh12 to Dh25.

Getting There & Away Minibuses leave from the Deira taxi and minibus station and cost Dh25. Long-distance taxis cost Dh25 shared, or Dh150 engaged. In Fujairah the taxi station is on the road to Sharjah and Dubai. Minibuses don't go any farther along the coast. A shared/engaged taxi costs Dh5/20 from Fujairah to Khor Fakkan and Dh20/100 to Dibba, though you should be able to negotiate a discount.

Masafi
☎ 09

This small town, 35km from Fujairah, is at the junction where the road from Dubai to the east coast splits into two and heads north to Dibba and south to Fujairah. Known as the location of Masafi water-bottling factory, the town is also famous for its **Friday market**, confirmed by the number of tour buses that have recently begun to stop here on their way to the east coast. The market is actually open every day of the week and has an enormous number of carpets, plants and souvenirs for sale. You are sure to get a bargain here, but you have to work at it – aim to pay 40% to 50% of the asking price. The stall-holders here are becoming more shrewd as more bus loads of tourists come past each week, eager to buy something, but with little time to haggle over the price.

Kalba
☎ 09

This traditional fishing village, just south of Fujairah, is a real slice of what life would have been like on the Gulf coast earlier this century. *Shasha* boats (small, canoe-shaped fishing boats made from stripped palm fronds) and crayfish baskets line the beach, and fishermen can be seen setting out and pulling in their nets each morning and evening.

Kalba is part of the Sharjah Emirate. The khor, just south of town, is also the site of the oldest mangrove forest in Arabia. This conservation reserve has abundant bird life and is the only home in the world to the Khor Kalba white collared kingfisher. It's possible to hire boats from the local fishermen and paddle up the inlets into the mangroves.

Breeze Motel (☎ 778 877, fax 776 769) is the only place to stay. Run-down cabins are a ridiculous Dh250/300, but those rates can drop by up to Dh100 if things are slow. A taxi from Fujairah should cost you about Dh10 to Dh12.

Al-Hayl Castle

You'll need a 4WD to get to these ruins set among mountain peaks in Wadi Hayl, 13km from Fujairah. They were once the site of the summer palace of the ruling sheikhs of Fujairah. The ruins of the palace look quite stunning set against the green mountains with its freestanding pillars and watchtowers.

Coming from Fujairah towards Dubai, the signposted turn-off for Al-Hayl Castle is on the left about 2km past the main roundabout on the outskirts of town. The tarmac road goes for 7km to a village. Drive straight through the village and down into a wadi that goes off to the left. From here it's a 2.1km rough road to the castle. The track rises up and runs along the left bank of the wadi. After almost 2km it joins up with a graded track that veers to the right up a hill to the castle. Allow half a day for a trip here from Fujairah.

Khor Fakkan

☎ 09

One of Sharjah's enclaves, and the largest town on the east coast after Fujairah, Khor Fakkan must be the most beautiful spot in the UAE. It's also a trendy weekend resort, but while the port has proved to be a roaring success, the development of tourism has been somewhat held back by Sharjah's ban on alcohol.

The sweeping Corniche is bounded by the port and **fish market** at the southern end and the luxury Oceanic Hotel to the north, with a nice **beach** in between.

If you have your own transport it's worth a drive to **Rifaisa Dam**, in the mountains above the town. The dam resembles a Swiss mountain lake without the greenery. To get there, turn inland from the main street at the Select N Save store, just near the mosque. The road swings round to the right and over a bridge. Turn left immediately after the

bridge onto a dirt road. Follow this road for 4.7km to the dam. You'll notice a couple of ruined watchtowers atop hills along the way.

There's really only one place to stay here. The *Oceanic Hotel* (☎ 238 5111, fax 238 7716) at the northern end of the Corniche costs Dh460/575 for singles/doubles, but it is much better value than *Al-Khaleej Hotel* (☎ 238 7336). This place is on the right as you enter Khor Fakkan from Fujairah and has shabby and dusty rooms with shared bath for Dh150. You also don't get the magnificent views that the Oceanic does.

On the Corniche there are two restaurants worth trying. *The Lebanon Restaurant* is the better of the two, with both Lebanese mezze and the usual cheap Indian fare of biryanis and tikka dishes. The mezze cost Dh5 to Dh15 and main dishes cost around Dh20 apiece. Farther north is the *Green Beach Cafeteria & Restaurant*, which has similar fare. Avoid the appealing *Irani Pars Restaurant* at the roundabout on the Corniche, near the souq. It is overpriced and the food is average at best.

Badiyah

☎ 09

Badiyah, 8km north of Khor Fakkan (but in the Fujairah emirate), is one of the oldest towns in the Gulf. Archaeological digs have shown that the site of the town has been settled more or less continuously since the 3rd millennium BC. Today it is known mainly for its **mosque**, a small whitewashed structure of stone, mud-brick and gypsum, which is still in use. It was built around 640 AD and is the oldest mosque in the UAE. It is built into a low hillside along the main road just north of the village, and on the hillside above and behind it are several ruined **watchtowers**.

There is no place to stay in Badiyah, but 6km to the north, near the village of Al-Aqqa, there's the *Sandy Beach Motel* (☎ 445 555, fax 445 200). Hotel rooms cost Dh267.50 and one-bedroom chalets cost Dh399. There is a diving centre here where you can organise dives or just hire snorkelling gear to explore the coral reef 100m from the beach. The stretch of beach next to the hotel is a popular unofficial *camp site*.

AL-AIN & BURAIMI
☎ 03 & 00968

These two towns lie within the Buraimi Oasis, which straddles the border between Abu Dhabi and Oman. In the days before the oil boom, the oasis was a five day overland journey by camel from Abu Dhabi. Today the trip takes 1½ hours on a tree-lined freeway. It's best to make an overnight trip, but if you are really pressed for time you could get there, zip around the sites and get back to Dubai in a day, as long as you get an early start. Once in the oasis, you can cross freely between the UAE and Oman – the border is 50km from Buraimi. UAE currency is accepted in Buraimi at a standard rate of OR1 = Dh10 (at the time of writing).

One of Al-Ain's main attractions during summer is its dry air – a welcome change from the humidity of the coast. The fact that many sheikhs from around the Emirates have their summer palaces here is a function of the temperate climate. The cool and quiet date-palm oases all over town are nice to wander through at any time of the year.

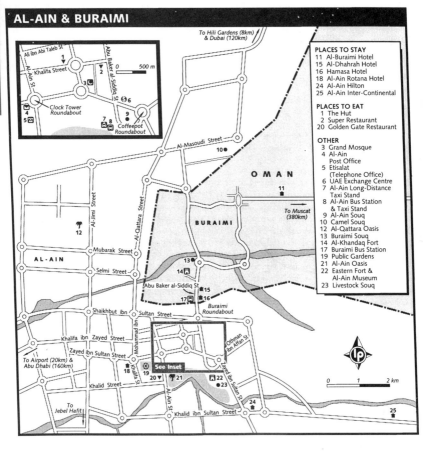

AL-AIN & BURAIMI

PLACES TO STAY
11 Al-Buraimi Hotel
15 Al-Dhahrah Hotel
16 Hamasa Hotel
18 Al-Ain Rotana Hotel
24 Al-Ain Hilton
25 Al-Ain Inter-Continental

PLACES TO EAT
1 The Hut
2 Super Restaurant
20 Golden Gate Restaurant

OTHER
3 Grand Mosque
4 Al-Ain
Post Office
5 Etisalat
(Telephone Office)
6 UAE Exchange Centre
7 Al-Ain Long-Distance
Taxi Stand
8 Al-Ain Bus Station
& Taxi Stand
9 Al-Ain Souq
10 Camel Souq
12 Al-Qattara Oasis
13 Buraimi Souq
14 Al-Khandaq Fort
17 Buraimi Bus Station
19 Public Gardens
21 Al-Ain Oasis
22 Eastern Fort &
Al-Ain Museum
23 Livestock Souq

Orientation & Information

The main streets in Al-Ain are Khalifa ibn Zayed St and Zayed ibn Sultan St. The main north-south streets are Abu Baker al-Siddiq St, which extends into Buraimi, and Al-Ain St. The two landmarks you need to know for navigational purposes are the Clock Tower and Coffeepot roundabouts. Distances in both Al-Ain and Buraimi are large, but taxis are abundant and cheap. It's fairly easy to find most of the things worth seeing in Al-Ain by following the big purple tourist signs.

There are lots of banks in Al-Ain near the Clock Tower roundabout; the area around the Grand Mosque has several money-changers. Al-Ain's main post and telephone offices are at the Clock Tower roundabout. The post office is open Saturday to Wednesday from 8 am to 1 pm and 4 to 7 pm; Thursday from 8 am to 4.30 pm and Friday from 8 to 11 am. The Etisalat office is open from 7 am to 3 pm Saturday to Wednesday and from 8 am to 1 pm on Thursday.

Eastern Fort & Al-Ain Museum

The museum and fort are in the same compound, south-east of the overpass near the Coffeepot roundabout. This is one of the best museums in the country and is a highlight of a visit to Al-Ain. The fort was the birthplace of the UAE's current ruler, Shaikh Zayed. As you enter the museum, take a look at the *majlis* (formal meeting room) and be sure to see the display of photographs of Al-Ain in the 1960s – it's unrecognisable. Other exhibits cover traditional education, flora, fauna, weapons and Bedouin life. A large portion of the museum is dedicated to the archaeology of the area.

The museum is open Sunday to Wednesday from 8 am to 1 pm and 3.30 to 5.30 pm (4.30 to 6.30 pm from May to October). On Thursday it's open from 8 am to noon and Friday from 9 to 11.30 am. It's closed all day Saturday. Admission is 50 fils.

Livestock Souq

You can see the entrance to the livestock souq from the museum/fort parking lot. The souq, which sells everything from Brahmin cows to Persian cats, attracts people from all over the southern UAE and northern Oman. Don't be surprised if you see an Emirati loading newly bought goats into the back seat of his newly bought Mercedes. The best time to be there is early in the morning (before 9 am) when the trading is at its heaviest.

Camel Souq

The camel market is in Buraimi, on a large vacant block off Al-Masoudi St. It's quite a small market, but worth visiting for local colour. You may have to fight off the camel merchants, however, who seem to think that tourists will actually buy a camel from them if the price is right. It is open from early morning until about noon every day, then from about 4 pm until dusk. To get there go 4km up the main street of Buraimi from the Buraimi roundabout. Then turn right onto a paved road just after a red and white transmitter tower. Continue on for 1.5km and the camels will be on your left.

Al-Khandaq Fort

This fort in Buraimi is said to be about 400 years old. If you're coming from the centre of Al-Ain you'll see it about 200m off the road to your left, about 750m past the border. It is open Saturday to Wednesday from 8 am to 6 pm and Thursday and Friday from 8 am to 1 pm and 4 to 6 pm. Admission is free.

The fort's restoration (which took several years) has been impressively thorough. Even the dry moat around the structure has been restored to its former glory. Be sure to climb one of the battlements for a view of the surrounding oasis. Unusually for an Omani fort, there are both inner and outer defence walls. Once you get into the courtyard head directly across it and slightly to the left to reach a large, well-restored room. This was the majlis, where the fort's commander would have conducted his official business.

The large enclosed yard just east of the fort is Buraimi's Eid prayer ground, where people gather to pray during the holidays marking the end of Ramadan and the end of the pilgrimage season.

Buraimi Souq

Buraimi's main souq is housed in the large brown building at the Horse roundabout and sells fruit, vegetables, meat and household goods. The enclosed (concrete) part of the souq includes a few stores that sell Omani silver jewellery and *khanjars*, the ornate daggers worn by many Omani men (see the boxed text 'Khanjars' in the Shopping chapter for more information), though the selection is not great.

Hili Gardens & Archaeological Park

This combination public park and archaeological site is about 8km north of the centre of Al-Ain, off the Dubai road. The site is open daily from 4 to 11 pm (holidays from 10 am to 10 pm). Admission is Dh1.

The main attraction is the **Round Structure**, a 3rd millennium BC building, possibly connected with the Umm al-Nar civilisation, the oldest in the Abu Dhabi Emirate. It has two porthole entrances and is decorated with relief carvings of animals and people. Even though this structure is referred to as a tomb, it may not have been a tomb at all. No bones were ever found here, just remnants of pottery; there are suggestions that it may have been a temple.

At the time of writing there were further excavations taking place on a **tomb** that dates back to somewhere between 2300 and 2000 BC. This tomb is 8m in length and adjoins the older round structure. More than 250 skeletons were found here.

The park can be reached by bus Nos 80, 100 and 203. The fare is Dh1. A taxi from the centre costs about Dh6.

Jebel Hafit

The views from the top of this mountain and on the winding drive up are well worth the effort of getting here. The summit is about 30km by road from the centre of Al-Ain. At the time of writing a luxury hotel was under construction about halfway up the mountain.

To get there, head south from the Clock Tower roundabout and turn right at Khalid ibn Sultan St. From there follow the purple tourist signs. There are no buses to Jebel Hafit. A taxi will cost around Dh50 for the round trip.

Places to Stay & Eat

If you're on a budget you'll want to stay in Buraimi. *Hamasa Hotel (☎ 651 200; in the UAE call ☎ 050-619 4248, fax 651 210)* is the better of the two cheap hotels. It sits almost smack on the border, and will be on your right as you enter Buraimi from Al-Ain. Clean and bright singles/doubles are Dh150/200. *Al-Dhahrah Hotel (☎ 650 492, fax 650 881)* has rooms for Dh130/160. It is a few doors north of the Hamasa Hotel. *Al-Buraimi Hotel (☎ 652 010, 050-474 954, fax 652 011)* can be found easily enough by following the signs strategically positioned throughout the Omani part of the oasis. Singles/doubles are Dh420/500. None of the hotels in Buraimi serve alcohol.

Back in the UAE, your only choices are five star hotels. *Al-Ain Hilton (☎ 686 666, fax 686 888)* charges Dh535/585 for singles/doubles, and *Al-Ain Inter-Continental (☎ 686 686, fax 686 766)* charges Dh464/580 for singles/doubles. *Al-Ain Rotana Hotel (☎ 515 111, fax 515 444)* opened at the beginning of 1999 and is the only new hotel in Al-Ain. Singles/doubles cost Dh550/600.

You won't have any trouble finding cheap eats in the centre. *Super Restaurant* is a very popular Indian restaurant with expats, both western and Indian. It has a large menu and meals are between Dh10 and Dh12.

Golden Gate Restaurant on Al-Ain St is a little more upmarket and serves very good Chinese and Filipino food. Main dishes cost between Dh15 and Dh25.

The Hut is a western-style coffee shop on Khalifa St. It offers good cappuccino, latte and other coffee drinks as well as a wide selection of cakes, pastries and sandwiches. At Dh5 for a cappuccino the prices are a bit high, but the comfortable surroundings make up for it.

In Buraimi your options are limited to the standard cheap fare of a helping of biryani for about Dh10.

Getting There & Away

Minibuses to Al-Ain leave from Al-Ghubaiba bus station in Bur Dubai. It costs Dh30; a shared/engaged taxi costs Dh30/150. To return to Dubai you'll need to catch a taxi, as the minibuses don't take passengers in the other direction.

Getting Around

All of Al-Ain's buses run roughly on the half hour from 6 am to midnight. Most fares are Dh1. There are no local buses in Buraimi. Almost everyone travels by taxi in Al-Ain as they are so cheap. Most trips around the centre will only cost you Dh3. It's better to use the gold-and-white Al-Ain taxis than the orange-and-white Buraimi ones, which don't have meters.

RAS AL-KHAIMAH

☎ 07

Ras al-Khaimah is about 90km from Dubai city and is the northernmost emirate in the UAE. It has a lovely setting at the foot of the Hajar Mountains, although the town itself is a bit of a dump. The only real reason for an overnight trip up this way is to visit the numerous archaeological sites just north of Ras al-Khaimah. The town has a fairly interesting museum, which you should visit while you're here.

Orientation & Information

Ras al-Khaimah is really two cities: Ras al-Khaimah proper, which is the old town on a sandy peninsula along the Gulf coast, and Al-Nakheel, the newer business district farther inland on the other side of Ras al-Khaimah's creek.

You can change money at any of the banks along Al-Sabah St in Ras al-Khaimah or Oman St in Al-Nakheel. The main post office is a red brick building on King Faisal St, about 4km north of the Bin Majid Beach Hotel. The Etisalat office is on Al-Juwais Rd in Al-Nakheel.

Ras al-Khaimah Museum

Ras al-Khaimah's museum is in the old fort on Al-Hosen Rd, next to the police headquarters. The fort was built in the mid-18th century. Until the early 1960s it was the residence of the ruling Al-Qasimi sheikhs. The courtyard of the fort is paved with stones from the fossil-bearing strata of Wadi Haqil in the emirate. The museum is open daily except Tuesday from 8 am to noon and from 4 to 7 pm. Admission is Dh2.

Places to Stay & Eat

Al-Sana Resthouse (☎ 229 004, fax 223 722) on Oman St is the cheapest place to stay in town at Dh70/120, including breakfast. *Al-Nakheel Hotel* (☎ 222 822, fax 222 922) on Muntaser St in Al-Nakheel has the cheapest bar in town and rooms cost Dh140/190. *Bin Majid Beach Hotel* (☎ 352 233, fax 353 225) is the favoured haunt of Russian and German tour groups. Rooms are Dh250/350, including breakfast. The beach here is lovely. *Ras al-Khaimah Hotel* (☎ 362 999, fax 362 990) has rooms for Dh330/440, but is overpriced compared with the Bin Majid.

For a good, cheap meal, try *Punjab*, a Pakistani and north Indian restaurant in the souq area of Al-Nakheel. A chicken curry costs Dh6, dahl costs Dh3 and all meals include bread and salad. *Al-Sana Restaurant* next to Al-Sana Resthouse is highly recommended. It has western, Chinese, Indian and Filipino food. Meals should not run to more than Dh20. You should definitely drop in at the barasti *coffeehouse* near Mina Saqr and overlooking the creek. Sheeshas costs Dh10.

Getting There & Away

Minibuses to Ras al-Khaimah cost Dh20 and leave from the Deira minibus and taxi station. Shared/engaged taxis cost Dh20/100. To get back to Dubai you'll need to catch a taxi from the station on King Faisal St, just south of the Bin Majid Beach Hotel. A shared/engaged taxi costs Dh15/70.

AROUND RAS AL-KHAIMAH
Shimal

☎ 07

The village of Shimal, 5km north of the town of Ras al-Khaimah, is the site of some of the most important archaeological finds in the UAE. The area has been inhabited

EXCURSIONS

since the late 3rd millennium BC. The main attraction is the **Queen of Sheba's Palace**, a set of ruined buildings and fortifications spread over two small plateaus overlooking the village. Despite its name, the palace was not built by the Queen of Sheba, who is generally thought to have come from what is now Yemen. It may, however, have been visited by Queen Zenobia who ruled a sizeable chunk of the Near East in the 4th century AD from Palmyra in modern Syria. The fortifications are known to have been in use as recently as the 16th century AD. What is visible today apparently sits on top of a much older structure, and pottery found here dates from that time. You will notice a large well and walls around the ruins.

To reach the site, travel north from the Hospital roundabout in Al-Nakheel for 4.3km and turn right onto a paved road where there are a number of signs. One has a red arrow, another has red Arabic script on a white background and another has the falcon crest on it. Follow this road for 1.5km until you reach a roundabout. Turn right at the roundabout and drive for another 2.3km through a village until you come to the People Heritage Revival Association, a new building made to look like a fort. Turn left. After about 400m the paved road ends. Continue along this dirt track through the village. You'll pass a small green and white mosque on the left. Keep going straight, heading for the base of the hills and get onto the paved road to your left. Continue along this road for about 1km until you see a track leading to a large green water tank. At this point you will see a gap in the fence on your right. Park the car and walk through the gap in the fence and follow a faint track to the base of the closest hill. At the top of this hill (which will be on your right) you should see the remains of a stone wall. The 15 minute climb is a little strenuous due to the loose rocks underfoot.

A taxi from Ras al-Khaimah to Shimal costs Dh15. Note that Dh15 only gets you there. Going to Shimal, waiting while you climb the hill and then taking you back is definitely going to cost more. Decide on a fare before you set out and don't pay the driver until you get back again.

Dhayah
☎ 07

Dhayah, a small village beneath a ruined fort, is 15.5km north of Ras al-Khaimah. It was here that the people of Rams, from the coast just 3.5km away, retreated in the face of the advancing British in 1819 and surrendered after a four day siege. The fort sits atop a sharp, cone-shaped hill behind the modern village. It takes 15 to 20 minutes to climb the hill, longer if you stop to collect some of the numerous sea shells that blanket the slopes. Be careful, however, the rocks are very loose and it's easy to slip. The easiest approach is from the west side of the hill (facing the sea), moving towards the south side as you ascend. Once you get to the top the only easy way into the fort is through the south wall. There are some more ruined fortifications just south of the hill.

To reach the hill, turn right off the road from Ras al-Khaimah immediately after you pass Dhayah's new white mosque and the grocery store (the turn is exactly 14.5km north of the Hospital roundabout). If you pass a sign saying 'Sha'm 15km', you've gone too far. The dirt track swings around to the right behind the village. After about 500m you'll see the Al-Adal grocery. Keep to the left of this. The road forks just past the grocery. Take the track to the right (the one that runs along the fence). You'll pass an old watchtower on the left. From the watchtower the track twists and turns for another 450m. When you get to a white wall turn right and head towards the hill. You'll only be able to drive for about another 80m.

Language

English is widely spoken throughout the Gulf, but a few words of Arabic can do a lot to ease your passage through the region.

There are several different varieties of Arabic. Classical Arabic, the language of the Quran (Koran), is the root of all of today's dialects of spoken and written Arabic. A modernised and somewhat simplified form of classical Arabic is the common language of the educated classes in the Middle East. This language, usually known as Modern Standard Arabic (MSA), is used in newspapers and by TV and radio newsreaders. It's also used as a medium of conversation by well-educated Arabs from different parts of the region. Such a written language is necessary because the dialects of spoken colloquial Arabic differ to the point where a few of them are mutually unintelligible. Mercifully, the words and phrases a traveller is most likely to use are fairly standard throughout the Gulf. The words and phrases in this chapter should be understood anywhere in the region.

Transliteration

It's worth noting here that transliterating from Arabic script into English is at best an approximate science. The presence of sounds unknown in European languages, and the fact that the script is 'incomplete' (most vowels are not written), combine to make it nearly impossible to settle on one method of transliteration. A wide variety of spellings is therefore possible for words when they appear in roman script – and that goes for places and people's names as well.

The matter is further complicated by the wide variety of dialects and the imaginative ideas Arabs themselves often have on appropriate spelling in, say, English: words spelt one way in a Gulf country may look very different in Syria, heavily influenced by French (not even the most venerable of western Arabists have been able to come up with an ideal solution).

Pronunciation

Pronunciation of Arabic can be tongue-tying for someone unfamiliar with the intonation and combination of sounds. Pronounce the transliterated words slowly and clearly.

This language guide should help, but bear in mind that the myriad rules governing pronunciation and vowel use are too extensive to be covered here.

Vowels

a	as in 'had'
e	as in 'bet'
i	as in 'hit'
o	as in 'hot'
u	as in 'put'

A macron over a vowel indicates that the vowel has a long sound:

ā	as the 'a' in 'father'
ē	as in 'ten', but lengthened
ī	as the 'e' in 'ear', only softer
ō	as in 'for'
ū	as the 'oo' in 'food'

You may also see long vowels transliterated as double vowels, eg 'aa' (ā), 'ee' (ī) and 'oo' (ū).

The Transliteration Dilemma

TE Lawrence, when asked by his publishers to clarify 'inconsistencies in the spelling of proper names' in *Seven Pillars of Wisdom* – his account of the Arab Revolt in WWI – wrote back:

Arabic names won't go into English. There are some "scientific systems" of transliteration, helpful to people who know enough Arabic not to need helping, but a washout for the world. I spell my names anyhow, to show what rot the systems are.

The Arabic Alphabet

Final	Medial	Initial	Alone	Transliteration	Pronunciation
ـا			ا	ā	as the 'a' in 'father'
ـب	ـبـ	بـ	ب	b	as in 'bet'
ـت	ـتـ	تـ	ت	t	as in 'ten'
ـث	ـثـ	ثـ	ث	th	as in 'thin'
ـج	ـجـ	جـ	ج	g	as in 'go'
ـح	ـحـ	حـ	ح	H	a strongly whispered 'h', almost like a sigh of relief
ـخ	ـخـ	خـ	خ	kh	as the 'ch' in Scottish *loch*
ـد			د	d	as in 'dim'
ـذ			ذ	dh	as the 'th' in 'this'
ـر			ر	r	a rolled 'r', as in the Spanish word *caro*
ـز			ز	z	as in 'zip'
ـس	ـسـ	سـ	س	s	as in 'so', never as in 'wisdom'
ـش	ـشـ	شـ	ش	sh	as in 'ship'
ـص	ـصـ	صـ	ص	ṣ	emphatic 's'
ـض	ـضـ	ضـ	ض	ḍ	emphatic 'd'
ـط	ـطـ	طـ	ط	ṭ	emphatic 't'
ـظ	ـظـ	ظـ	ظ	ẓ	emphatic 'z'
ـع	ـعـ	عـ	ع	'	the Arabic letter 'ayn; pronounce as a glottal stop – like the closing of the throat before saying 'Oh oh!' (see Other Sounds on p.143)
ـغ	ـغـ	غـ	غ	gh	a guttural sound like Parisian 'r'
ـف	ـفـ	فـ	ف	f	as in 'far'
ـق	ـقـ	قـ	ق	q	a strongly guttural 'k' sound; in Egyptian Arabic often pronounced as a glottal stop
ـك	ـكـ	كـ	ك	k	as in 'king'
ـل	ـلـ	لـ	ل	l	as in 'lamb'
ـم	ـمـ	مـ	م	m	as in 'me'
ـن	ـنـ	نـ	ن	n	as in 'name'
ـه	ـهـ	هـ	ه	h	as in 'ham'
ـو			و	w	as in 'wet'; or
				ū	long, as the 'oo' on 'food'; or
				aw	as the 'ow' in 'how'
ـي	ـيـ	يـ	ي	y	as in 'yes'; or
				ī	as the 'e' in 'ear', only softer; or
				ay	as the 'y' in 'by' or as the 'ay' in 'way'

Vowels Not all Arabic vowel sounds are represented in the alphabet. See Pronunciation on p.141.

Emphatic Consonants To simplify the transliteration system used in this book, the emphatic consonants have not been included.

Consonants

Pronunciation for all Arabic consonants is covered in the alphabet table on the preceding page. Note that when double consonants occur in transliterations, both are pronounced. For example, *al-Hammam* (toilet/bath), is pronounced 'al-ham-mam'.

Other Sounds

Arabic has two sounds that are very tricky for non-Arabs to produce: the 'ayn and the glottal stop. The letter 'ayn represents a sound with no English equivalent that comes even close. It is similar to the glottal stop (which is not actually represented in the alphabet) but the muscles at the back of the throat are gagged more forcefully – it has been described as the sound of someone being strangled. In many transliteration systems, 'ayn is represented by an opening quotation mark, and the glottal stop by a closing quotation mark. To make the transliterations in this language guide (and throughout the rest of the book) easier to use, we have not distinguished between the glottal stop and the 'ayn, using the closing quotation mark to represent both sounds. You'll find that Arabic speakers will still understand you.

Pronouns

I	*ānē*
you (sg)	*inta/inti* (m/f)
he	*huwa*
she	*hiya*
we	*nahnu*
you (pl)	*untum/inti* (m/f)
they	*uhum*

Greetings & Civilities

Hello.	*as-salāma alaykum*
Hello. (response)	*wa alaykum e-salām*
Goodbye. (person leaving)	*ma'al salāma*
Goodbye. (person staying)	*alla ysalmak* (to a man)
	alla ysalmich (to a woman)
	alla ysallimkum (to a group)

Goodbye.	*Hayyākallah* (to a man)
	Hayyachallah (to a woman)
	Hayyakumallah (to a group)
Goodbye. (response)	*fi aman ullah* or *alla yHai'īk* (to a man)
	alla yHai'īch (to a woman)
	alla yHai'īkum (to a group)
Good morning.	*sabaH al-kheir*
Good morning. (response)	*sabaH an-nur*
Good afternoon/ evening.	*masa' al-kheir*
Good afternoon/ evening. (response)	*masa' an-nur*
Good night.	*tisbaH ala-kheir* (to a man)
	tisbiHin ala-kheir (to a woman)
	tisbuHun ala-kheir (to a group)
Good night. (response)	*wa inta min ahlil-kheir* (to a man)
	wa inti min ahlil-kheir (to a woman)
	wa intu min ahlil-kheir (to a group)
Welcome.	*ahlan wa sahlan* or *marHaba*
Welcome to you.	*ahlan fīk* (to a man)
	ahlan fīch (to a woman)
	ahlan fīkum (to a group)
Pleased to meet you. (also said on leaving)	*fursa sa'ida*
Pleased to meet you. (response)	*wa ana as'ad* (by an individual)
	wa iHna as'ad (by a group)

Basics

Yes.	*aiwa/na'am*
No.	*lā*

Maybe.	*mumkin*
Please.	*min fadhlik* or *lō tsimaH* (to a man) *min fadhlich* or *lō tsimiHīn* (to a woman) *min fadhelkum* or *lō tsimiHūn* (to a group)
Thank you.	*shukran* or *mashkur* (to a man) *mashkura* (to a woman) *mashkurin* (to a group)
You're welcome.	*afwan/al-afu*
Excuse me.	*lō tsimaH* (to a man) *lō tsimiHīn* (to a woman) *lō tsimiHūn* (to a group)
I'm sorry/ Forgive me.	*ānē āsef*
After you.	*atfaddal* or *min badik* (to a man) *min badak* (to a woman)
OK.	*zein/kwayyis/tayib*
No problem.	*mafī mushkila*
Impossible.	*mish mumkin*
It doesn't matter/ I don't mind.	*ma'alish*

Small Talk

How are you?	*kef Halak?* (to a man) *kef Halik ?* (to a woman) *kef Halkum?* (to a group)
Fine, thanks.	*(zein) al-Hamdulillah* (by a man) *(zeina) al-Hamdulillah* (by a woman) *(zeinin) al-Hamdulillah* (by a group)

What's your name?	*shismak?* (to a man) *shismich?* (to a woman) *shisimkum?* (to a group)
My name is ...	*ismi ...*
Do you like ...?	*tahabi ...?*
I like ...	*ahib ...*
I don't like ...	*la ahib ...*
God willing.	*inshallah*

I'm from ...	*ana min ...*
Australia	*usturālyē*
Canada	*kanadē*
Egypt	*masur*
Ethiopia	*ithyūbyē*
Europe	*ōrobba*
France	*faransa*
Germany	*almania*
Jordan	*elerdon*
Netherlands	*holanda*
New Zealand	*nyūzilande*
South Africa	*jinūb afrīqye*
Switzerland	*swissra*
Syria	*sūriye*
Tunisia	*tūnis*
UK	*britania*
USA	*amrika*

Language Difficulties

I understand.	*ana fahim* (by a man) *ana fahma* (by a woman)
We understand.	*iHna fahmīn*
I don't understand.	*ana afHām*
We don't understand.	*iHna nafHām*
Please repeat that.	*lō simaHt ti'id hādtha*

I speak ...	*ana atkallam ...*
Do you speak ...?	*titkallam ...?*
English	*inglīzi*
French	*fransawi*
German	*almāni*
I don't speak Arabic.	*ma-atkallam arabi*
I speak a little Arabic.	*atkallam arabi shwayē*

What does this mean?	*shu ya'ani?*
How do you say ... in Arabic?	*kef igūl ... bila'arabi?*
I want an interpreter.	*urīd mutarjem*

Getting Around

I want to go to ...	*abga arouH li ...*
When does the ... leave?	*mata yamshi il ...?*
When does the ... arrive?	*mata tosal il ...?*
What is the fare to ...?	*cham il tadhkara li ...?*
Which bus/taxi goes to ...?	*ai bas/tax yrouH il ...?*
Does this bus/taxi go to ...?	*Hadhal bas yrouH il ...?*
How many buses go to ...?	*cham bas yrouH li ...?*
Please tell me when we arrive at ...	*lau samaHtit goul li mata nosal li ...*
May I sit here?	*mumkin ag'id hina?*
May we sit here?	*mumkin nag'id hina?*
Stop here, please.	*'ogaf hina, law samaHt*
Please wait for me.	*law samaHt, intidherni*

Where is the ...?	*wein al ...?*
How far is the ...?	*cham yibe'id ...?*
airport	*al-matār*
bus stop	*mokaf al-bas*
bus station	*maHattat al-bas*
taxi stand	*maHattat tax/ maHattat ajara*
train station	*maHattat al-qatar*

boat	*markab*
bus	*bas*
camel	*jamal*
car	*sayyara*
donkey	*Hmār*
horse	*Hsan*
taxi	*tax/ajara*

daily	*kil yōm*
ticket office	*maktab al-tadhāker*
ticket	*tadhkara/bitāq*
first class	*daraje ūlā*

second class	*daraje thānye*
crowded	*zaHme/matrūs*
Where can I rent a ...?	*min wein agdar asta'ajir ...?*
bicycle	*saikel*
motorcycle	*motorsaikel*

Directions

Where is the ...?	*wein al ...?*
Is it near?	*uhwe girīb?*
Is it far?	*uhwe bi'īb?*
How many kilometres?	*kam kilometer?*
Can you show me the way to ...?	*mumkin tdallini mukān ...?*

address	*onwān*
street	*shāri'*
number	*raqam*
city	*madina*
village	*qaria*

here	*hnī*
there	*hnāk*
next to	*yam*
opposite	*gbāl/mgābel*
behind	*warā/khaif*
to	*min*
from	*ile*
left	*yasār*
right	*yimīn*
straight	*sīda*

Signs

ENTRY *dukhūl*		مدخل
EXIT *khurūj*		خروج
TOILETS (Men) *Hammam lirrijal*		حمام للرجال
TOILETS (Women) *Hammam linnisa'a*		حمام للنساء
HOSPITAL *mustashfa*		مستشفى
POLICE *shurta*		الشرطة
PROHIBITED *mamnu'u*		ممنوع

north	shimāl
south	jinūb
east	sharug
west	gharub

Around Town

I'm looking for the ...	ga'ed adawwēr ala ...
Where is the ...?	wein al ...?
bank	al-bank
barber	al-Hallaq
beach	il-shatt/il-shāt'i
city centre	wasat al-balād
customs	aljamarek
embassy	al-safara
mosque	al-masjid
museum	al-matHaf
old city	al-madina il-qadima
palace	al-qasr
passport & immigration office	markaz aljawazat welhijrā
police station	al-makhfar
post office	maktab al-barīd
telephone	al-telefon/al-hataf
telephone centre	maqsam al-hatef
toilet	al-Hammam
tourist office	isti'ilāmāt al-suyyaH
university	il-jam'a
zoo	Hadiqat il-Haywan

What time does it open?	mita tiftaH?
What time does it close?	mita tsaker?
I'd like to make a telephone call.	abgyi attisel telefōn/ abi akhaber
I want to change money.	abga asrif flūs
I want to change travellers cheques.	abga asrif sheikat syaHīa

Accommodation

Where is the hotel?	wein al-funduq/el-ōtel?

I'd like to book a ...	abgyi aHjiz ...
bed	sarīr/frāsh
cheap room	ghurfa rikhīsa
single room	ghurfa mifred
double room	ghurfa mijwīz

room with a bathroom	ghurfa ma'Hammam
room with air-con	ghurfa mukhayyafa

for one night	la leila wiHdē
for two nights	la leiltein thintein
May I see the room?	mumkin ashuf al-ghurfah?
May I see other rooms?	mumkin ashuf ghuraf dhānia?
How much is this room per night?	cham ujrat hādhil ghurfah fil-leila?
How much is it per person?	shtiswa ala eshshakhs al-āhed?
Do you have any cheaper rooms?	fih ghuraf arkhas?
This is fine.	hadha zein.

This is very ...	hādhi wāhed ...
noisy	muzi'ije
dirty	waskha
expensive	ghalye

address	al-unw
blanket	battaniyye
camp site	emakan al-mukhayyam
electricity	kahruba
hotel	funduq/ōtel
hot water	māi Hār
key	miftaH
manager	al-mudīr
shower	al-dūsh
soap	sābūn
toilet	Hammam

Food

I'm hungry.	āne jūda'ān
I'm thirsty.	āne atshān
I'd like ...	aHib/abghi ...
Is service included in the bill?	al-fatūra fihā qīmat al-khidma?
What is this?	shinū hādhe
Another one, please.	ba'ad wiHde min fadhlik?

breakfast	riyūg/ftūr
lunch	al-ghade
dinner	al-ashe
restaurant	mata'ām
set menu	qa'imat al-akel muHaddada

Emergencies

Call the police!	khaber eshurta!
Call a doctor!	khaber ettabīb!
Help me please!	sa'idnī lō simaHt!
Where is the toilet?	wein al-Hammam?
Go away!	rūh wallī!/isref!
Go/Get lost!	imshi!
Thief!	Harāmi!/bawwāg!
They robbed me!	bagonī!
Shame on you! (woman to man)	yā eibak!/yal mā tistiHi!

bread	khubz
chicken	dajaj
coffee	qahwa
fish	samak
meat	laHma
milk	laban/halīb
pepper	felfel
potatoes	batatas
rice	roz
salt	sel/melaH
sugar	suker
tea	chai
water	mayya

Shopping

I want ...	abga ...
Do you have ...?	indik ...? (to a man)
	indich ...? (to a woman)
Where can I buy ...?	wein agdar ashtiri ...?
How much is this?	kam hadha?
How much is that?	kam hadhak?
How much are those?	kam hadhol?
How much ...?	kam ...?
It costs too much.	ghalia wai'd
bookshop	al-maktaba
chemist/pharmacy	saydaliyya
laundry	masbagha
market	souq
newsagents/ stationers	maktabet-al-qurtāsiyye
big	chibīr
bigger	akbar

Numbers

Arabic numerals are simple to learn and, unlike the written language, run from left to right. Pay attention to the order of the words in numbers from 21 to 99.

0	٠	sifir
1	١	waHid
2	٢	idhnīn
3	٣	dhaladha
4	٤	arba'a
5	٥	khamsa
6	٦	sitta
7	٧	sab'a
8	٨	dhimania
9	٩	tis'a
10	١٠	ashra
11	١١	Hda'ash
12	١٢	dhna'ash
13	١٣	dhaladhta'ash
14	١٤	arba'ata'ash
15	١٥	khamista'ash
16	١٦	sitta'ash
17	١٧	sabi'ta'ashr
18	١٨	dhimanta'ash
19	١٩	tisi'ta'ash
20	٢٠	'ishrīn
21	٢١	waHid wa 'ishrīn
22	٢٢	idhnīn wa 'ishrīn
30	٣٠	dhaladhīn
40	٤٠	arbi'īn
50	٥٠	khamsīn
60	٦٠	sittīn
70	٧٠	saba'īn
80	٨٠	dhimanīn
90	٩٠	tis'īn
100	١٠٠	imia
101	١٠١	imia wa-waHid
200	٢٠٠	imiatayn
300	٣٠٠	dhaladha imia
1000	١٠٠٠	alf
2000	٢٠٠٠	alfayn
3000	٣٠٠٠	dhaladha-alaf

Ordinal Numbers

first	awwal
second	dhānī
third	dhālidh
fourth	rābi'
fifth	khāmis

small	*sighīr*	When?	*mita?*
smaller	*asghar*	now	*alHīn*
cheap	*rikhīs*	after	*ba'ad*
cheaper	*arkhas*	daily	*kil yom*
expensive	*ghāli*	today	*al-yom*
open	*āmaftūH*	yesterday	*ams*
closed	*msakkar/mughlaq*	tomorrow	*bukra*
money	*flūs*	morning	*es-subāH*
		afternoon	*ba'ad ezzuhur/*

Health

I need a doctor.	*abi tabīb*		*edhuhur*
My friend is ill.	*sidiji marīd/ayyān*	evening	*al-masa*
headache	*wija' rās*	day	*nahār*
hospital	*mustashfa*	night	*leil*
pharmacy	*saydaliyye*	week	*esbū'u*
prescription	*wasfa tibbiyā*	month	*shahar*
stomachache	*wija' batun*	year	*sine*
tampons	*fuwat siHiyya lalHarīm*	early	*mbach'ir/badri*
		late	*mit'akhir*

Time & Dates

What time is it?	*as-sa'a kam?*	on time	*alwaqit*
It is ...	*as-sa'a ...*		
one o'clock	*waHda*	Monday	*yom al-idhnīn*
1.15	*waHda wa rob'*	Tuesday	*yom al-dhaladh*
1.20	*waHda wa tilt*	Wednesday	*yom al-arbā'*
1.30	*waHda wa nus*	Thursday	*yom al-khamis*
1.45	*idhnīn illa rob'* (lit:	Friday	*yom al-jama'a*
	'quarter to two')	Saturday	*yom as-sabt*
		Sunday	*yom al-Had*

Glossary

Here, with definitions, are some unfamiliar words and abbreviations you might meet in this book or while you are in Dubai:

abaya – woman's full-length black robe
abba – sheikh's black or gold cloak worn over the *dishdasha* on formal occasions
abra – small, flat-decked motorboat
abu – father; saint
acropolis – high city; hilltop citadel and temples of a classic Hellenistic city
agal – headropes used to hold a *kufeyya* or *gutra* in place
ahwa – see *qahwa*
ain – spring
Allah – God
areesh – palm leaves
attar – Arabic oil-based perfume
Ayyalah – traditional Bedouin dance
azzan – call to prayer

bahoor – generic term for incense
bait – house
barasti – traditional method of building palm-leaf houses and the name of the house itself
barjeel – windtowers
Bedouin – also called Bedu; desert dweller of Arabia
birnah – ceramic pot used to store milk
biryani – very common Indo-Pakistani dish consisting of spiced meat with rice
burj – tower
burqa – stiff material face mask worn by women in the UAE to cover eyebrows, nose and mouth

caliph – Islamic ruler
chai – tea

dalla – traditional copper coffeepot
dhow – traditional sailing vessel of the Gulf
dishdasha – name of man's shirt-dress worn in Kuwait and the UAE
diwan – Ruler's Office; highest administrative body of an emirate

dosa – flat, grilled bread made from flour and water

Eid al-Adha – Feast of Sacrifice marking the pilgrimage to Mecca
Eid al-Fitr – Festival of Breaking the Fast; celebrated at the end of Ramadan
emir – Islamic ruler, military commander or governor; literally, prince

falaj – traditional irrigation system used in the Gulf States
Farsi – official language of Iran
felafel – deep-fried balls of chickpea paste with spices, served in a piece of flat bread with tomatoes or pickled vegetables
fuddel – literally 'come in', but is used more as an invitation to share food
fuul – dish made from stewed fava beans

GCC – Gulf Cooperation Council: membership includes Saudi Arabia, Kuwait, Bahrain, Qatar, Oman and the UAE
gutra – headcloth worn by men in the Gulf States

habban – Arabic goatskin bagpipes
hadith – a saying by the Prophet Mohammed, or a story about his life
haj – annual Muslim pilgrimage to Mecca
halal – religiously acceptable or permitted (usually refers to meat)
hamour – common species of fish found in Gulf waters
Hanbali – the strictest of the Islamic schools of thought
hareem – the women of the household or family
haram – forbidden by Islam; religiously unacceptable
Hejira – migration; also name of Islamic calendar
hibb – ceramic pot used to keep water cold
housh – a courtyard

imam – prayer leader, Muslim cleric
inshallah – literally 'god willing'

iwan – vaulted hall, opening into a central court in the *madrassa* of a mosque

jebel – hill, mountain
jefeer – shopping basket woven from palm leaves
jihad – literally 'striving in the way of the faith'; holy war

kandoura – casual shirt-dress worn by men and women
khanjar – (also *khanja*) Omani curved dagger
khir – ceramic pot used to store dates
kufeyya – cotton headcloth worn by men
kuttab – school where children were taught to recite *Quran* by rote

Liwa – traditional Emirati dance with its roots in East Africa. Also an oasis region in the south of the UAE.
luban – frankincense

madrassa – Muslim theological seminary; also modern Arabic word for school
mafraj – room with a view; top room of a tower house
majlis – formal meeting room or reception area; also parliament
Maliki – one of the Islamic schools of thought
manior – traditional percussion instrument that is tied around the waist
manzar – attic
masayf – a traditional summer house incorporating a windtower
mashait – a traditional winter house incorporating a courtyard
mashrabiyyah – ornately carved wooden panel or screen; a feature of Islamic architecture
mehaffa – hand fan woven from palm leaves
mihrab – niche in a mosque indicating the direction of Mecca
mimzar – traditional wind instrument like a small oboe
minaret – the spire or tower of a mosque
minbar – pulpit used for sermons in a mosque
mosque – the Muslim place of worship

muezzin – cantor who sings the *azzan* (call to prayer)
Muslim – one who submits to God's will; follower of Islam

Qaaba – (also *Kaaba*) the rectangular structure at the centre of the Grand Mosque in Mecca (containing the Black Stone) around which haj pilgrims circumambulate
qahwa – (also *ahwa*) coffee; coffeehouse
qasr – castle
qibla – the direction of Mecca
Quran – the holy book of Islam; also spelt Koran

rakats – cycles of prayer, during which the *Quran* is read and bows and prostrations are performed
Ramadan – the Muslim month of fasting
ras – cape or headland

salat – prayer
sawm – fasting
semma – woven palm mat on which food is placed
shahadah – a Muslim's profession of his or her faith
shaikh – (also sheikh) a venerated religious scholar
sharia'a – Islamic law
shasha – small fishing boat made out of palm fronds
shayla – woman's headscarf
sheesha – tall, glass-bottomed smoking implement
sheikh – see *shaikh*
Shi'ite – sect of Islam which believes that the line of a caliph descends through the Prophet Mohammed's son in law, Ali
shwarma – grilled meat sliced from a spit and served in pitta bread with salad
sirwal – women's trousers, worn under the *kandoura*
souq – market or shopping centre
sultan – the absolute ruler of a Muslim state
Sunnah – body of work recording the sayings and doings of the Prophet and his family
Sunni – follower of the faction of Islam that holds that any Muslim who rules with

justice and according to the *Sharia'a* (Islamic law) can become a caliph

surood – cone-shaped, woven palm mat used to cover food

tabl – Middle Eastern drum

talli – different coloured cotton, silver and gold threads interwoven to make decorative ankle, wrist and neck bands

tamboura – traditional harp-like stringed instrument

taqia – men's lace skull-cap worn under the *ghutra*

Tawminah – festival carried out on completion of the recitation of the *Quran* by school children

tell – an ancient mound created by centuries of urban rebuilding

tolah – a measurement of weight used in the UAE – 12g or 12mL

Umayyads – (also Omayyad) first great dynasty of Arab Muslim rulers, based in Damascus (661-750 AD)

umm – mother

umrah – pilgrimage to Mecca that is not *haj*

wadi – dried up river bed; seasonal river

wusta – influence gained by way of connections in high places

zakat – alms or charity

LONELY PLANET

Phrasebooks

Lonely Planet phrasebooks are packed with essential words and phrases to help travellers communicate with the locals. With colour tabs for quick reference, an extensive vocabulary and use of script, these handy pocket-sized language guides cover day-to-day travel situations.

- handy pocket-sized books
- easy to understand Pronunciation chapter
- clear & comprehensive Grammar chapter
- romanisation alongside script to allow ease of pronunciation
- script throughout so users can point to phrases for every situation
- full of cultural information and tips for the traveller

'... vital for a real DIY spirit and attitude in language learning'
— *Backpacker*

'the phrasebooks have good cultural backgrounders and offer solid advice for challenging situations in remote locations'
— *San Francisco Examiner*

Arabic (Egyptian) • Arabic (Moroccan) • Australian *(Australian English, Aboriginal and Torres Strait languages)* • Baltic States *(Estonian, Latvian, Lithuanian)* • Bengali • Brazilian • British • Burmese • Cantonese • Central Asia (Uyghur, Uzbek, Kyrghiz, Kazak, Pashto, Tadjik • Central Europe *(Czech, French, German, Hungarian, Italian, Slovak)* • Eastern Europe *(Bulgarian, Czech, Hungarian, Polish, Romanian, Slovak)* • Ethiopian (Amharic) • Fijian • French • German • Greek • Hebrew • Hill Tribes • Hindi & Urdu • Indonesian • Italian • Japanese • Korean • Lao • Latin American Spanish • Malay • Mandarin • Mediterranean Europe *(Albanian, Croatian, Greek, Italian, Macedonian, Maltese, Serbian, Slovene)* • Mongolian • Nepali • Pidgin • Pilipino (Tagalog) • Quechua • Russian • Scandinavian Europe *(Danish, Finnish, Icelandic, Norwegian, Swedish)* • South-East Asia *(Burmese, Indonesian, Khmer, Lao, Malay, Tagalog Pilipino, Thai, Vietnamese)* • South Pacific Languages • Spanish (Castilian) *(also includes Catalan, Galician and Basque)* • Sri Lanka • Swahili • Thai • Tibetan • Turkish • Ukrainian • USA *(US English, Vernacular, Native American languages, Hawaiian)* • Vietnamese • Western Europe *(Basque, Catalan, Dutch, French, German, Greek, Irish, Italian, Portuguese, Scottish Gaelic, Spanish (Castilian), Welsh)*

Lonely Planet Journeys

Journeys is a unique collection of travel writing – published by the company that understands travel better than anyone else. It is a series for anyone who has ever experienced – or dreamed of – the magical moment when they encountered a strange culture or saw a place for the first time. They are tales to read while you're planning a trip, while you're on the road or while you're in an armchair in front of a fire.

These outstanding titles explore our planet through the eyes of a diverse group of international writers. JOURNEYS books catch the spirit of a place, illuminate a culture, recount a crazy adventure or introduce a fascinating way of life. They always entertain, and always enrich the experience of travel.

MALI BLUES
Traveling to an African Beat
Lieve Joris (translated by Sam Garrett)

Drought, rebel uprisings, ethnic conflict: these are the predominant images of West Africa. But as Lieve Joris travels in Senegal, Mauritania and Mali, she meets survivors, fascinating individuals charting new ways of living between tradition and modernity. With her remarkable gift for drawing out people's stories, Joris brilliantly captures the rhythms of a world that refuses to give in.

THE GATES OF DAMASCUS
Lieve Joris (translated by Sam Garrett)

This best-selling book is a beautifully drawn portrait of day-to-day life in modern Syria. Through her intimate contact with local people, Lieve Joris draws us into the fascinating world that lies behind the gates of Damascus. Hala's husband is a political prisoner, jailed for his opposition to the Assad regime; through the author's friendship with Hala we see how Syrian politics impacts on the lives of ordinary people.

THE OLIVE GROVE
Travels in Greece
Katherine Kizilos

Katherine Kizilos travels to fabled islands, troubled border zones and her family's village deep in the mountains. She vividly evokes breathtaking landscapes, generous people and passionate politics, capturing the complexities of a country she loves.

'beautifully captures the real tensions of Greece' – *Sunday Times*

KINGDOM OF THE FILM STARS
Journey into Jordan
Annie Caulfield

Kingdom of the Film Stars is a travel book and a love story. With honesty and humour, Annie Caulfield writes of travelling in Jordan and falling in love with a Bedouin with film-star looks.

She offers fascinating insights into the country – from the tent life of traditional women to the hustle of downtown Amman – and unpicks tight-woven western myths about the Arab world.

Lonely Planet Travel Atlases

L onely Planet has long been famous for the number and quality of its guidebook maps. Now we've gone one step further and produced a handy companion series: Lonely Planet travel atlases – maps of a country produced in book form.

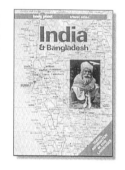

Unlike other maps, which look good but lead travellers astray, our travel atlases have been researched on the road by Lonely Planet's experienced team of writers. All details are carefully checked to ensure the atlas corresponds with the equivalent Lonely Planet guidebook.

- full-colour throughout
- maps researched and checked by Lonely Planet authors
- place names correspond with Lonely Planet guidebooks
- no confusing spelling differences
- legend and travelling information in English, French, German, Japanese and Spanish
- size: 230 x 160 mm

Available now: Chile & Easter Island ● Egypt ● India & Bangladesh ● Israel & the Palestinian Territories ● Jordan, Syria & Lebanon ● Kenya ● Laos ● Portugal ● South Africa, Lesotho & Swaziland ● Thailand ● Turkey ● Vietnam ● Zimbabwe, Botswana & Namibia

Lonely Planet TV Series & Videos

L onely Planet travel guides have been brought to life on television screens around the world. Like our guides, the programs are based on the joy of independent travel and look honestly at some of the most exciting, picturesque and frustrating places in the world. Each show is presented by one of three travellers from Australia, England or the USA and combines an innovative mixture of video, Super-8 film, atmospheric soundscapes and original music.

Videos of each episode – containing additional footage not shown on television – are available from good book and video shops, but the availability of individual videos varies with regional screening schedules.

Video destinations include: Alaska ● American Rockies ● Argentina ● Australia – The South-East ● Baja California & the Copper Canyon ● Brazil ● Central Asia ● Chile & Easter Island ● Corsica, Sicily & Sardinia – The Mediterranean Islands ● East Africa (Tanzania & Zanzibar) ● Cuba ● Ecuador & the Galapagos Islands ● Ethiopia ● Greenland & Iceland ● Hungary & Romania ● Indonesia ● Israel & the Sinai Desert ● Jamaica ● Japan ● La Ruta Maya ● London ● The Middle East (Syria, Jordan & Lebanon ● Morocco ● New York City ● Northern Spain ● North India ● Outback Australia ● Pacific Islands (Fiji, Solomon Islands & Vanuatu) ● Pakistan ● Peru ● The Philippines ● South Africa & Lesotho ● South India ● South West China ● South West USA ● Trekking in Uganda & Congo ● Turkey ● Vietnam ● West Africa ● Zimbabwe, Botswana & Namibia

The Lonely Planet TV series is produced by: Pilot Productions
The Old Studio
18 Middle Row
London W10 5AT, UK

Lonely Planet Online

Whether you've just begun planning your next trip, or you're chasing down specific info on currency regulations or visa requirements, check out Lonely Planet Online for up-to-the-minute travel information.

As well as miniguides to more than 250 destinations, you'll find maps, photos, travel news, health and visa updates, travel advisories and discussion of the ecological and political issues you need to be aware of as you travel. You'll also find timely upgrades to popular guidebooks that you can print out and stick in the back of your book.

There's an online travellers' forum (The Thorn Tree) where you can share your experience of life on the road, meet travel companions and ask other travellers for their recommendations and advice.

There's also a complete and up-to-date list of all Lonely Planet travel products including travel guides, diving and snorkeling guides, phrasebooks, atlases, travel literature and videos, and a simple online ordering facility if you can't find the book you want elsewhere.

Lonely Planet Diving & Snorkeling Guides

Beautifully illustrated with full-colour photos throughout, Lonely Planet's Pisces books explore the world's best diving and snorkeling areas and prepare divers for what to expect when they get there, both topside and underwater.

Dive sites are described in detail with specifics on depths, visibility, level of difficulty, special conditions, underwater photography tips and common and unusual marine life present. You'll also find practical logistical information and coverage on topside activities and attractions, sections on diving health and safety, plus listings for diving services, live-aboards, dive resorts and tourist offices.

LONELY PLANET

Guides by Region

L onely Planet is known worldwide for publishing practical, reliable and no-nonsense travel information in our guides and on our Web site. The Lonely Planet list covers just about every accessible part of the world. Currently there are thirteen series: travel guides, shoestring guides, walking guides, city guides, phrasebooks, audio packs, city maps, travel atlases, diving & snorkeling guides, restaurant guides, first-time travel guides, healthy travel and travel literature.

AFRICA Africa on a shoestring • Africa – the South • Arabic (Egyptian) phrasebook • Arabic (Moroccan) phrasebook • Cairo • Cape Town • Cape Town city map• Central Africa • East Africa • Egypt • Egypt travel atlas • Ethiopian (Amharic) phrasebook • The Gambia & Senegal • Healthy Travel Africa • Kenya • Kenya travel atlas • Malawi, Mozambique & Zambia • Morocco • North Africa • South Africa, Lesotho & Swaziland • South Africa, Lesotho & Swaziland travel atlas • Swahili phrasebook • Tanzania, Zanzibar & Pemba • Trekking in East Africa • Tunisia • West Africa • Zimbabwe, Botswana & Namibia • Zimbabwe, Botswana & Namibia travel atlas
Travel Literature: The Rainbird: A Central African Journey • Songs to an African Sunset: A Zimbabwean Story • Mali Blues: Traveling to an African Beat

AUSTRALIA & THE PACIFIC Auckland • Australia • Australian phrasebook • Bushwalking in Australia • Bushwalking in Papua New Guinea • Fiji • Fijian phrasebook • Healthy Travel Australia, NZ and the Pacific • Islands of Australia's Great Barrier Reef • Melbourne • Melbourne city map • Micronesia • New Caledonia • New South Wales & the ACT • New Zealand • Northern Territory • Outback Australia • Out To Eat – Melbourne • Out to Eat – Sydney • Papua New Guinea • Pidgin phrasebook • Queensland • Rarotonga & the Cook Islands • Samoa • Solomon Islands • South Australia • South Pacific Languages phrasebook • Sydney • Sydney city map • Sydney Condensed • Tahiti & French Polynesia • Tasmania • Tonga • Tramping in New Zealand • Vanuatu • Victoria • Western Australia
Travel Literature: Islands in the Clouds • Kiwi Tracks: A New Zealand Journey • Sean & David's Long Drive

CENTRAL AMERICA & THE CARIBBEAN Bahamas, Turks & Caicos • Bermuda • Central America on a shoestring • Costa Rica • Cuba • Dominican Republic & Haiti • Eastern Caribbean • Guatemala, Belize & Yucatán: La Ruta Maya • Jamaica • Mexico • Mexico City • Panama • Puerto Rico
Travel Literature: Green Dreams: Travels in Central America

EUROPE Amsterdam • Amsterdam city map • Andalucía • Austria • Baltic States phrasebook • Barcelona • Berlin • Berlin city map • Britain • British phrasebook • Brussels, Bruges & Antwerp • Budapest city map • Canary Islands • Central Europe • Central Europe phrasebook • Corsica • Croatia • Czech & Slovak Republics • Denmark • Dublin • Eastern Europe • Eastern Europe phrasebook • Edinburgh • Estonia, Latvia & Lithuania • Europe on a shoestring • Finland • France • French phrasebook • Germany • German phrasebook • Greece • Greek Islands • Greek phrasebook • Hungary • Iceland, Greenland & the Faroe Islands • Ireland • Italian phrasebook • Italy • Krakow • Lisbon • London • London city map • London Condensed • Mediterranean Europe • Mediterranean Europe phrasebook • Norway • Paris • Paris city map • Poland • Portugal • Portugal travel atlas • Prague • Prague city map • Provence & the Côte d'Azur • Romania & Moldova • Rome • Russia, Ukraine & Belarus • Russian phrasebook • Scandinavian & Baltic Europe • Scandinavian Europe phrasebook • Scotland • Slovenia • Spain • Spanish phrasebook • St Petersburg • Switzerland • Trekking in Spain • Ukrainian phrasebook • Vienna • Walking in Britain • Walking in Ireland • Walking in Italy • Walking in Spain • Walking in Switzerland • Western Europe • Western Europe phrasebook
Travel Literature: The Olive Grove: Travels in Greece

INDIAN SUBCONTINENT Bangladesh • Bengali phrasebook • Bhutan • Delhi • Goa • Hindi & Urdu phrasebook • India • India & Bangladesh travel atlas • Indian Himalaya • Karakoram Highway • Kerala • Mumbai (Bombay) • Nepal • Nepali phrasebook • Pakistan • Rajasthan • Read This First: Asia & India • South India • Sri Lanka • Sri Lanka phrasebook • Trekking in the Indian Himalaya • Trekking in the Karakoram & Hindukush • Trekking in the Nepal Himalaya
Travel Literature: In Rajasthan • Shopping for Buddhas

LONELY PLANET

Mail Order

Lonely Planet products are distributed worldwide. They are also available by mail order from Lonely Planet, so if you have difficulty finding a title please write to us. North and South American residents should write to 150 Linden St, Oakland, CA 94607, USA; European and African residents should write to 10a Spring Place, London NW5 3BH, UK; and residents of other countries to PO Box 617, Hawthorn, Victoria 3122, Australia.

ISLANDS OF THE INDIAN OCEAN Madagascar & Comoros • Maldives • Mauritius, Réunion & Seychelles

MIDDLE EAST & CENTRAL ASIA Arab Gulf States • Central Asia • Central Asia phrasebook • Hebrew phrasebook • Iran • Israel & the Palestinian Territories • Israel & the Palestinian Territories travel atlas • Istanbul • Istanbul to Cairo • Jerusalem • Jordan & Syria • Jordan, Syria & Lebanon travel atlas • Lebanon • Middle East on a shoestring • Syria • Turkey • Turkey travel atlas • Turkish phrasebook • Yemen
Travel Literature: The Gates of Damascus • Kingdom of the Film Stars: Journey into Jordan

NORTH AMERICA Alaska • Backpacking in Alaska • Baja California • California & Nevada • Canada • Chicago • Chicago city map • Deep South • Florida • Hawaii • Honolulu • Las Vegas • Los Angeles • Miami • New England • New Orleans • New York City • New York city map • New York, New Jersey & Pennsylvania • Pacific Northwest USA • Puerto Rico • Rocky Mountain • San Francisco • San Francisco city map • Seattle • Southwest USA • Texas • USA • USA phrasebook • Vancouver • Washington, DC & the Capital Region • Washington DC city map
Travel Literature: Drive Thru America

NORTH-EAST ASIA Beijing • Cantonese phrasebook • China • Hong Kong • Hong Kong city map • Hong Kong, Macau & Guangzhou • Japan • Japanese phrasebook • Japanese audio pack • Korea • Korean phrasebook • Kyoto • Mandarin phrasebook • Mongolia • Mongolian phrasebook • North-East Asia on a shoestring • Seoul • South-West China • Taiwan • Tibet • Tibetan phrasebook • Tokyo
Travel Literature: Lost Japan

SOUTH AMERICA Argentina, Uruguay & Paraguay • Bolivia • Brazil • Brazilian phrasebook • Buenos Aires • Chile & Easter Island • Chile & Easter Island travel atlas • Colombia • Ecuador & the Galapagos Islands • Healthy Travel Central & South America • Latin American Spanish phrasebook • Peru • Quechua phrasebook • Rio de Janeiro • Rio de Janeiro city map • South America on a shoestring • Trekking in the Patagonian Andes • Venezuela
Travel Literature: Full Circle: A South American Journey

SOUTH-EAST ASIA Bali & Lombok • Bangkok • Bangkok city map • Burmese phrasebook • Cambodia • Hanoi • Healthy Travel Asia & India • Hill Tribes phrasebook • Ho Chi Minh City • Indonesia • Indonesia's Eastern Islands • Indonesian phrasebook • Indonesian audio pack • Jakarta • Java • Laos • Lao phrasebook • Laos travel atlas • Malay phrasebook • Malaysia, Singapore & Brunei • Myanmar (Burma) • Philippines • Pilipino (Tagalog) phrasebook • Singapore • South-East Asia on a shoestring • South-East Asia phrasebook • Thailand • Thailand's Islands & Beaches • Thailand travel atlas • Thai phrasebook • Thai audio pack • Vietnam • Vietnamese phrasebook • Vietnam travel atlas

ALSO AVAILABLE: Antarctica • The Arctic • Brief Encounters: Stories of Love, Sex & Travel • Chasing Rickshaws • Lonely Planet Unpacked • Not the Only Planet: Travel Stories from Science Fiction • Sacred India • Travel with Children • Traveller's Tales

FREE Lonely Planet Newsletters

W e love hearing from you and think you'd like to hear from us.

Planet Talk

Our FREE quarterly printed newsletter is full of tips from travellers and anecdotes from Lonely Planet guidebook authors. Every issue is packed with up-to-date travel news and advice, and includes:

- a postcard from Lonely Planet co-founder Tony Wheeler
- a swag of mail from travellers
- a look at life on the road through the eyes of a Lonely Planet author
- topical health advice
- prizes for the best travel yarn
- news about forthcoming Lonely Planet events
- a complete list of Lonely Planet books and other titles

To join our mailing list, residents of the UK, Europe and Africa can email us at go@lonelyplanet.co.uk; residents of North and South America can email us at info@lonelyplanet.com; the rest of the world can email us at talk2us@lonelyplanet.com.au, or contact any Lonely Planet office.

Comet

O ur FREE monthly email newsletter brings you all the latest travel news, features, interviews, competitions, destination ideas, travellers' tips & tales, Q&As, raging debates and related links. Find out what's new on the Lonely Planet Web site and which books are about to hit the shelves.

Subscribe from your desktop: www.lonelyplanet.com/comet

Index

Text

A

abras 77
accidents 75
accommodation 96-104
    budget 96-9
    mid-range 99-101
    top end 101-3
air travel 64-9
    airline offices 68-9
    departure tax 64
    duty free 72
    travel agencies 68
    travel glossary 66
airline offices 68-9
Al-Ain & Buraimi 136-9, **136**
    Al-Khandaq Fort 137
    Buraimi Souq 138
    Camel Souq 137
    Eastern Fort 137
    Hili Gardens & Archaeo-
        logical Park 138
    Livestock Souq 137
    museum 137
Al-Ahmadiya School 85-6
Al-Ain Museum 137
Al-Boom Tourist Village 89
Al-Hayl Castle 135
Al-Hisn Fort 129-30
Al-Khandaq Fort 137
Al-Maktoum Family 11, 12,
    14, 18
Al-Mamzar Beach Park 89
Al-Qusais 10
ambulance 55
animals, see fauna
Aquapark Dreamland 58
Arabian souvenirs 122
Arabic 34, 141-8
    courses 95
arcades, see computer
    arcades
architecture 23-8
    modern 26-8
    traditional 23-6
art galleries 84
    Dubai International Arts
        Centre 84

Bold indicates maps.

    Majlis Gallery 84
    Orient Gallery 84
    Profile Gallery 84
arts 21-2, 29

B

Badiyah 135-6
Bani Yas 11
barasti houses 24-5
bargaining 45
bars 114-15
Bastakia Quarter 85, see also
    architecture
beaches 90
Bedouin
    hospitality 132
    jewellery 122-3
bicycle travel 77
boat trips, see Creek cruises
boat travel, see abras
books 47-8, see also literature
bookshops 125
Buraimi, see Al-Ain
bus travel 69-70, 72-4
    around Dubai 73
    to/from Dubai 69-70
business 39, 61-3, see also
    cultural considerations
    etiquette 63
    facilities 62
    hours 60
    useful organisations 62

C

camels 117
    racing 117-18
    souq 137
camping 96
car travel 70, 74-6, 94
    accidents 75
    insurance 128
    rental 74-6
    road rules 76-8
    to/from Dubai 70
carpets 120-2
children, travel with 57-8
cinemas 116-17
climate 14
clothing, see traditional dress
clubs, see nightclubs

coffee 108-9
coffeehouses 116
computer arcades 119
computer games, see computer
    arcades
concerts 117, see also theatre
conduct, see cultural
    considerations
conservation 15-16
    desertification 15
consulates 42-3
costs 44-5
courses 95
    desert safaris 95
    diving 95
    language 95
crafts 29
credit cards 44
Creek cruises 93
Creekside Park 89
cricket 118
cultural centres 59
cultural considerations 29-31,
    39, 49-50, 108
    avoiding offense 31-2
currency 43
customs 43

D

dance 21
date palm 16
Deira Covered Souq 126
dentists 55
departure tax 64
desert rallies 118
desert safaris 94
    4WD desert driving 95
Dhayah 140
Dhow Building Yard 88-9
dhow wharfage 81-2
dhows 88
disabled travellers 57
discos, see nightclubs
diving 91-2
    safety guidelines 92
    course 95
doctors 55
drinks 107-9
    coffee 108-9
driving, see car travel

Bold indicates maps.

Boxed Text

The commercial hub of the UAE: modern skyscrapers line Shaikh Zayed Road.

Camels, the ships of the desert, prepare for a race at Nad al-Sheba Race Track.

MAP 1 – DUBAI

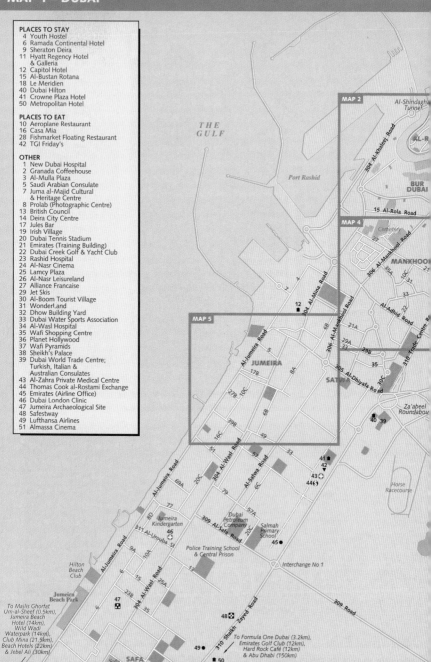

PLACES TO STAY
4 Youth Hostel
6 Ramada Continental Hotel
9 Sheraton Deira
11 Hyatt Regency Hotel
   & Galleria
12 Capitol Hotel
15 Al-Bustan Rotana
18 Le Meridien
40 Dubai Hilton
41 Crowne Plaza Hotel
50 Metropolitan Hotel

PLACES TO EAT
10 Aeroplane Restaurant
16 Casa Mia
28 Fishmarket Floating Restaurant
42 TGI Friday's

OTHER
1 New Dubai Hospital
2 Granada Coffeehouse
3 Al-Mulla Plaza
5 Saudi Arabian Consulate
7 Juma al-Majid Cultural
   & Heritage Centre
8 Prolab (Photographic Centre)
13 British Council
14 Deira City Centre
17 Jules Bar
19 Irish Village
20 Dubai Tennis Stadium
21 Emirates (Training Building)
22 Dubai Creek Golf & Yacht Club
23 Rashid Hospital
24 Al-Nasr Cinema
25 Lamcy Plaza
26 Al-Nasr Leisureland
27 Alliance Francaise
29 Jet Skis
30 Al-Boom Tourist Village
31 WonderLand
32 Dhow Building Yard
33 Dubai Water Sports Association
34 Al-Wasl Hospital
35 Wafi Shopping Centre
36 Planet Hollywood
37 Wafi Pyramids
38 Sheikh's Palace
39 Dubai World Trade Centre;
   Turkish, Italian &
   Australian Consulates
43 Al-Zahra Private Medical Centre
44 Thomas Cook al-Rostami Exchange
45 Emirates (Airline Office)
46 Dubai London Clinic
47 Jumeira Archaeological Site
48 Safestway
49 Lufthansa Airlines
51 Almassa Cinema

THE GULF

Port Rashid

MAP 2
Al-Shindagha
Tunnel

AL-R

BUR
DUBAI

306 Al-Khaleej Road

15 Al-Rola Road

MAP 4
Cemetery

306 Al-Mankhool Road

MANKHOO

35A

10C

31

33

306 Al-Mankhool Road

Al-Adhid Road

21A
6B
29A
33
29B

305 Al-Dhiyafa Road

310 Trade Centre Rd

304 Al-Mina Road

306 Al-Mankhool Road

MAP 5

Al-Jumeira Road

JUMEIRA

17B

27B

10C

39B

16C

6B

49

35
9C

12

4

7

5

8A

SATWA

Za'abeel
Roundabou

40 39

41
42
43
44

Horse
Racecourse

51

304 Al-Wasl Road

Al-Jumeira Road

69A
20C

Al-Satwa Road

77
6C

79

57A

20C

309 Al-Safa Road

Dubai
Petroleum
Company

Salmah
Primary
School

Police Training School
& Central Prison

45

Interchange No 1

8D
Jumeira
Kindergarten

311 Al-Usquba St

46

9A

10C

6

15

23B

25A

304 Al-Wasl Road

35

13

Hilton
Beach
Club

Jumeira
Beach Park

47

To Majlis Ghorfat
Um-al-Sheef (0.5km),
Jumeira Beach
Hotel (14km),
Wild Wadi
Waterpark (14km),
Club Mina (21.5km),
Beach Hotels (22km)
& Jebel Ali (30km)

UMM SUQEIM

SAFA

Safa
Park

310 Sheikh Zayed Road

To Formula One Dubai (3.2km),
Emirates Golf Club (12km),
Hard Rock Café (12km)
& Abu Dhabi (150km)

48

49

50

51

309 Road

MAP 2 – DEIRA & BUR DUBAI

PLACES TO STAY
2 Shiraz Hotel
3 Green Line Hotel
4 Metro Hotel
6 Gold Plaza Hotel
8 Al-Noor Hotel
9 Deira Palace Hotel
10 Al-Khail Hotel
11 Al-Karnak Hotel
13 Sina Hotel
14 New Avon Hotel
15 Royal Prince Hotel
17 Mariana Hotel
18 Vienna Hotel
22 Hotel Delhi Darbar
25 Arbella Hotel
26 Landmark Hotel
27 Ramee International Hotel
30 Phoenicia Hotel
32 Piccadilly Hotel
34 Swiss Hotel
38 Dubai Inter-Continental Hotel
41 Carlton Tower Hotel
42 Riviera Hotel
53 Al-Khaleej Hotel
55 Victoria Hotel
56 Al-Sheraa Hotel
57 Shams al-Sahraa Hotel
60 St George Hotel
71 Ambassador Hotel
73 New Penninsula Hotel
74 Swiss Plaza Hotel
79 Admiral Plaza
79 Astoria Hotel
81 Time Palace Hotel
96 Heritage International Hotel
102 Rolla Residence
103 Royal Imperial Apartments
104 Dubai Marine Hotel
105 Bourivage Residence

PLACES TO EAT
5 Sarovar Restaurant
7 Al-Burj Cafeteria
16 Gulf Restaurant & Cafeteria
21 Bab al-Sabkha
28 Swagath Restaurant
29 Entezary Restaurant
31 Golden Fork
43 Cafe Mozart
45 Popeye
45 Hatam Restaurant
49 Pizza Corner
50 Cafeteria al-Abra
78 Emirates Restaurant
83 Bhavna Deluxe Restaurant
84 India House
101 Kowloon

OTHER
1 Gold Souq Bus Station
12 Emirates (Airline Office)
19 Al-Sabkha Rd Bus Station
20 Windtower
23 Golden Laundry
24 Police Station (Old Fort)
33 Tide Dry Cleaners & Laundry
35 DTCM Welcome Bureau
36 Deira Tower
37 Dubai Tower
39 Pick-up & Drop-off for Creek Cruises
40 Twin Towers Shopping Centre
46 Pearl Building
47 British Bank of the Middle East
48 Thomas Cook al-Rostami Exchange
51 Deira Post Office
52 Sheesha Cafe
54 Emirates Bank International
58 Heritage House
59 Al-Ahmadiya School
61 Public Library
62 MMI Travel Centre; Air New Zealand Office
63 Diving Village
64 Heritage Village
65 Shaikh Saeed al-Maktoum House
66 Bin Suroor Mosque
67 Shindagha Tower
68 Public Seating Area
69 British Bank of the Middle East
70 Emirates Bank International
72 Al-Ghubaiba Bus Station
75 Meraj Typing Centre & Internet
77 Al-Warda al-Ahmar Laundry
80 Thomas Cook al-Rostami Exchange
82 Mosque
85 Sharaf Building; German Consulate
86 Dubai Museum
87 Grand Mosque
88 Hindu Temple
89 Diwan (Ruler's Office)
90 Majlis Gallery
91 Al-Musalla Post Office
92 British Embassy
93 Fatafeet Cafe
94 National Bank of Umm al-Qaiwain; Malaysia Airlines
95 ABN-Amro Bank; Dutch Consulate
97 Etisalat (Telephone Office)
98 Spinney's Supermarket
99 Choitram's (24 Hours)
100 Bordertown
106 Port Rashid Customs Authority

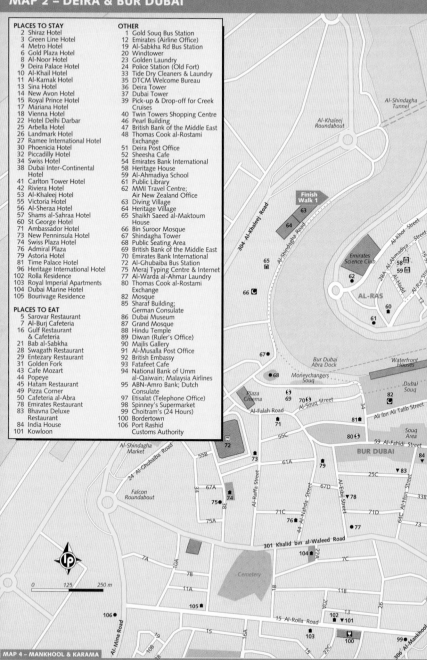

MAP 4 – MANKHOOL & KARAMA

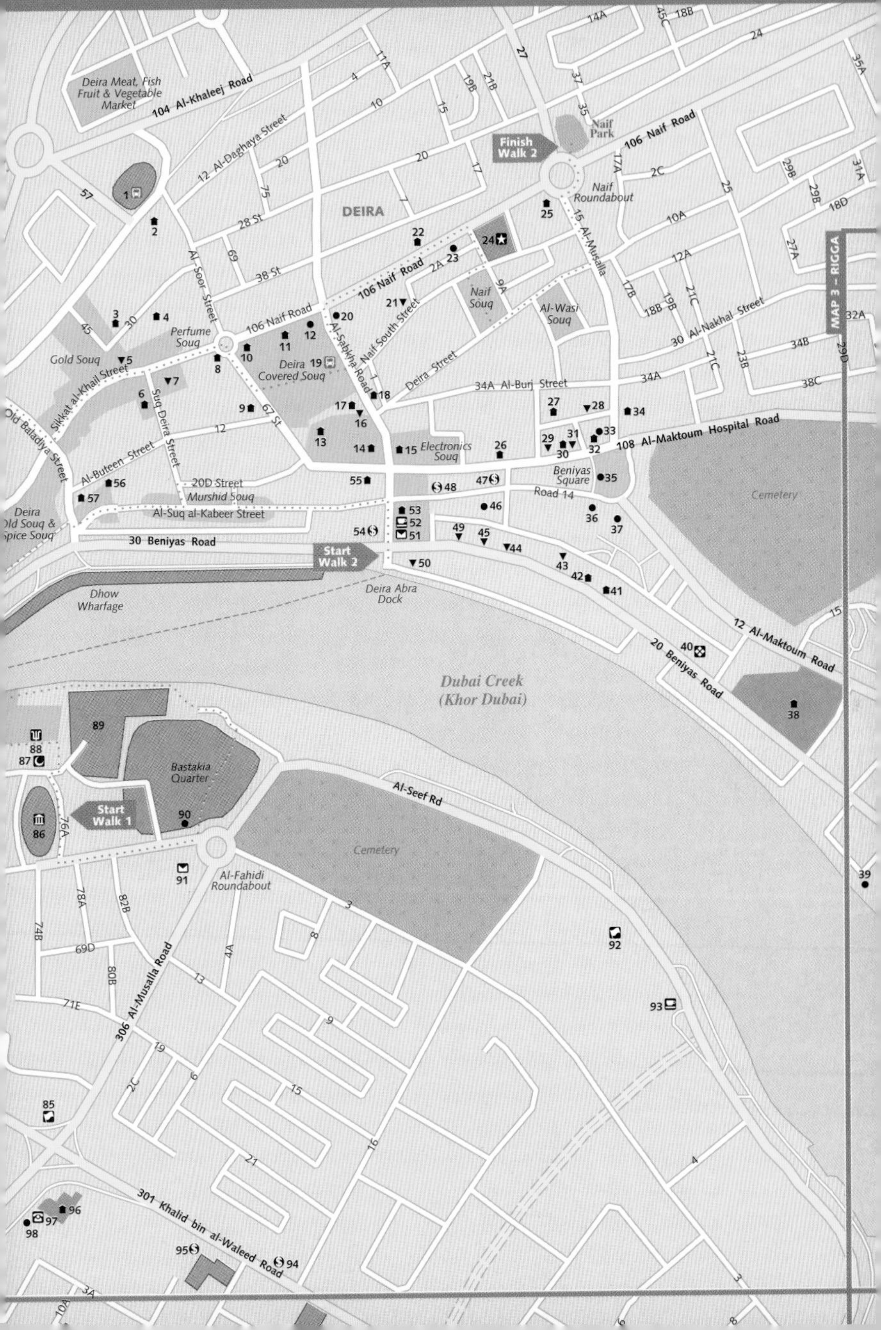

MAP 2 – DEIRA & BUR DUBAI

Deira Meat, Fish
Fruit & Vegetable
Market

104 Al-Khaleej Road

14A
16B 18B
27
24
35A

12 Al-Daghaya Street

Naif
Park

106 Naif Road

Finish
Walk 2

Naif
Roundabout

2C

28 St
38 St

DEIRA

25

10A

29B 29B

32A

MAP 3 – RIGGA

Perfume
Souq

106 Naif Road

3
30
4
12

22
24

106 Naif Road
2A 23
21
Naif
Souq

Al-Musalla

17A
17B
18B
21C

30 Al-Nakhal Street

21C
23B

34B
38C

Gold Souq

5
6
7
8

Al-Sabkha Road

20

19
Deira
Covered Souq

Deira Street

9
12
16
17
16
13
14
18

34A Al-Buri Street

27
28
34

108 Al-Maktoum Hospital Road

29
31
30
32
33

Al-Butteen Street
Suq Deira Street

Al-Wasl
Souq

Gold Souq

Sikkat al-Khail Street

Old Baladiya Street

57

56

20D Street
Murshid Souq

15
Electronics
Souq

26

Beniyas
Square

35

Cemetery

Al-Suq al-Kabeer Street

55

48
47

Road 14

Deira
Old Souq &
Spice Souq

30 Beniyas Road

54
51

53
52

46
49
45
44

36
37

Start
Walk 2

50

43
42
41

Dhow
Wharfage

Deira Abra
Dock

40

12 Al-Maktoum Road

20 Beniyas Road

15

38

Dubai Creek
(Khor Dubai)

89

88
87

Bastakia
Quarter

Al-Seef Rd

86

Start
Walk 1

90

Cemetery

91

Al-Fahidi
Roundabout

3

39

92

8

306 Al-Musalla Road

9

93

85

301 Khalid bin al-Waleed Road

96
97
98

95
94

MAP 3 – RIGGA

MAP 2 – DEIRA & BUR DUBAI

MAP 4 – MANKHOOL & KARAMA

30 Al-Nakhal Street

Omar ibn al-Khattab Rd

108 Salah al-Din Road

18 Al-Muraqqabat Road

Omar ibn al-Khattab Road

Union Square

Deira Cinema

30 Al-Rigga Road

RIGGA

110 Al-Maktoum Road

105 Abu Baker al-Siddiq Road

Clock Tower Roundabout

10 Beniyas Road

Dhow Wharfage

Dubai Creek (Khor Dubai)

314 Tariq ibn Ziyad Road

Al-Maktoum Bridge

0   125   250 m

MAP 3 – RIGGA

PLACES TO STAY
2 Mariedas Hotel
4 Renaissance Dubai Hotel
6 JW Marriott Hotel
11 Holiday Inn Downtown
13 Quality Inn Horizon
24 Sheraton Dubai
27 Al-Khaleej Palace Hotel
30 Lords Hotel
32 Metropolitan Palace Hotel
39 Mayfair Hotel
42 Nihal Hotel
43 Orchid Hotel
46 Royalton Plaza
48 Avari Dubai Hotel

PLACES TO EAT
10 King Pastries
12 Automatic Restaurant
14 Harry Ramsden's
15 Curry House
17 Barrio Fiesta
18 Iranian Sweets
33 Sadaf Restaurant

OTHER
1 Al-Maktoum Hospital
3 Gulf Air
5 Spinney's Supermarket
7 Hamarain Centre;
   Al-Firdoos Travel;
   Afghan Carpet Palace
8 The Travel Market
9 Arab Link
16 Al-Ghurair Centre;
    Books Gallery
19 Deira Minibus & Taxi Stand
20 Ghawar Sheesha & Coffeeshop
21 Etisalat (Headquaters)
22 French Consulate; Arbift Tower
23 Kuwaiti Consulate
25 National Bank of Dubai
26 Dubai Chamber of
    Commerce & Industry
28 Nasser Air Travel & Shipping;
    Alitalia
29 Qatar Airways
31 Air France
34 Sadaf Carpet
35 Emirates Bank International
36 Al-Majid Travel Agency
37 EgyptAir
38 Air India
40 Al-Ghaith & Al-Moosa
    Travel Agency
41 Avis
44 White Falcon
45 Saudi Arabian Airlines
49 Al-Rigga Post Office
49 Patriot Rent-A-Car
50 Airline Centre
51 Hertz
52 Budget
53 Cargo Village

HOR
AL-ANZ

Dubai
Cinema

108 Salah al-Din Road

105 Abu Baker al-Siddiq Road

202 Al-Ittihad Rd

202 Al-Ittihad Road

Airport Road

MAP 4 – MANKHOOL & KARAMA

MAP 2 – DEIRA & BUR DUBAI

MAP 5 – JUMEIRA & SATWA

PLACES TO STAY
4 Ramada Hotel
5 Al-Hina Residence
6 Baisan Residence
7 Savoy
8 Pearl Residence
19 Regent Palace Hotel
26 President Hotel

PLACES TO EAT
22 Chhappan Bhog
23 Thai Terrace
24 Puranmal
25 All Spice Fast Food
33 Shezan
34 Fiesta Filipino

OTHER
1 Al-Khaleej Shopping Centre
2 Al-Rais Travels
3 Rais Hassan Saadi; Royal Brunei Airlines
9 Canadian Consulate; United Bank
10 Citibank
11 Orient Gallery
12 Kinko's Copying Centre
13 Iranian Consulate
14 Indian Consulate
15 Egyptian Consulate
16 Omani Consulate
17 Jordanian Consulate
18 Strand Cinema
20 Bur Juman Centre
21 Pyramid Building; Archie's Library
27 Karama Centre
28 AmEx
29 Main Post Office
30 Car Rental Companies
31 Sana Building; Scubatec
32 Qatar Consulate

MANKHOOL

Cemetery
Cemetery
Cemetery

306 Al-Mankhool Road

D.E.C. Gas Power Station

Al-Adhid Road

310 Trade Centre Road

Department of Health & Medical Services

0   125   250 m

MAP 4 – MANKHOOL & KARAMA

MAP 3 – RIGGA

10A

5A

1

8

18B

2B

5

7

22A

26A

5B

9A

11B

13C

75B

26B

17B

27B

9B

22B

301 Khalid bin al-Waleed Road

12

9

10

11

13

7B

20

19

14

15

16

17

Iranian School

2A

4A

16B

18

5

A'ishat Intermediate School

Al-Karama Kindergarten

Islamic Studies College

11

21

13A

9A

8A

10A

14A

7A

Ministry of Health

22

23

24

25

2B

4B

6A

8B

10B

13B

Sheikha Latifa Bint Hamdan School

18A

20A

21

17A

17C

12C

10C

24

22 Za'abeel Road

310 Trade Centre Road

310 Trade Centre Road

26

2C

KARAMA

25 A

27

28

Al-Sae Divyat International School

27A

Romania

29

29A

30

31

33A

35

37B

39

41

45B

47A

16

33

2D

4C

16

29B

33B

20B

Al-Karama Shopping Centre

34

18B

47B

45B

47C

Al-Qatalyat Road

13a

4

10

15

17a

12A

Umm Hureir Road

314

MAP 5 – JUMEIRA & SATWA

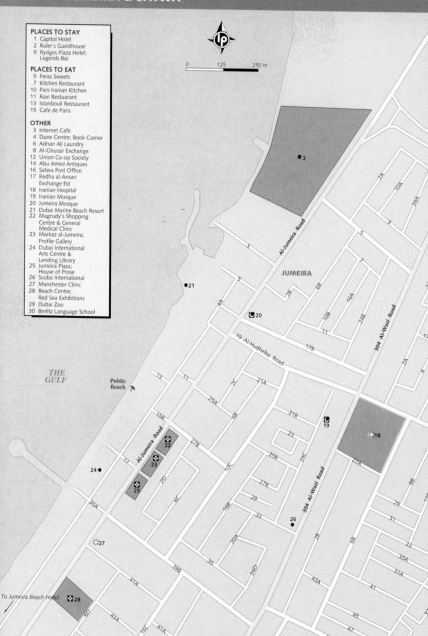

PLACES TO STAY
1 Capitol Hotel
2 Ruler's Guesthouse
9 Rydges Plaza Hotel;
   Legends Bar

PLACES TO EAT
5 Feras Sweets
7 Kitchen Restaurant
10 Pars Iranian Kitchen
11 Ravi Restuarant
13 Istanbouli Restaurant
15 Cafe de Paris

OTHER
3 Internet Cafe
4 Dune Centre; Book Corner
6 Adnan Ali Laundry
8 Al-Ghurair Exchange
12 Union Co-op Society
14 Abu Amed Antiques
16 Satwa Post Office
17 Redha al-Ansari
   Exchange Est
18 Iranian Hospital
19 Iranian Mosque
20 Jumeira Mosque
21 Dubai Marine Beach Resort
22 Magrudy's Shopping
   Centre & General
   Medical Clinic
23 Markaz al-Jumeira;
   Profile Gallery
24 Dubai International
   Arts Centre &
   Lending Library
25 Jumeira Plaza;
   House of Prose
26 Scuba International
27 Manchester Clinic
28 Beach Centre;
   Red Sea Exhibitions
29 Dubai Zoo
30 Berlitz Language School

0   125   250 m

THE GULF

Public Beach

JUMEIRA

Al-Jumeira Road

304 Al-Wasl Road

19 Al-Hudheiba Road

To Jumeira Beach Hotel

MAP 5 – JUMEIRA & SATWA

Al-Dhiyafa Road

306 Al-Manhool Road

Satwa
Roundabout

SATWA

Satwa
Souq

Al-Satwa Road

Soft corals from the reef off Dubai's coast.

CHRIS MELLOR

Some of the day's catch from the waters
around the Gulf.

CHRIS MELLOR

MAP LEGEND

CITY ROUTES

Freeway `- - - - - - - -` Freeway
Highway `- - - - -` Primary Road
Road `- - -` Secondary Road
Street `- - - - - - - - - -` Street
Lane `- - - - - - - - -` Lane
`- - - -` On/Off Ramp

`- - - -` Unsealed Road
`- - -` One Way Street
`- - -` Pedestrian Street
`- - -` Stepped Street
`- - - - - - - - - -` Tunnel
`- - - - - - -` Footbridge

REGIONAL ROUTES

`- - -` Tollway, Freeway
`- - - - -` Primary Road
`- - -` Secondary Road
`- - - - -` Minor Road

BOUNDARIES

`- - - - -` International
`- - - - - - - - - - -` State
`- - - - - - - -` Disputed
`- - - -` Fortified Wall

HYDROGRAPHY

`- - - - - - -` River, Creek
`- - - - - - - - - -` Canal
`- - - - - - - - - - -` Lake

Dry Lake, Salt Lake
`- - - -` Spring, Rapids
`- - - - - - -` Waterfalls

TRANSPORT ROUTES & STATIONS

`├─┼─○- - - - - - - - - - -` Train
`├─┼─┼-` Underground Train
`- - - -Ⓜ- - - - - - - -` Metro
`- - - - - - - - - - -` Tramway
`├─┼─┼─┤.` Cable Car, Chairlift

`- - - -◻- - - - - - - - - -` Ferry
`- - - - - - - -` Walking Trail
`• • • • • • • •` Walking Tour
`- - - - - - - - - -` Path
`- - - - - -` Pier or Jetty

AREA FEATURES

`- - - - - - - - -` Building
`- - - - -` Park, Gardens

`- - - - - - - - -` Market
`- - - -` Sports Ground

`- - - - - - - - - -` Beach
`- - - - - - -` Cemetery

`- - - - - - - - -` Hotel
`- - - - - - - - -` Plaza

POPULATION SYMBOLS

✪ **CAPITAL** `- - - - - -` National Capital
◉ **CAPITAL** `- - - - - - - - -` State Capital

● **CITY** `- - - - - - - - - - - -` City
● **Town** `- - - - - - - - - - -` Town

● Village `- - - - - - - - - - - -` Village
`- - - - - - - - -` Urban Area

MAP SYMBOLS

■ `- - - - - - - - - - - -` Place to Stay

▼ `- - - - - - - - - - - -` Place to Eat

● `- - - - - - - - - - -` Point of Interest

✈ `- - - - - - - - -` Airport		▯ `- - - - - - - -` Embassy		🏛 `- - - - - - - -` Museum		⛏ `- - - - - - - - - - -` Ruins
ⓢ `- - - - - - - - - - -` Bank		⚐ `- - - - -` Golf Course		🏞 `- - - - -` National Park		⊗ `- - -` Shopping Centre
🚌 `- - - - -` Bus Terminal		✚ `- - - - - - - - -` Hospital		▣ `- - - - - - - - -` Parking		🚕 `- - - - - - - -` Taxi Rank
🚏 `- - - - - - - -` Bus Stop		▣ `- - - - -` Internet Cafe		⊙ `- - - - - - - - -` Petrol		☎ `- - - - - -` Telephone
✝ 🏢 `- - - - - - - - -` Church		✳ `- - - - - - - - -` Lookout		✚ `- - - - -` Police Station		⛩ `- - - - - - - - -` Temple
🎬 `- - - - - - - - -` Cinema		⚱ `- - - - - -` Monument		✉ `- - - - - - -` Post Office		❶ `-` Tourist Information
☕ `- - - - - -` Coffeeshop		☪ `- - - - - - - - -` Mosque		🍺 `- - - - - - -` Pub or Bar		🐾 `- - - - - - - - - - -` Zoo

Note: not all symbols displayed above appear in this book

LONELY PLANET OFFICES

Australia
PO Box 617, Hawthorn, Victoria 3122
☎ 03 9819 1877 fax 03 9819 6459
email: talk2us@lonelyplanet.com.au

USA
150 Linden St, Oakland, CA 94607
☎ 510 893 8555 TOLL FREE: 800 275 8555
fax 510 893 8572
email: info@lonelyplanet.com

UK
10a Spring Place, London NW5 3BH
☎ 020 7428 4800 fax 020 7428 4828
email: go@lonelyplanet.co.uk

France
1 rue du Dahomey, 75011 Paris
☎ 01 55 25 33 00 fax 01 55 25 33 01
email: bip@lonelyplanet.fr
minitel: 3615 lonelyplanet *(1,29 F TTC/min)*

World Wide Web: www.lonelyplanet.com *or* AOL keyword: lp
Lonely Planet Images: lpi@lonelyplanet.com.au